CENTER
ON
GOD

# LITERARY CURRENTS IN BIBLICAL INTERPRETATION

## EDITORS

Danna Nolan Fewell
*Perkins School of Theology,*
*Southern Methodist University, Dallas TX*
David M. Gunn
*Columbia Theological Seminary, Decatur GA*

## EDITORIAL ADVISORY BOARD

# CENTERING
# ON
# GOD

---

## method
## and
## message
## in
## luke-acts

---

## ROBERT L. BRAWLEY

**Westminster/John Knox Press**
Louisville, Kentucky

CENTERING ON GOD: METHOD AND MESSAGE IN LUKE-ACTS

© 1990 Robert L. Brawley

*First edition*

Published by Westminster/John Knox Press
Louisville, Kentucky

PRINTED IN THE UNITED STATES OF AMERICA
2 4 6 8 9 7 5 3 1

**Library of Congress Cataloging-in-Publication Data**

Brawley, Robert L. (Robert Lawson)
  Centering on God : method and message in Luke-Acts / Robert L. Brawley. — 1st ed.
      p.    cm. — (Literary currents in biblical interpretation)
  Includes bibliographical references and indexes.
  ISBN 0-664-25133-1

  1. Bible. N.T. Luke—Criticism, interpretation, etc.  2. Bible. N.T. Acts—Criticism, interpretation, etc.  I. Title.  II. Series.
BS2589.B72  1990
226.4'.06—dc20                                                    90-38427

To my brother Boyce,

δίδυμος καὶ συνδρομεὺς
ἐν τῇ ἀγωνίᾳ

# CONTENTS

# SERIES
# PREFACE

New currents in biblical interpretation are emerging. Questions about origins—authors, intentions, settings—and stages of composition are giving way to questions about the literary qualities of the Bible, the play of its language, the coherence of its final form, and the relations between text and readers.

Such literary criticism is rapidly acquiring sophistication as it learns from major developments in secular critical theory, especially in understanding the instability of language and the key role of readers in the production of meaning. Biblical critics are being called to recognize that a plurality of readings is an inevitable and legitimate consequence of the interpretive process. By the same token, interpreters are being challenged to take responsibility for the theological, social, and ethical implications of their readings.

Biblical interpretation is changing on the practical as well as the theoretical level. More readers, both inside and outside the academic guild, are discovering that the Bible in literary perspective can powerfully engage people's lives. Communities of faith where the Bible is foundational may find that literary criticism can make the Scripture accessible in a way that historical criticism seems unable to do.

Within these changes lie exciting opportunities for all who seek contemporary meaning in the ancient texts. The goal of the series is to encourage such change and such search, to breach the confines of traditional biblical criticism, and to open channels for new currents of interpretation.

—THE EDITORS

# PREFACE

Many of my debts for assistance in completing this book will go unpaid. But acknowledging some of them may serve as a token of my gratitude. Memphis Theological Seminary provided me with a sabbatical leave in order that I might devote full time to the project. Dean Jack Forstman, the Divinity School, Vanderbilt University, helped me secure an appointment as a Visiting Scholar. Vanderbilt University then opened its library facilities to me. Robert Tannehil allowed me access to *The Literary Unity of Luke-Acts*, vol. 2, *The Acts of the Apostles*, in manuscript form. David Gowler gave me advanced copies from his dissertation. The documentation reveals my dependence upon others, but I am certain that it does so inadequately. Colleagues gave me suggestions, encouragement, and support. My wife, Jane, made sacrifices on my behalf, and although I am proud to thank her here, the public forum is unsuitable to express my full appreciation. I am grateful to Editors Danna Nolan Fewell and David Gunn and to General Editor Davis Perkins for accepting my work for publication. I have discovered that editors help us to say some of the things we intend and not to say some of the things we do not intend, although in keeping with my own literary theory my intentions now offer little control over the interpretation of this book.

Portions of my article, "Paul in Acts: Aspects of Structure and Characterization," in *Society of Biblical Literature Seminar Papers*, edited by David J. Lull (Atlanta: Scholars Press, 1988) 90-105, appear in revised form in chapters 4 and 6. They are used by permission of Scholars Press.

—ROBERT L. BRAWLEY

9

# 1

# THE
# CHALLENGE
# OF
# ANALYSIS

Put dramatically, to analyze interpretation is to undermine it. Interpretation is understanding, and understanding is itself incomprehensible. Part of being human is that we can contemplate ourselves as if from another's perspective. But mind transcending itself and turning back on itself—like a mirror reflecting inward and toward another—ultimately stands alienated by its own complexity. Or to switch to a technological metaphor, mind contemplating itself is comparable to a television camera focusing on the same picture it is transmitting.

In the case of both the mirror and the television, with each phase the distance between the primary and secondary images increases until the image dissolves into infinity. That too is comparable to mind considering itself. Mind and mind reflecting on mind may have a unitary origin. But reflection moves toward estrangement as mind distances itself and views itself as if another.

Julian Jaynes has the provocative if unprovable thesis that prior to about 1000 BCE human beings reacted to voices from the right side of the brain, which they perceived as audible, telling them what to do in specific situations, a kind of original schizophrenia that denies the unitary nature even of the origin of consciousness (1977:67-99). If mind contemplating mind does not have a unified origin, analyzing interpretation, as a kind of understanding, splinters understanding all the more.

In understanding, a variety of operations intersect at a unitary point, a point that may move as elements behind the operations vary, but nevertheless a unitary point. But this unitary character conceals the complexity of the intersection. In contrast, analysis gives partial explanations of partial processes. Analytical methods neglect some elements and overemphasize others.[1] Therefore, interpretation as a kind of understanding is incomprehensible for two primary reasons: (1) the complexity proves insurmountable and (2) analytical methods fragment the point of intersection.

Is this a book that overcomes the awesome complexity and escapes the fragmentation of analysis? Would that it were! Alas, it is largely analytical. How, in light of the complexity of interpretation and the shattering of the point of intersection by analysis, is it defensible? Ultimately it is not. But penultimately analysis has its merits. Even partial understanding of partial processes enables us to critique interpretations. Checking one interpretation against another analytically can be a step toward richer discernment. Further, critiques enable us to evaluate interpretation. Every interpretation is a "metatext," that is, a text about a text. The basic criterion for the value of an interpretation is that the metatext have a convincing correspondence to the text (Ingarden 1973:241, 337, 383, 386-90). In that sense, interpretation possesses a self-authenticating quality.

Does this claim for a criterion of self-authenticating correspondence to the text render any further word senseless? On the basis of such a criterion Augustine's allegory of the Good Samaritan (Luke 10:29-37) might appear to carry a convincing correspondence to the text. For Augustine, the man who goes down from Jerusalem to Jericho is Adam who falls into sin when the thieves, that is the devil and his angels, attack, and who is saved by the Samaritan, none other than Jesus. But Augustine's allegory lacks the power of convincing correspondence to the text because it substitutes a secondary text for the original. By switching allegedly equivalent items, allegory transforms the text. The same is true for all "spiritual" interpretations. They do not correspond to the text because they rewrite it.[2]

What may come as a surprise to biblical interpreters schooled in historical critical methodology is that source criticism, form criticism, and redaction criticism often also rewrite the text. The two-document hypothesis partitions Luke into special L, Mark, and Q. Form criticism isolates individual units of tradition and understands them against an ecclesiastical and sociological context rather than within their literary context. Redaction criticism distinguishes between tradition and redaction, only the latter, allegedly, being fully Lucan. Further, today interest in reconstructing historical events, particularly those depicted in Acts, is reviving (Hengel 1980, Luedemann 1988: 109-125). Although historical critical methods may offer indispensable contributions to interpretation, interpretation they are not, inasmuch as they substitute a secondary text for the original.

To return my defense of this, another analytical book—approaching a text with a wide variety of methods can compensate for the partial understandings of partial processes deriving from isolated analytical methods (Ingarden 1973:356). It is true that method and world view are inextricable (McKnight 1988: 55), and inasmuch as some world views are incompatible, so are some of the methods that grow out of them. But even if methods have limited validity, they may complement each other, and the complementarity helps to offset the problem of complexity in interpretation.

Furthermore, analysis, for all its fragmentation, can be part of a synthesis. Human beings not only differentiate but integrate as well. Integration is, after all, the unitary point of intersection which is understanding.[3] Synthesis draws estranged analytical fragments back together like train rails merging into a point in the distance. But we can arrive at the unitary point of intersection more or less informed with more or less internal consistency. Employing wide-ranging methods is a part of the attempt to be more informed. In addition, to integrate the results of analysis into a unitary point of intersection is also a part of the attempt to be coherent, that is, to produce a metatext that is self-authenticating by virtue of its genuine correspondence to the text. To interpret Luke-Acts, according to the aspirations of this book, is to come to an informed, coherent understanding (Hayes and Holladay 1982:112).

## COMPLEXITY IN INTERPRETATION

Interpretation demands notoriously complicated mental procedures, although even children accomplish many of them with astounding ease.

To illustrate, it is difficult to produce computers with the capacity to decipher oral speech. Meaning sometimes rests on minute variations in pronunciation that are difficult for a computer to catch. A computer finds it troublesome to differentiate "recognize speech" from "wreck a nice peach." Or ambiguities inhere in language. The simple words "time beats" can be construed in two distinct ways. If time is a noun and beats is a verb, then the sentence means something like "time pulsates." But if time is a verb in the imperative and beats is a noun in the objective case, then it is a command (perhaps instructions to a nurse taking a pulse).[4] With longer, more complicated texts, the task assumes astronomical proportions. But that is little cause to despair, because anyone reading, comprehending, and reflecting on this paragraph is already engaged in these complicated operations.

There is, however, a tendency in some circles to assume that biblical interpretation avoids conundrums. Because of its alleged simplicity, some readers of the Bible casually dismiss additional information. In a Bible study in a Presbyterian church a participant suggested that Josephus relates incidents about Theudas and Judas that may add to the understanding of Acts 5:36-37. A county medical examiner objected, "Josephus is a notorious liar." Most of us would probably expect a county medical examiner to weigh evidence even if it does come from a notorious liar. In like manner, should not readers of the Bible weigh evidence rather than summarily dismissing it?

On another level some interpreters reject secondary information as irrelevant. Kenneth R. R. Gros Louis argues, for example, that a literary approach to the Bible means placing emphasis on the text itself rather than on such things as historical backgrounds (1982:14-15). Importing extra-textual information rewrites the text and misplaces the emphasis, a fallacy against which I have just argued. But information from Theudas and Judas in Josephus may correspond to information in the repertoire upon which Luke-Acts draws, in the same way that stories of the Hebrew patriarchs form a part of the repertoire. In this regard the problem lies not in using extra-textual information but in importing *irrelevant* extra-textual information.[5]

The problem of the "intentional fallacy" is quite similar. It grows out of the conviction that the interpreter must understand the mind of the author lying behind the text. This falsifies interpretation in that external intentions have no existence in the text. One could not assume, therefore, that the Lucan portrait of Paul grows out of the author's personal relationships with Paul. On the other hand, the intentions of the narrator inscribed in the text are vital for interpretation (Ingarden 1973: 349-50).[6]

Another obstacle to interpretation is reliance upon traditional, cultural interpretations. When there was a liquor-by-the-drink referendum in a county in Tennessee, some churches made contributions to finance lobbying against it. The state ruled that they were political action committees, and that as such they would have to reveal the identities of the contributors. They balked and maintained that churches were exempt from laws regulating political action committees. A judge ruled against them. He claimed that the churches had become political action committees by overstepping the boundary between church and state. Further, he argued that the churches should understand because Jesus said, "Render to Caesar the things that are Caesar's and to God the things that are God's."

According to a southern tradition, this text supports the separation of church and state. In Luke, however, a literary framing device characterizes Jesus' opponents (Luke 20:20 & 26). They are spies and insincere. They wish to catch him in a compromising position worthy of arrest (20:20). But Jesus turns the question back on the opponents and challenges them to make their own decision about paying tribute to Caesar. Far from teaching separation of church and state, the text leaves the question of what belongs to Caesar and to God disarmingly open, and the incident reveals Jesus' perspicuity (20:26). Here relying on tradition is a simplification that interpretation with a genuine correspondence to the text can ill afford.

Far more subtle, but equally detrimental, are interpretations distorted by the structures of power that legitimate oppression on the basis of their exegesis. Biblical interpretation often serves the dominant society against the marginalized. Even the translators of the King James Version were in service to a king.

This concealed agenda has led to a modern hermeneutics of suspicion, that is, suspicion of vested interests behind interpretation (Brown 1984:13, Fiorenza 1983:6-36, González and González 1980:11-18). According to conventional understanding, Jesus' admonitions to turn the other cheek and not to withhold the undergarment from one demanding the outergarment (Luke 6:29) are actions of submissive acquiescence to the power structure as a sign of reliance upon God (Danker 1988:145). Quite a different meaning emerges, however, when these texts come under the suspicion of the disenfranchised who find a third way that neither submits to nor assaults the power structure—a subversive assertiveness that robs the oppressive powers of their initiative (Wink 1988:210-224).[7]

The previous section established that the goal of interpretation in this book is an informed, coherent understanding. Even the "an" in that formulation is important. Modern linguistics has shown that language inherently stimulates a plurality of understandings. Both ways of construing "time beats" in the illustration above have a genuine correspondence to the text, and neither is a superior or more correct reading.

Moreover, all texts contain indeterminacies. For example, in the parable of the prodigal son, the text does not report the Jewish cultural norm against feeding swine. Such gaps allow interpreters to fill in texts with multiple meanings (Ingarden 1973: 50-54, 241, 298-99, 354-55, 368, 374-75, 386-87).

Further, working with the Greek often increases ambiguity because translations choose from a variety of possible meanings. To take a simple case, when Mary and Joseph find the twelve year old Jesus in the temple, he asks them: *ouk êdeite hoti en tois tou patros mou dei einai me?* (Luke 2:49). In this question the referent of the word *tois* is uncertain. It could mean: (1) "the affairs of my Father"; (2) "the people of my Father"; or (3) "the house of my Father" (Fitzmyer 1981:443-44).[8] English translations make a choice and reduce the plurality of meanings. The conspicuous ambiguity in this text is but a miniature of the multiplicity of meanings evoked by the whole of Luke-Acts. Therefore, the goal of interpretation in this book is *an* informed, coherent understanding.

For all the complexity of interpretation, texts are composites of elements that analysis can name with a degree of precision, if not finality. According to Roland Barthes, texts are woven out of at least five voices, and it is in the plurality of the possibilities of integrating these voices into a unitary point of intersection that varieties of interpretation have their origin.

Barthes's names for the voices may be as imposing as they are stimulating: (1) *the hermeneutic voice*, (2) *the voice of semes*, (3) *the proairetic voice*, (4) *the cultural voice*, and (5) *the symbolic voice* (Barthes 1974:17-18, see Martin 1986:163-64). The remaining chapters of this book appropriate Barthes's five voices as categories for the analysis of Luke-Acts. Such a strategy warrants further introduction.

(1) *The hermeneutic\* voice* consists of the elements of the text that formulate a question and its responses. This voice also includes the variety of events which either formulate the question, delay its answer, or constitute an enigma, and lead to its resolution.

At the beginning of Acts the risen Jesus speaks of ". . . the promise of the Father which you heard from me" (Acts 1:4). A question arises: "Which promise?" This part of the hermeneutic voice reaches both back into Luke and forward to the future fulfillment of the promise in Acts. Conventional interpretations

---

\* "Hermeneutic" here is a technical term referring to what is true in the literary world. The use in this sense is quite distinct from the meaning of "hermeneutical" elsewhere as a reference to the process of appropriating the meaning of a text.

have taken Acts 1:5 as the content of the promise, which, according to 1:4, Jesus has declared unto his disciples. This implies that Luke has taken a saying of John the Baptist (Luke 3:16), reformulated it, and placed it on the lips of Jesus (Haenchen 1971:141-42, cf. 142, n. 2).

But Robert Tannehill gives a refreshingly new appraisal. The phrase ". . . which you heard from me . . ." in 1:4 employs the aorist tense and is Jesus' documentation of his own previous words rather than a reference to what is to follow in 1:5. This means that rather than quoting his own words in 1:5, Jesus picks up the theme of the superiority of baptism with the Holy Spirit over John's baptism from Luke 3:16. The aorist in Acts 1:4 then stretches back to Jesus' promise in Luke 11:13: "If you then, who are evil, know how to give good gifts to your children, how much more will the heavenly Father give the Holy Spirit to those who ask him" (Tannehill 1990:12, Pesch 1986: 1.66-67, Schneider 1980:200).

There is still mystery about the promise, however, because it is yet to be fulfilled. Therefore, the hermeneutic voice extends forward. It is picked up quickly in Acts 1:8 where Jesus attaches power for witness to the coming of the Spirit. Because, however, the plot development in Acts discloses witness to the ends of the earth only partially, this trajectory never reaches its complete resolution. But given that it does attain an assured degree of partial disclosure, the witness to the ends of the earth extends beyond the end of Acts—in the jargon of literary criticism, ✓ an external "prolepsis," that is, a foreshadowing that anticipates fulfillment beyond the end of the literary work.[9]

(2) A seme is a unit of a signifier (a minimal element of a *semeion*, a sign). Of course everything in a literary work signifies, but for Barthes, *the voice of semes* has to do particularly with characters, that is, persons as signifiers. The voice of semes is the combination of individual elements that coalesce into a character. The repeated combination of appropriate semes such as emotions, personal traits, and thoughts under a proper name creates a character. The character is then a signifier, a carrier of meaning, the combination of the units of signification; or rather,

the character is the signified—what the semes signify for the reader (Barthes 1974:190).

Barthes derived his categories from modern fiction. Modern literature portrays characters from the perspective of their internal conflicts, and such characters do not exist in the literature of antiquity (cf. Auerbach 1953). For the study of Luke-Acts, therefore, Barthes's categories require some emendation. In Luke-Acts units of information, action, traits, and evaluation coalesce to create characters.[10] Significantly, for Luke-Acts, God is a character—the most important at that—an interplay of information, actions, traits, and evaluations.[11] Jesus, Peter, and Paul are the other dominant characters.

(3) Perhaps initially intimidating, "proairetic" derives from Greek for "course of action." In reference to *the proairetic voice* Barthes also uses the terms "empirics," "actions," and "behavior." That is, it is the network of actions tied together by cause and effect. Any reader who is aware may note that the previous paragraph names action as one of the semes for characterization. Furthermore, action is implicated in the hermeneutic voice (Barthes 1974:62).

The actions of the witnesses in Acts partially realize Jesus' prediction in Acts 1:8. But the proairetic voice has to do with actions in a causal nexus that can be subsumed under generic titles for actions (e.g., Paul's conversion). Both Luke and Acts can be episodic. Relatively independent incidents may be juxtaposed by themes or catchwords. Themes of proper use of possessions structure Luke 16, and the catchword "mammon" ties 16:9 to 16:10-13 (Talbert 1982:153). On the other hand, Acts 3:1-5:42 contains a chain of events linked together causally in a proairetic sequence. The encounter of Peter and John with a lame man leads to his healing, providing opportunity for proclamation, provoking opposition, providing opportunity for proclamation, bringing the proclaimers under threats, and so forth (Tannehill 1990:48-79). The proairetic voice has to do with actions in sequence and the behavior that causes or results from these actions.

(4) Barthes also uses the "voice of science" and "reference codes" as synonyms for *the cultural voice*. This is the repertoire

of knowledge upon which the text draws. This can be the ordinary presuppositions of everyday experience, such as the implicit antipathy between Jews and Samaritans in the parable of the good Samaritan (Luke 10:30-35), or allusions to the scriptures or to Greek poets (Acts 17:28). The cultural voice consists of the proverbial (Barthes 1974:100).

(5) *The symbolic voice* develops out of antitheses. This voice focuses on mediation between antitheses. In the magnificat, because of the promise attached to the fruit of Mary's womb, her low estate stands over against her blessedness, the mighty God opposes mighty rulers, the hungry are set in contrast to the rich (Luke 1:42-55). Similarly, after the birth of Jesus, Simeon announces that the child is set for the fall and rising of many in Israel (2:34). Mary and the child mediate the antipodes. Jesus himself stands in between the oppositions like a double sided mirror reflecting each extreme of the antitheses.[12] In fact, Luke 2:34 explicitly designates Jesus a *sêmeion antilegomenon*—a sign that is opposed. Mediation developing out of antitheses are utterances of the symbolic voice.

These five voices are a part of the network of complexity that constitutes a text, and, therefore, they are also a part of the plurality that constitutes understanding. A skeptic could demur that the number five is quite finite even if it does allow for a wide variety of combinations. But the complexity of interpretation ranges far beyond the exponential possibilities. Because of the complexity and the reader's subjectivity, some elements may lack complete definition, while others may dominate disproportionately. Thus, as the balance of the elements from the five voices changes, the unitary point of intersection, which is interpretation, may slide along an infinite number of points.

To compound the problem, additional factors make understanding even more labyrinthine. One is the point of view. The voices are not naked but clothed with perspective—that of a narrator or character. Point of view, however, has its own complexity. In a seminal work on the subject, Boris Uspensky details five levels: (1) ideological, (2) phraseological, (3) spatial, (4) temporal, and (5) psychological (1973).[13]

(1) There are in texts ideological points of view that evaluate the literary world, its aspects, and its characters—a further complicating factor in that narrators and characters may represent conflicting points of view. Acts 19:26 demonstrates such a complicating factor. Demetrius the silversmith accuses Paul of turning people away from the veneration of Artemis and claims that Paul has said ". . . that gods made with hands are not gods." Here there are two evaluative points of view with respect to Paul. Demetrius is an opponent, the narrator views Paul positively. Therefore, is Demetrius's saying accurate? In Acts 17:24 Paul has said that God does not live in shrines made by hands. Thus, that Paul opposes belief in idols appears accurate enough. Is Demetrius also accurate in his claim that Paul has dissuaded a considerable crowd of devotees? With intricate interweavings of points of view, even a character who opposes the narrator ideologically may unwittingly express the truth from the narrator's perspective.[14]

(2) There is inference of point of view in phraseology. Although characters and the narrator apply the title "Lord" to Jesus from quite different perspectives, opponents never use it to address Jesus. Thus the phraseology indicates point of view, and even when the narrator uses it, it reflects a special relationship with Jesus.

(3 & 4) At the beginning of Luke, there is a self-referential intrusion of the narrator. This differentiates the narrator from the events of the narrative. The point of view is retrospective. The narrator stands distanced from the events by a line of tradition coming from eyewitnesses and ministers of the word, and the narrator stands outside and beyond the characters and events of the story both temporally and spatially (Luke 1:1-4). Thereafter, the narrator forsakes the intrusion, with the exception of the prologue to Acts, and becomes, in literary terms, omniscient. The narrator is able to move spatially from the account of Elizabeth's pregnancy in the hill country of Judah to the simultaneous annunciation of Gabriel to Mary in Nazareth (Luke 1:24-38). The narrator can also anticipate future events out of sequence, thereby revealing a temporal omniscience. In

the transfiguration, Moses and Elijah confer with Jesus about his "departure" which he is to accomplish at Jerusalem.

(5) Uspensky uses the term "psychological" to refer to the relationship of the point of view to a character. If the narrator portrays a character and the character's actions from an external perspective, then the point of view is objective. A subjective view is internal to the character. In Acts 10 the narrator first relates the conversion of Cornelius as an observer external to Peter. In the following chapter there is an essential difference in that Peter's words grant access to his interior. And so, according to Peter's own account, he objected to the voice in the vision, ". . . nothing common or unclean has ever entered my mouth" (11:8). According to the narrator's account Peter protested, "I have never eaten anything that is common or unclean" (10:14). The shift in point of view toward Peter's interior leads the reader to deduce that Peter's own words convey what was actually spoken whereas the first account represents the narrator's close equivalent. A similar but more involved case occurs with the narrator's version of Paul's call in Acts 9 (external) and Paul's own accounts in Acts 22 and 26 (internal).

To trace the intricacies of texts one step further, there is an intimate link between the point of view and reliability. The discussion above of the case of Demetrius the silversmith in Acts 19 has already raised the issue of credibility. Unreliable narrators and characters may convey untrustworthy information. But there is no direct equivalent between unreliability and inaccuracies. Rather, the degree of reliability throws the reader into a range of possibilities for the degree of certainty.

According to Robert Alter's hierarchy of the degree of certainty, the actions of a character alone leave the reader in the realm of inference, direct speech from characters allows the reader to judge their claims, interior speech leads to relative certainty, and a reliable narrator's explicit statements imply the highest level of certainty (Alter 1981:117).

For Luke-Acts, however, there is one emendation of Alter's hierarchy. Divine speech reported by a reliable narrator or character conveys the highest level of certainty. To illustrate, Acts 4:36-37 relates Barnabas's action—he sold a field and brought the proceeds to the apostles for distribution according to need. The action stands on its own for the reader to infer what the reader can or will. Or to take another case, in the temptation of Jesus, because the devil is an unreliable character, even the citation of scripture is duplicitous (Luke 4:1-13).

By now my case for complexity has itself taken on an air of complexity. The multiplicity of meanings in an ambiguous term is but a microcosm of the plurality in texts. But beyond ambiguity, this discussion has spelled out five voices that constitute texts. It has added five levels of point of view and five levels of reliability that progressively complicate the problems of interpretation. This kind of complexity stands guard over analytical methods as a watch dog against overemphasizing the partial results of analysis and calls for an ultimate synthesis into an informed, coherent interpretation.

My procedure is to analyze each voice separately. In so doing, I violate Barthes's method. He cautions that the plurality in a text implies a gradual analysis that constantly interweaves the plurality of the voices (Barthes 1974:11-13). I take a further analytical step in that I abstract the voices in order to associate a variety of interpretive methods with them. I do so only with the ultimate expectation of a genuine synthesis—an interweaving of the voices. (See chapter 9.)

## APPROPRIATING MEANING

Luke 1:4 makes an astonishing declaration: ". . . that you may know the certainty concerning the things about which you have been informed." With this introduction Luke-Acts announces not only that it is an accurate narrative, but that it offers access to the truth. Not the truth of scientific propositions—Luke-Acts makes very few direct assertions open to the judgment "true or false." Perhaps ". . . the Most High does not dwell in houses made with hands" (Acts 7:48, cf. 17:24) qualifies, but hardly "Blessed are you poor, for yours is the kingdom of God" (Luke 6:20). Rather, the narrative offers a view of the world for which it makes a truth claim.

✓Roman Ingarden distinguishes between apprehension of literary works of art and scientific works (1973:149-62, 360).

Scientific works make assertions about reality independent of the work. To illustrate, all interpretations of the Bible (including this one) belong to the scientific category because they make assertions about a reality (the biblical text) outside the interpretation itself. In contrast, literary works of art portray a presumed reality, a fictive world. The fictive world is self-contained and can even conflict with the outside world. In fairy tales bears, pigs, goats, and wolves speak our language. Readers may actually forsake their own view of reality temporarily in order to participate in the fictive world of the literary work.

But Ingarden's alternatives fail to account adequately for Luke-Acts. On the one hand, Luke-Acts rarely makes assertions in Ingarden's scientific category. Moreover, Luke-Acts is narrative, and narrative portrays a literary world like Ingarden's literary work of art. On the other hand, whereas Ingarden's literary work of art portrays a world that is self-contained, independent of external reality, Luke-Acts claims to represent a world of reality outside and beyond the text. Initially the claim is that the narrative grants access to the truth ("certainty," Luke 1:1-4). This has led to attempts to evaluate Luke-Acts with the criteria of history, that is, as if it were in Ingarden's scientific category. The issue for Luke-Acts, however, is not merely the accuracy of an account of events, but the relationship of the events to divine reality beyond the ordinary categories of history. And so in Ingarden's classification Luke-Acts is a hybrid. Like a literary work of art it portrays a literary world. But beyond a literary work of art, it claims that its literary world corresponds to authentic reality.[15]

Appropriating meaning in the case of Luke-Acts involves a clash of worlds. The world of the text comes into conjunction with the interpreter's construct of the world. Each has its own way of organizing experience, which would otherwise be chaotic, into a system of meaning (Funk 1988:286-99).

The limits of such a system of understanding comprise what Hans-Georg Gadamer calls a horizon. In the appropriation of meaning the horizon of the text breaks into the horizon of the interpreter's world. Equally, the horizon of the interpreter's world breaks into the horizon of the text. The world of the text takes its shape for the interpreter in terms of the interpreter's world. But the world of the text also challenges the interpreter's construct of the world so that there is a fusion of horizons (1975:269-73). Part of the problem of appropriating meaning, then, is, to borrow from Robert McAfee Brown: Dare we venture ". . . the initially bizarre gamble that 'the strange new world within the Bible' is a more accurate view of the world than our own"? (Brown 1984:13, cf. Auerbach 1953:15). Luke-Acts is profoundly theological. The divine plan dominates the personages and events of Luke-Acts. Does such a view of the world demand that we adjust our construct of reality?

To repeat an earlier argument, interpretation has a self-authenticating character by virtue of correspondence to the text. With appropriation, there is another correspondence, although it is less self-authenticating. In the case of interpretation the correspondence is capable of verification by comparison to an established text. In the case of appropriation, the correspondence is to one's own understanding of existence, ambiguities and all. To test the correspondence between the world of the text and our own construct of reality is an existential matter, a decision of faith, hardly subject to external verification. But if Luke-Acts is preeminently theological, and if it portrays a world under divine sovereignty, then correspondence logically prescribes that the methods of appropriation be theocentric and world-encompassing.

Unhappily, some popular hermeneutical methods are neither. Nineteenth century liberalism attempted to derive general truth from the Bible. Because it was striving for universal truth, it may have created the illusion that the truth was world-encompassing. But general truth surprisingly can have little to do with concrete existence. Some indigenous people of Latin America, who still live quite primitively, now know the formula $E=mc^2$.

In addition, the general truth of nineteenth century liberalism could get on well without serious theological attachments. ✓Adolf Jülicher interpreted the good Samaritan as teaching that self-sacrificing love without regard to status and birth is of the highest value in the eyes of God and human beings (1910: 2.596). Such interpretation lacks any compelling identification

with the Jewish traveler who fell among thieves and who perhaps would rather die than be the object of a hated Samaritan's
compassion. Similarly, Jülicher's interpretation fails to confront
the reader with the radical reversal of world under the rule of
God (Crossan 1973:62-66). In this case the methods of appropriation are neither theocentric nor world-encompassing.

Surprisingly, many at the conservative end of the spectrum
have fared little better and in many ways have shared the same
agenda. Their concern for biblical "principles," that is, a kind of
universal truth, aligns them closely with the general truth of
nineteenth century liberalism (Barr 1980:76).

As a case in point, when a federal grand jury indicted television evangelist Jim Bakker for soliciting funds for one purpose
and diverting them for personal use, columnist Cal Thomas,
who designates himself a born again Christian, tried his hand at
appropriating meaning from the Bible. Thomas argued that
according to biblical principles, the proper penalty for Bakker
was restitution. He found the principle of restitution in the story
of Zacchaeus: ". . . if I have defrauded any one of anything, I
restore it fourfold" (Luke 19:8) (1988). But abstracting such a
principle from the narrative neglects that Jesus includes Zacchaeus in the people of God on the basis of his repentance
whereas the crowd implies that Jesus ought to exclude him on
the basis of his status as a sinner. Moreover, Thomas's principle
has to do with one aspect of life—what to do in the case of
fraud. And other than perhaps viewing God as the originator of
the principle, Thomas's appropriation of the text gives God
short shrift. Thus, mining "principles" from the text is neither
theocentric nor world-encompassing.

Another impediment to theocentric, world-encompassing
appropriation of meaning is a popular appetite for biblical
characters as role models. In a blatantly crass case of role model
hermeneutics, Christus Gardens in the resort area of Gatlinburg,
Tennessee, periodically picks an All-Bible football team—it is
difficult to miss the parody on All-America selections. Some of
the 1988 picks include Joshua, who was a talented field general, at quarterback; Paul, who could cover ground as a missionary, at running back; and John the Baptist, who showed his

abilities to block in preparing the way for Jesus, at fullback. Of course Christus Gardens operates for profit, but general manager Joe E. Waggoner says that it seriously attempts to call attention to some of the special qualities of characters in the Bible (Dunning 1988). For role model hermeneutics that appears to be warrant enough. But it is clear that the interest is only in some of *our* values supposedly exemplified by the characters, and there is not as much as a hint of God. This kind of role model hermeneutics is neither theocentric nor world-encompassing.

Not only does role model hermeneutics hold up heroes as examples to emulate, it also frequently psychologizes the text. Psychologizing is to attribute motives to the characters where the text does not. It is almost proverbial to attribute Peter's confession of Jesus as the Christ to his observation of Jesus' mighty works. Luke provides no information about Peter's motivation (9:18-22). On the other hand, the text informs the reader that at the descent from the Mount of Olives a multitude of disciples acclaim Jesus the king who comes in the name of the Lord because of all the mighty works they had seen (19:37-38). Peter's motives are unavailable whereas the motives of the crowd are inscribed in the text.

In considering homiletical options on Acts 1:12-24, Charles Talbert suggests that the posture of the disciples waiting in prayer for empowerment for ministry can be exemplary of avoiding distractions and receiving power for modern ministry through prayer. Here Talbert takes the disciples as role models and therefore emphasizes an anthropocentric demand for human activity (prayer) (1984:8-9). In contrast, the events of the entire first two chapters of Acts emphasize divine initiative. The period of waiting and the coming of the Spirit at Pentecost are theocentric.

In a monograph on Paul's Miletus address (Acts 20:18-35) Lars Aejmelaeus contends that Paul appeals to himself as an example to emulate in a way comparable to imitation of Jesus (1987:87).[16] The elements of exhortation in Paul's speech are unmistakable,[17] but they are as subordinate as they are obvious. There are but three imperatives, and they are quite general: "Take heed . . . to care for the church of God" (20:28); ". . . be alert . . ." (20:31); and ". . . it is necessary to help the weak" 20:35). To be sure, in 20:35 Paul says specifically that he has modeled helping the weak through his own labor. But far more dominant is the defense of Paul's past. Not only does Paul's past dominate the first half of the speech, it continues to do so even when the verbs change to the imperative. The focus on the past corresponds to the rhetorical species "judicial"—rhetoric designed to persuade the audience to make judgments about the past (Kennedy 1984:19). What appears to be exhortation for the future actually serves to vindicate Paul's past. Rather than present Paul as a model to emulate, the speech vindicates him. But even if the speech appeals to Paul's exemplary behavior, it is quite theocentric. The theme of serving God pervades the address (20:19, 24, 27).

Clearly, there are cases where Luke-Acts makes characters role models. When Peter confesses that Jesus is God's Messiah (Luke 9:20), Jesus responds with a call for anyone to deny self, take up the cross daily, and to follow (9:23). Later in 18:28 Peter picks up the same theme: "We have left our homes and followed you." This time Jesus replies with a promise that those who have done so will receive much more both in the present and in the age to come. Peter and the twelve, then, are models for following Jesus. As noted in the previous paragraph, in Acts 20:35 Paul professes to have exemplified benevolence toward the weak. Further, when Paul defends himself before Agrippa, he makes himself an exemplary convert by saying, "I would to God that . . . all who hear me this day might become such as I am" (Acts 26:29).

These cases, however, are rare and limited. Luke-Acts implies little imitation of the characters as such—not even of Jesus. Following Jesus is something quite different from imitating his ethical behavior, though following certainly does mean identifying with him. Further, is some cases specific details exclude the reader from taking the characters as role models. For example, even though the twelve are examples of identifying with Jesus in his trials, only they will sit on twelve thrones judging the twelve tribes of Israel (Luke 22:28-30). Role model hermeneutics breaks down where the reader cannot expect a similar destiny. In addition, notices that focus on God enclose cases where the characters are models. The Lord has anointed Jesus as Spirit-filled Messiah and prophet for divine purposes that cover his entire ministry (Luke 4:16-30). Jesus' call to follow, then, always carries with it submission to the consummate plan of God. It is in this sense that Jesus proclaims that disciples when *fully* taught will be like their teacher.

In a comparable way, Acts makes Paul subservient to God (Acts 9:15; 13:2; 19:11). Additionally, Paul makes explicit statements that draw attention away from himself and refocus it on God. When the Lycaonians, impressed by the healing of a lame man, call Barnabas Zeus and Paul Hermes, the two confess to be human beings like the Lycaonians and issue a call to turn to the living God (14:8-18). Or when Paul and Barnabas return from a successful mission that includes Gentiles, they relate what God has done through them (15:4,12).

One might be able to speak of role model hermeneutics where the characters of Luke-Acts become examples of submitting their lives to divine purposes that would possess a self-authenticating correlation to the text. But such characters would no longer be anthropocentric role models. Rather, they would be models of God accompanying humanity, and the corresponding method of appropriating meaning would be theocentric and world-encompassing. Thus, characters are points where the reader can buy into the world of God in relation to humanity by identification.

If searching for general truth, biblical principles, and role models impedes an appropriation which corresponds to the text, what are the alternatives? One, not to exclude others, is analogy: that is, a kind of comparison between the theocentric world of Luke-Acts and our own construct of the world.

Analogy means first of all similarity—parallel, likeness, resemblance. But sooner or later analogies break down. That is, there is always some distinction between the members of an analogy. And so analogy also means distinction—contrast, difference, antithesis. Appropriating meaning by way of analogy means that the comparison between the theocentric world of

Luke-Acts and our own view of the world convinces us that there is a resonance between the two. But the friction between them challenges us. The encounter of these two worlds forces the question: Dare we venture the initially bizarre gamble that the literary world of Luke-Acts makes demands upon us to alter our own?

To illustrate, the scandal of a crucified Messiah creates severe tension in Luke-Acts. The birth and infancy narratives carry heavy overtones of a nationalistic restoration of Israel. The angel Gabriel announces to Mary that her promised son, Jesus, will sit on the throne of David and rule over the house of Jacob forever (Luke 1:32-33). With that kind of promise in the foreground, Mary's exclamation that God has put down the mighty from their thrones (1:52) and Zechariah's inspired prophecy ". . . that we should be saved from our enemies" (1:71) strongly imply a political, nationalistic restoration. The same goes for the expectations of Simeon, who looks for the consolation of Israel, and of Anna, who is one of those looking for the redemption of Jerusalem (2:25, 38). But Jesus' claim to a ministry to the poor, captives, blind, and oppressed (4:18-21) nulls out the political overtones. The crucifixion is a final blow that devastates the hopes of Jesus' followers that he would be the Messiah (24:21).

Luke-Acts transforms this potential disconfirmation of messianism into its confirmation. The scriptures, properly interpreted, anticipate that the Messiah must suffer (Luke 24:26-27, 45-47). Further, the restoration of Israel is not political. Rather, it is the gathering of believers first under Jesus and then the twelve apostles (Lohfink 1975). The messianic expectations of the early chapters of Luke are fulfilled only by means of an ironic reinterpretation of the redemption of Israel (see Tiede 1988, and Moessner 1988a). Messianic restoration has to do with gathering the people of God, but not with reestablishing the nation.

It is relatively easy to detect some similarities and antitheses to modern life in the United States. A resurgence of religious nationalism has marked the decade of the 80s. Jerry Falwell once vowed to stay in politics until the United States became a

Christian nation. But an analogy with the theocentric world of Luke-Acts calls into question our religious nationalism. In a rather sobering way, however, at the moment that I make that judgment, I am sitting in a rather comfortable position. I am a client of a consumer economy where even middle class opulence and leisure outstrip the glories of the kingdom of David. And I remain a client of this consumer economy even though I know that, in spite of my own hard work, its structure rests on the backs of oppressed people, the type of people Jesus pledges to liberate in his messianic ministry. Rather than threaten my own advantages, I passively consent to the social structure, though this confession is at least hushed testimony to my encounter with the theocentric Lucan literary world.

This kind of hermeneutic, however, involves what James Sanders calls a "dynamic" analogy. The analogy side of his formulation assumes that there is something abiding about the divine reality of the Bible. We can expect encounters with God today to be similar to such encounters in the Bible. But the dynamic side means that God works in believing communities today ". . . to weave these texts to God's own purposes and truth" (1984:xvii, cf. xvii-xviii, 70-71). Dynamic analogy suggests that the appropriated meaning may be quite different as the conditions of the analogy vary.

For James Sanders, a major aspect of the dynamic analogy is identification with characters in biblical narrative. As a matter of honesty Sanders advocates identifying with all the characters in the narrative rather than with just the heroes. In the case of Jesus' parable of the good Samaritan, a reader appropriating meaning should identify with the priest and Levite as well as with the Samaritan and the man who fell among thieves. From the standpoint of a hermeneutics of suspicion, perhaps that reader should identify even with the thieves.

But does not James Sanders confuse two distinct methods of appropriation? Analogy is particularly appropriate for historical situations. For all its present ambiguities, we may expect the modern world to stand in relation to God in a way analogous to God's relation with the biblical world. But identification with characters is a way not of comparing but of buying into the portrayed world of the Bible. In *The Sound and the Fury*, when William Faulkner describes events through the eyes of the developmentally handicapped Benjy, the reader identifies with Benjy and experiences the sound and the fury coming not from the idiot, as in Shakespeare's *Macbeth*, but from the people of higher intelligence who present him with such a perplexing world. In a similar way readers can buy into the theocentric literary world of Luke-Acts by identifying with characters.

Jack Sanders's *The Jews in Luke-Acts* provides a case for illustration. His thesis is that Luke-Acts is anti-Semitic. He argues that there is a pernicious portrayal of Jewish authorities as those who rejected and crucified Jesus (1987:3-16). For him, Luke-Acts burdens the Jews with this guilt and retributively transfers divine salvation to the Gentiles. Granted, Luke-Acts has been used to sanction anti-Semitism. It is possible, however, for a modern reader to identify even with the opponents of Jesus, as James Sanders suggests, in such a way as to experience an exhortation to fidelity. The narrative of the last supper clearly designates Judas the betrayer before the meal (Luke 22:3-6). Nevertheless, Judas is with Jesus at the table (22:21-22). Modern readers who identify with Judas might sense deeply their own infidelities and answer yes to the question of the spiritual: "Were you there when they crucified my Lord?" Vulnerable as we are, we might identify with the opponents rather than bear malice toward them.

Beyond analogy and identification yet a third way of appropriating meaning is by extending the story to include us. The temporal frames of Luke-Acts limit its chronological range from the announcement of the birth of John the Baptist until Paul's preaching and teaching under house arrest in Rome. But Luke-Acts also sees itself as a segment of the larger divine plan stretching from Abraham to the parousia, if not from creation to the parousia.

Moreover, Acts ends with a sense both of closure and openness.[18] There is closure in that Paul has fulfilled his mission and the predictions that he would go to Jerusalem and Rome (Acts 19:21). Further, there is powerful finality to Paul's announcement that the rejection of his message by Jews warrants a Gentile mission (28:28). But there is also openness. Paul has not yet gone to trial. He is still preaching and teaching. Moreover, the witness to the ends of the earth (1:8) is still incomplete. And the promise of the parousia (1:11) awaits fulfillment. The ending of Acts faces the problem of the division among the Jews in Rome caused by Paul's proclamation of the gospel. There is a similar division during the ministry of Jesus, in the first half of Acts, and throughout Paul's ministry.

Thus, Luke-Acts projects toward the future so that by extension its story can include modern readers. The problem of Judaism in the face of the gospel may appear now not only as analogous, and not only as something in Paul's experience with which we may identify, but also as a part of the story from Abraham to the parousia of which we are a part. Similarly, Jesus' prediction of witness to the ends of the earth may extend to us as actors in an implied narrative. And when Luke-Acts predicts the parousia without realizing its fulfillment, by extension the story includes modern believers.

Such methods of appropriating meaning, by no means exhaustive, may nevertheless be effective for modern interpreters who encounter the theocentric literary world of Luke-Acts.

# 2

# PROGRESSIVE DISCOVERY: TRUTH IN THE NARRATIVE WORLD

Suspense pulls readers forward in narrative like the proverbial carrot before the horse. Readers make sense of narrative by anticipating the outcome and then constantly revising their expectations as the narrative unfolds. Narrative proceeds not so much by fulfilling anticipations as by modifying them (Iser 1974:278, Brook 1984:23). Suspense is usually achieved by foreshadowing even though foreshadowing may give away the ending. When foreshadowing and outright predictions make the ending a foregone conclusion, the narrative's enticement shifts from what will happen to how it will happen (Chatman 1978: 59, Rimmon-Kenan 1983:48). Components that contribute to the suspense by articulating questions and to the resolution of the suspense by formulating responses to the questions constitute what Roland Barthes calls the hermeneutic voice.

In moving toward its goal narrative does not follow a linear development as if to confirm that the shortest distance between two points is a straight line. Otherwise, it would achieve resolution prematurely, and the goal would rob the narrative of its sense of dynamic progression. Therefore, delay in moving toward resolution is also part of literary anticipation. Narrative paradoxically moves toward its solution and yet delays it (Barthes 1974:75). The hidden identity of the risen Jesus on the road to Emmaus is an essential part of creating expectation and desire for his recognition (Luke 24:16).

Erich Auerbach demurs that digression does not increase suspense but prevents the reader from concentrating too heavily on a crisis in order to keep the suspense from being overwhelming (Auerbach 1953:4-11). But Auerbach ignores the reader's Nietzschian "will to power." We seek to dominate the text by knowing how the text orchestrates our most urgent impasses and gropings (Wilder 1983:353-64), a desire spurred on by delay.

Moreover, the story simply cannot continue once it arrives at its resolution, and delay is a strategy to stimulate the reader's interest without arriving at an untimely end. Barthes analyzes five specific strategies of delay: (1) evasion of truth (a "snare"), (2) equivocation (a mixture of truth and evasion), (3) partial answer, (4) suspended answer (the process of disclosure stops), and (5) jamming (acknowledgement of the insolubility of a problem) (1974:75-76).

To illustrate, Jesus' prediction in Luke 9:44 foreshadows the passion, and in 9:51 Jesus sets his face to go to Jerusalem. But the central section of Luke portrays Jesus as itinerating without arriving at the goal until 19:45. This is a suspended movement toward a goal. To employ a technological metaphor, Jerusalem and the passion are still on the line, but they are on hold for a long time.

Texts are also pocked with gaps. Intentionally or unintentionally narratives do not supply all the information necessary for them to be understood. The parable of the good Samaritan does not specify that the man who falls among thieves is a Jew, and it says nothing about the animosity between Jews and Samaritans. But the coherence of the text provides some clues to fill in these gaps (Iser 1974:38, Rimmon-Kenan 1983:123-28). That is, Jesus narrates from a Jewish point of view that assumes the Jewishness of a personage unless otherwise indicated. And even if the reader knows nothing of the conflict between Jews and Samaritans, Jesus' remarks about the grateful Samaritan ("this foreigner") whose leprosy is cleansed in Luke 17:16-19 point to nationalistic antipathy.

Not only do delays and gaps restrict linear development, but narration does not always follow chronological order. Some points of Gérard Genette's discussion of anachronies in narrative have significance for understanding the revision of anticipations (1980:35-83).

Genette analyzes foreshadowing (prolepsis) and retrospection (analepsis), preview and review in narratives. External analepses supply information prior to the temporal limits of the story. Jesus provides an external analepsis in Luke 11:51 when he speaks of the blood of all the prophets from Abel to Zechariah. Internal analepses allude back to something within the time frame of the narrative. A completing internal analepsis fills in an earlier gap within the narrative. To give a case in point, in Acts 22:17-21 Paul relates a vision in the temple in which the Lord told him to leave Jerusalem and to go to the Gentiles. But at the corresponding point in Acts 9 there is no mention of such a vision in the temple. A mixed (internal and external) analepsis begins within the narrative time and extends to a time antecedent to the story.

Prolepses can likewise be internal or external or mixed. Acts 1:8 is a mixed prolepsis in that the mission it anticipates is inaugurated in Acts but extends beyond the end of Acts. There are also completing prolepses, anticipations of events not described in the narrative such as the parousia.

But even if the resolution of foreshadowing does not follow a linear chronology, it is syntagmatic. That is, it follows an irreversible order logically and temporally (Barthes 1974:30, cf. Ingarden 1973:94-95). Questions arise and are settled in logical and temporal networks so that reading is a process of progressive discovery (Iser 1978:222). This dictates that the progressive discovery is quite distinct from Genette's category of "story," which is essentially the plot.

For Genette the story is the narrated events abstracted and reconstructed in chronological order (1980:27 and passim, cf. Rimmon-Kenan 1983:3). But progressive discovery follows the sequential order of the text. Thus, it is a prospective rather than a retrospective reading, a reading having to do with suspense and mystery (Culler 1975:210).

In the Cornelius incident, for example, Peter is perplexed about the meaning of: "What God has cleansed, you must not call common" (Acts 10:15). His own confusion raises a hermeneutic question for the reader about what is problematic. Peter informs Cornelius that it is unlawful for a Jew to associate with a Gentile (10:28). But not until 11:3 does the reader discover that the circumcision party objects to Peter's table fellowship with Gentiles. In the first account of events in Cornelius's house in Acts 10 the narrator makes no mention of table fellowship. Thus, a completing internal analepsis fills in an earlier gap (cf. Genette 1980:51). When the reader maps out the plot, the table fellowship comes in a proper chronological order. But in the progressive discovery, it follows the irreversible order of the text. The text holds the answer in abeyance until the resolution in 11:3.

## GENRE

The first constraint that qualifies interpretation is genre (Kermode 1979:18). Literary works raise an immediate question for the reader: What kind of literature am I reading? So, part of the progressive discovery is the question of genre. Meaningful communication is possible because literature is a communal convention (Fish 1980:10). That is to say, out of the history of literature interpretive communities share assumptions about how writing and interpreting texts takes place, or as Wayne Booth puts it, genre is shared grooves or tracks that direct interpretation (1974:100). But the strategy for reading a poem varies significantly from the strategy for interpreting a scientific treatise.

Further, genre itself is a matter of interpretation (Fish 1980:164-71, 265). How does the reader discern whether a text is a poem or a scientific treatise? During the death of God controversy in 1966, *Christian Century* published a satire entitled "Sex Is Dead!" (Brill 1966:957-59). It implied that God is no more dead than sex. But letters to the editor showed that many readers took it at face value. The genre is not given as an objective set of formal features. Rather, the reader is already interpreting in trying to decide the genre of the text.

Discerning the genre is a question of the relationship of the old and the new. Literary works repeat typical elements and therefore manifest an affinity to an archetype. But variations also transform the genre (Iser 1974:34, 288, Kort 1988:99-100, Kawin 1972:7, 94, Damrosch:1987:2). Percy Bysshe Shelly makes the point when he claims that poetry "creates anew the universe, after it has been annihilated in our minds by the recurrence of impressions blunted by reiteration" (quoted by Frye 1972:129). Repetition of the old is also part of shared presuppositions, and, for this reason, genre crops up again in chapter 7. But the way in which the reader raises and resolves the question of genre pertains to the progressive discovery of what is true in the narrative world.

The inscribed author of Luke-Acts identifies his work as a *diêgêsis* ("account," "narrative," Luke 1:1). The *diêgêsis* concerns happenings that have come down to him from eyewitnesses and ministers of the word—tradition that has stood up to the inscribed author's investigation. How does this answer the reader's question: What kind of literature am I reading? Modern historical consciousness provided a climate for a communal convention to regard Luke-Acts as hellenistic historiography. And the notion that history gives a descriptive account led to reading Luke-Acts as a bank of data about events. Thus, judgments about Luke-Acts revolved around historical reliability, and historical events became the focus for interpretation.

## THE LITERARY WORLD

Are such phenomena the proper focus for the interpreter? Paul Ricoeur has a provocative thesis that indicates that they are not. Ricoeur classifies biblical texts as poetic. He does so (1) in order to make the point that their primary reference is not to objectively described phenomena; he also does so (2) in order to recover a non-descriptive reference to the world.

For Ricoeur, a text unfolds a world. That world is the reference of the literary work, not the author's intention nor the structures of the text, but that about which a text speaks. Moreover, human beings participate in their world not by cognitive descriptions of phenomena but through other quite distinct referential functions of language. A literary work is referential not by virtue of factual descriptions but by virtue of the world it creates. Thus, poetic texts give readers access to an order of things in which they participate. In this sense biblical texts propose a world, a world of God in relation to human beings, a world that cannot be reduced to descriptive knowledge. Rather, the world of God in relation to human beings comes to expression through models that produce figures of God accompanying humanity.[1]

There is a measure of the world coming to expression in models even in scientific descriptive language. Physics uses the model of wave motion to describe certain phenomena of light. If the world of the behavior of light comes to expression through the model of a wave, how much more will the world of God in relation to human beings comes to expression through models?

Is the narrative world of Luke-Acts such a model? There is some evidence in the preface to Luke that it is. (1) The preface does not isolate events themselves as objects of interest but makes the events a part of the *diêgêsis*. (2) The preface makes a subtle distinction between the things Theophilus has been taught and certainty concerning those things. (3) The preface correlates the orderly account and the certainty promised to Theophilus. Further, the term *kathexês* ("orderly")in Luke 1:3 has a close parallel in Acts 11:4 where it likewise refers to the technique of narration.[2] In Acts 11 Peter's narration of events in the house of Cornelius in order (*kathexês*) is neither chronological nor complete, as comparison with Acts 10 shows. Rather, Peter creates a narrative world in which he invites his detractors to participate. When they do, they adopt a new construct of world and agree with Peter. Similarly, the preface to Luke anticipates the production of a narrative world that will offer certainty to readers.

The preface itself is completely atheological. It offers no hint that it anticipates a world of God in relation to humanity. But Luke 1 quickly fills that gap when a messenger sent from God gives Zechariah a promise and delivers an oracle. Moreover, the claim in Acts 2:16-21 that God has poured out the Spirit is the hermeneutical key to all prophecy, visions, signs, and wonders of Jesus (cf. 2:22) and of the disciples (3:1-12; 4:16). They are all theocentric. Therefore, in Luke-Acts the world of God in relation to humanity comes to expression, as Ricoeur says, in a model that produces figures of God accompanying humanity.

A further indication of this is that for Luke-Acts it is quite inadequate to give a descriptive account of the resurrection of Jesus as if it were a mere datum of history. Rather, the resurrection of Jesus is a part of the world created by the text in which God stands in relation to humanity. And so repeatedly Acts breaks out of the limits of scientific description by testifying that *God* raised Jesus from the dead.

To illustrate the progressive discovery of what is true in the literary world, a reader advancing through Luke-Acts might raise the question how a Jewish messianic sect began to include Gentiles. There is some evidence that believers scattered by the persecution that arose over Stephen were the first to include Gentiles (Acts 11:20-21) (Conzelmann 1987:87).[3] Historically true or not, it is not true for the literary world of Luke-Acts. Rather, in the literary world God causes Peter to initiate the Gentile mission. Progressive discovery has to do with what is true in the hermetically sealed universe of the literary work without recourse to the external world (Barthes 1975:264-65, cf. Ingarden 1973:81-82, Harvey 1965:213-14).

## WHAT THINGS?

Luke begins without a trace of Jesus. The prologue alludes only to "things" that have been fulfilled and "things" about which Theophilus has been taught. The indeterminacy generates a puzzle: What things? Because John the Baptist comes onto the stage first, the reader tests him as a possible resolution. But he fills in too few gaps. In addition, the narrative pairs him with Jesus, who occupies the foremost place. But Jesus does not fill in all the gaps either. "These things" encompass more than Jesus' world. Gabriel links Jesus to the Davidic dynasty, and

Mary and Zechariah connect their experiences of God's grace to the Abrahamic covenant (Luke 1:32-33, 55, 72-73).

Further, Jesus points beyond himself. When the twelve year old Jesus converses with the teachers in the temple, he informs his parents that he must be about the things of his father (2:49). In spite of Gabriel's prediction that Jesus will be called the Son of God, in the Lucan world the identity of this father is unclear at this point. But there is a hint of a divine father, and Jesus' baptism and genealogy identify the divine father unmistakably (3:22-38). Therefore, the things have to do with Jesus in relation to God and in relation to God's acts in biblical history. That is, Luke-Acts is a theocentric story, a model that produces figures of God accompanying humanity.

In Luke there are additional allusions to secrets and mysteries, things hidden, later to be revealed. Jesus explains the parable of the sower in order that his disciples will know the secrets of the kingdom of God, whereas for others the secrets are in parables (Luke 8:10). The secrets cannot remain esoteric, however, because Jesus gives an explanation to the disciples in order that what is secret may come to light (8:17). So, outsiders may become insiders. Moreover, the explanation of the parable establishes norms for judging an appropriate response to hearing the word (8:15). The seed in good soil corresponds to those who hold the word fast and bring forth fruit. And so once the disciples have heard the secrets in the explanation, they have a mandate to make them known. Otherwise, they correspond to the seed that bears no fruit. So, insiders may also become outsiders.

In Acts the disciples are those who heed the word and bring forth fruit. Not only the commission from Jesus but also the election of Matthias anticipates the task of witnessing (1:8, 22). Early Christian preaching produces astonishing results—3,000 believers on Pentecost (2:41). By Paul's final journey to Jerusalem, there are many myriads among the Jews who believe (21:20). The witnesses in Acts correspond to the seed that brings forth fruit, and so outsiders become insiders.

But there is also a close relationship between Luke 11:33; 12:2 and 8:16-17. In the first two texts, the context has to do with confessing Jesus. The implication is that failure to confess Jesus and apostasy are the way insiders become outsiders. As the story progresses Judas becomes a paradigm of one who commits apostasy (22:3-6, 47-48; Acts 1:15-25). The deaths of Ananias and Sapphira for lying to the Spirit of God are signal events of how insiders become outsiders (5:1-10).

A similar mystery surrounds Luke 10:21-22. Jesus thanks God for hiding things from the wise and understanding and for revealing them to babes. In the context, this means that Jesus reveals his own relationship to God and brings those to whom he chooses to reveal God into a relationship with God (Tannehill 1986:238). That, however, creates mystery. Who are the wise and understanding from whom God has hidden these things? When one receives revelation, does one become wise and understanding? Are the disciples who hear Jesus' explanation in 8:10 the babes who receive revelation? If so, the disciples relapse in 9:45 because they fail to understand Jesus' prediction of his passion. Or again, when Jesus speaks of his suffering in 18:34, the twelve do not understand.

The things that make for peace are hid—from the people of Jerusalem (Luke 19:42), and those who crucify Jesus act in ignorance (23:34 [textually disputed], Acts 3:17). And so they correspond to the wise and understanding from whom God withholds revelation. But so do the disciples. When the risen Jesus walks with two disciples toward Emmaus, their eyes are kept from recognizing him (24:16). Although this is the first resurrection appearance, there is a delay in recognition. Jesus asks them, "What is this conversation which you are holding with each other?" They respond with their own question: "Are you the only visitor . . . who does not know *these things* . . . ?" (emphasis added). That prompts another question on the part of Jesus: "Which things?" But the two companions are the ones who are mystified rather than Jesus. Their despair delays illumination of the mystery. Resolution comes only when Jesus interprets scripture and unravels the scandalous enigma of a crucified Messiah. The Messiah suffers as a divine necessity (Luke 24:18-27). Still, not until 24:45 does Jesus open the minds of the eleven and those with them to understand.

In brief, the prologue anticipates a story focusing on things concerning Jesus in relation to God. But it is clear that that story is a part of a larger story embracing the whole history of God's acts of mercy and deliverance. Echoing the way Gabriel, Mary, and Zechariah link Jesus to Abraham and David, the speeches of Acts correlate events surrounding Jesus with Abraham, Moses, David, and the hope of Israel.

Another mystery about what is hidden and revealed arises in Luke 17:22. In the future the disciples will be unable to see the days of the Son of man. But the Son of man will be revealed in a time double-pronged with salvation and destruction (17:26-30). The coming of the Son of man in power and glory in 21:27 implies the same two prongs. Significantly, Jesus predicts the coming of the Son of man in a cloud. And that corresponds precisely to the prophecy of the parousia in Acts 1:9-11.

When the resurrection infuses new life into Jesus' followers, and when Jesus promises the Spirit, the disciples' hope revives. They pose a question to the risen Jesus about the restoration of the kingdom to Israel (Acts 1:5-6). Hans Conzelmann contends that the promise of the Spirit supplants the expectation of the immediate parousia (1987:6). But Jesus' response is an evasion rather than a substitution. Although he refuses to provide a time table, he affirms a divine plan (1:7). That leaves the question of the restoration of the kingdom to Israel open. Further, Jesus implies that God has a mission for the disciples to the extremities of the earth (1:8). The ascension holds out the hope of fulfillment with the promise of the parousia, and inasmuch as that recalls the promise of redemption in Luke 21:28, the restoration of the kingdom to Israel remains viable.

Further, Acts 2:35 anticipates the conquest of the enemies of God, and 3:19-23 foreshadows fulfillment of the divine plan with the parousia. Like Luke 17:26-30 and 21:27, these texts imply the two prongs of redemption and destruction. Paul also speaks of Jesus as the agent of future judgment (Acts 17:31). Nevertheless, for all the future expectation, the message of the two men at the ascension drives the disciples back from gazing into the sky to the task Jesus has set for them (1:9-11). Therefore, although "these things" focus on Jesus in relation to God, they concern a theocentric story from Abraham to the parousia.

## GREAT EXPECTATIONS

Luke-Acts launches out into confident optimism. Happy parents and a supporting cast acclaim the birth of two babies who are auspicious with promise. Predictions usher the reader into an atmosphere of expectancy. Gabriel promises that Jesus will be called the Son of God and will reign over the house of Jacob forever (1:32-35). Zechariah prophesies that Israel will be saved from enemies (1:71-73). Simeon foresees salvation in Jesus for the glory of Israel (2:32). Anna links the infant Jesus to the redemption of Jerusalem (2:38). Therefore, Luke-Acts raises high hopes for Israel.

There is a hitch, however. Simeon stipulates that Jesus is set for the fall and rising of many in Israel (Luke 2:34). How do expectations of falling and rising play out in Luke-Acts?

Robert Tannehill thinks that the hopes for Israel go unfulfilled. In his terms, anticipations in Luke 1-2 are frustrated so that Acts ends with a stab of pathos. What should have been true fails because of the disbelief of Israel. But, Tannehill argues, the tragedy is not necessarily final because there is still hope that the rejection of Jesus by the Jews is temporary (1985:69-85, 1986:15-44).[4]

David Tiede is more optimistic than Tannehill. According to Tiede, the hopes of the reliable characters are nothing less than God's promises to Israel. For their expectations to fail would be for God to fail. Therefore, Simeon's prediction of the fall of many anticipates the unbelief of Jews in Acts whereas his prediction of the rising of many constitutes a mixed prolepsis— the rising of many is merely inaugurated and its fulfillment deferred beyond the end of the narrative time in Acts (1988:21-34).

David Moessner has made another effort to resolve this question. Against Tiede, he rebuts that anticipations early in Luke find fulfillment within, rather than beyond, Luke-Acts. But Zechariah, Mary, and John the Baptist yearn for God's salvation in terms of might and power. The fulfillment, therefore, involves an ironic reversal. Fulfillment comes in the form of suffering servanthood. For Moessner, such a resolution is a reality within the temporal limits of Luke-Acts. Nevertheless, there is an external prolepsis, namely, a universal judgment and restoration/vindication of all Israel. Therefore, with expectations thus redefined by the image of suffering servanthood, the promises of God shall prevail (1988a:35-50).[5]

In a sense Moessner is correct in his critique of Tiede and Tannehill that the promises in Luke 1-2 cannot be taken at "face value." If the promises of Luke 1-2 establish hope of a political, nationalistic Messiah, as Tannehill suggests, how is it possible to account for the absence of nationalistic overtones in Jesus' own preview and review of his ministry in 4:18-19 and 7:22-23? And if the expectations of Luke 1-2 are nothing other than divine promises, is it not problematic for Tiede that the rising of many in Israel is so meagerly inaugurated in the temporal frame of Luke-Acts?

But Moessner lays the onus on Zechariah, Mary, and John the Baptist as partially unreliable characters who do not share the narrator's (ideological) point of view and, therefore, erroneously anticipate a Messiah who will defeat the enemies of God's salvation. This leads Moessner, however, into problems which he himself notes. According to the narrator, Zechariah prophesies as one filled with the Holy Spirit (Luke 1:67). Gabriel, indisputably reliable for Moessner, promises that the Holy Spirit will come upon Mary (1:35). Gabriel also declares that John the Baptist will be filled with the Holy Spirit (1:15), and the narrator specifies that John the Baptist speaks the message of God (3:2). By the norms of the narrator, they are reliable.

To catch a better grip, I drop three methodological reminders: (1) Discovery in the narrative world is prospective, not retrospective. It proceeds by progressive development. (2) The reader construes the progressive discovery. It is not given independently from the reading. (3) Progressive discovery develops not so much by fulfilling as by revising expectations.

Thus, the expectations in Luke 1-2 seduce the reader into an equivocation, truth mixed with evasion. The onus is not on Zechariah, Mary, and John the Baptist but on the reader who (mis)construes their expectations. Progressive reading constantly reshapes expectations. The development of the narrative forces a transformed understanding of Gabriel's prediction that God will give Jesus the throne of David (1:32) in order to make room for a crucified Messiah who is rejected by a significant portion of the Jews.

However beneficial Moessner's emphasis on fulfillment of expectations within Luke-Acts may be, Tiede's case for external prolepsis is correct in at least two respects. (1) Simeon expects the consolation of Israel (Luke 2:25) and Anna waits expectantly for the redemption of Jerusalem (2:38). In 21:28 Jesus predicts the redemption of Jerusalem at the *parousia*. (2) Moessner dismisses Zechariah's prophecy that God's people will be saved from their enemies (1:71, 74) as unreliable. But Acts 2:34 envisions the ultimate subjection of enemies as the finale of the reign of the exalted Jesus. Both of these are patently external prolepses.

The early chapters of Luke spawn expectations not only for Israel but also for Jesus. In Luke 1-3 three episodes invite the reader to compare John the Baptist with Jesus, and each time the deck is stacked in favor of the superiority of Jesus (Talbert 1982:15). Before the promises regarding John come to fruition, Gabriel breaks into the sequence of the narrative with greater promises about Jesus. The portentous celebrations of angels, shepherds, Simeon, and Anna top the festivities at the birth of John. John closes his career by pointing to a superior one to come after him. In fact, Gabriel gives away the ending from the beginning by designating Jesus Son of God, and by predicting that he will reign over the house of Jacob forever (Luke 1:32-35).

As is the case with foreshadowing, the suspense then becomes not what but how. This includes progressive discovery of (1) the identity of Jesus and (2) the shape of his mission. In the temptations, Jesus maintains his identity as Son of God by serving only God (Luke 4:1-13). At Nazareth, Jesus forecasts his mission by claiming to be a Spirit-filled Messiah with a ministry of liberation (4:18-19). But the people of Nazareth also mold the identity of Jesus by rejecting him according to the adage:

"No prophet is acceptable in his own country" (4:24) (Brawley 1987:6-10). Their rejection confirms his prophetic identity. In his ministry, he liberates people oppressed by demons, and the demons add to his identity by recognizing his relationship with God.

Conflict stories also shape expectations of the Davidic Messiah destined to reign forever. When Jesus attempts to liberate a paralytic from his ailment and his sin, opponents raise the question of identity: "Who is this that speaks blasphemies? Who can forgive sins but God only?" (5:21). The answer is that Jesus has authority to forgive sins on earth. If on the basis of Mary's exultation in the power of God the reader anticipates the power of God to be manifested in Jesus (1:49-55), then power is being qualified sharply. Now it is authority over the powers of evil that oppress human beings. Such authority leads Jesus into table fellowship with toll collectors and sinners as a part of his mission (5:30-32).

Jesus further redefines norms of authority when, over against demands of the law, he claims to be lord of the sabbath (6:5). As lord of the sabbath, he revises law. For the scribes and Pharisees in 6:6-11 the issue is whether Jesus will practice healing on the sabbath or not. But Jesus restates the problem not as an issue of doing something or nothing but of doing either good or harm, saving life or destroying it. He thus rejects doing nothing as morally irresponsible. To fail to do good on the sabbath is to harm. That is what is unlawful. To do good on the sabbath is lawful in a positive sense (Schweizer 1984:113, Tannehill 1986:175-76).

The redefinition of norms provokes animosity against Jesus from scribes and Pharisees (Luke 6:11). Their discussion about what to do to Jesus carries proleptic overtones.[6] Expectations heighten the tension. On the heels of that incident Jesus selects the twelve, and at the end of the list the narrator informs the reader that Judas will become a traitor (6:16). But because the notice leaves up in the air whether Judas will betray his country, his vows, his parents, his peers, God, or Jesus, it leaves the reader hanging.

The so-called sermon on the plain continues the reversal of norms. The poor, the hungry, those who weep, and those who are hated on account of Jesus are blessed. The rich, the well-fed, those who laugh, and those about whom all speak well are under the curse of woe (Luke 6:20-26). Catching up the note of deliverance from enemies in Zechariah's prophecy (1:71, 74), Jesus now counsels love for enemies (6:29, 35). An understanding of love of enemies as passive acquiescence to those in power, would paralyze Zechariah's prophecy. But Walter Wink describes a third way between submission to, and assault on, those in power. To turn the other cheek and to give the undergarment to one demanding the outergarment are, as already noted, a subversive assertiveness that deprives those in power of initiative (1988:210-24). Zechariah's anticipation of deliverance from enemies, then, is taking on different contours.

Norms take on a new shape also when a Gentile centurion appeals to Jesus to heal his servant (Luke 7:1-10). Jesus never directly encounters the centurion. He communicates through messengers. But Jesus declares that the centurion is related to him through faith. And because Jesus compares the centurion with people of Israel, there is a strong hint that he is transcending ethnic norms. On the other hand, that Jewish elders appeal to Jesus for the centurion on the basis of his love for the nation and of his contribution to the construction of a synagogue implies a positive relationship between Jesus and the nation and synagogue. The healing of Jairus's daughter also assumes a positive relationship with a ruler of the synagogue (8:40-42, 49-56).

The remainder of Luke 7 renews the progressive development of Jesus' identity. After the raising of the widow's son in Nain, the funeral crowd declares Jesus a great prophet (7:16). In the context of this speculation about Jesus' identity, an episode follows immediately in which John the Baptist raises the question: "Are you the one who is to come?" (7:19, 20).

Joseph Fitzmyer argues that this question does not refer to the Messiah but alludes back to 3:15-17 where John predicts that one mightier than he is coming, an eschatological messenger of God—a role that Fitzmyer thinks Jesus rejects (1981:66).

But two factors weigh against Fitzmyer. First, the context in 3:15-17, raises the issue of whether John is the Messiah or not. Already, then, there is some implication that the stronger one who is to come is the Messiah. In addition, the title "the one who is to come" in 7:19, 20 links up with an even stronger allusion to the Messiah in 19:38: "Blessed is the king who comes in the name of the Lord" (Tannehill 1986:80). Thus, "the one who is to come" is a periphrasis for "Messiah," and Jesus does not reject it but molds the reader's understanding of it in terms of his ministry of liberation.

At the end of his reply to John the Baptist, Jesus adds, "Blessed is the one who takes no offense at me" (Luke 7:23). No sooner has he said that than he challenges his generation as those who do take offense. They complain that Jesus is a glutton and a drunkard, a friend of toll collectors and sinners (7:34). Whoever the detractors are, they are unreliable characters. And yet, in what sense do they express the truth? Elsewhere in Luke Jesus eats with toll collectors and sinners (5:29; cf. 15:1-2), but nowhere else does he fit the pattern of a glutton or a drunkard. Thus, the reader is able to establish norms for judging—although opponents lampoon Jesus as a glutton and drunkard, that he befriends toll collectors and sinners is essentially true.

The final episode of the chapter continues to round out Jesus' identity. Simon the Pharisee is another example of one who takes offense at Jesus (Luke 7:36-50). The offense is again occasioned by Jesus' relationship to outcasts, this time to a woman who is a notorious sinner.

The omniscient narrator opens Simon's interior to the reader so that his skepticism about the prophetic identity of Jesus establishes dramatic tension. In response, the parable and its application in the first instance vindicate the woman and censure the behavior of Simon. But primarily the vindication of the woman and the reproach of Simon vindicate Jesus. Jesus did know what sort of woman touched him (Drexler 1968:165). Simon establishes a social criterion for determining the identity of Jesus and, therefore, denies his prophetic nature because he refuses to reject the woman. Jesus' social relationships do indeed determine his identity. But it is his acceptance of the woman rather than his rejection that guides the progressive discovery of his nature. Jesus is the prophetic Messiah with a ministry of liberation who is a friend to sinners.

Chapter 8 furthers the progressive discovery of the identity of Jesus. After the calming of the storm, Jesus' disciples raise a question that contains its own answer: "Who then is this that he commands even wind and water, and they obey him?" (8:25). The context links that with the Gerasene demoniac's declaration that Jesus is Son of the Most High God (8:28).

Luke 9 picks up the same thread of identity. For Herod, the deeds of Jesus raise the question of who he is. Popular speculation that Jesus is John the Baptist, Elijah, or one of the old prophets mystifies Herod (Luke 9:7-9). That connects with Jesus' discussion with his disciples about his identity. The disciples report the popular speculation, and then Peter identifies Jesus as God's Messiah (9:18-20). Jesus' rebuke and command to silence indicate that it is a proper identification only if understood correctly. All thought of royal grandeur and political eminence go out the window as Jesus swaps messianic imagery for candid talk about suffering and about rejection by eminent politicos. Messianic identity with the restrictions of suffering, rejection, death, and resurrection then receives divine confirmation in the transfiguration. Such a Messiah is God's Son (9:35).

The delineation of Jesus as the suffering one is tied to the development of a geographical schema. Luke 9:51 links Jesus' resolute determination to go to Jerusalem to his "assumption" (Fitzmyer 1981:827-28). The reference to his assumption generates another enigma; meanwhile, the text implies that the way to it is severe (9:57-62). Luke 11:49 anticipates persecution and death as a typical destiny of prophets. When the journey motif surfaces again, it is correlated with the necessity of Jesus to die as a prophet in Jerusalem (13:22; 33-35). Prophetic identity means confronting Jerusalem, which kills prophets. And the final reference to the journey to Jerusalem reiterates Jesus' prediction of his passion (18:31-33).

The identity of Jesus demands renewed attention when a blind man twice addresses him as Son of David (Luke 18:

38,39). A careful reader remembers Gabriel's prediction that God would give Jesus the throne of his father David and recalls Jesus' descent from David according to Luke 2:4 and the genealogy (3:23-38). That sets the stage for the designation of Jesus as king in 19:38. And yet Jesus initiates a discussion in which he questions how the Messiah can be David's son (Luke 20:41-44). Jesus likely intimates that the Messiah is more than David's son, and the implication that David calls the Messiah "lord" reverses the ordinary veneration of a son for a father (Fitzmyer 1985:1313-15). And so Jesus claims his kingdom in 22:29, and the text comes back to several allusions to Jesus' kingship in his trial (23:2-3).

Scoffed and mocked, Jesus dies under an inscription that he is king of the Jews—ironically a king who cannot save himself (23:37-38) (Tannehill 1986:198). The crucifixion seals the identity of Jesus as the suffering one and substantiates the restricted meaning of Messiah and king. In fact, the redefinition is so sharp as potentially to disconfirm Jesus' messianic identity. But three particular strategies counter the disconfirmation:

(1) Jesus consistently predicts suffering in connection with his messianic identity so that by the time of the crucifixion the reader anticipates a suffering Messiah.

(2) Luke-Acts claims that scripture predicts that the Messiah must suffer (24:26, 46; Acts 3:18; 13:28-29). Therefore, rather than disconfirm Jesus' messiahship, his crucifixion precisely confirms it.

(3) Against the designs of Jesus' opponents to put an end to him, God raises him from the dead and vindicates him (Acts 2:23-24; 3:15; 4:10-11; 13:28-30). The resurrection is the prelude to the installation of Jesus on the throne of David (Acts 2:30-31). But in Luke-Acts Jesus' kingship receives such qualification that understanding it as a political threat is a misunderstanding (Acts 17:7; 25:8).

## THE DESTINY OF DISCIPLES

Not only does Simeon's prediction of the fall and rising of many in Israel evoke questions of the place of unbelieving Jews in Luke-Acts, it also stimulates speculation about those destined to rise. Simeon associates the rising of many in Israel with revelation to the Gentiles, although it is premature to speak of anticipations of a Gentile mission (Luke 2:32-34). After Luke 4:18-19 there can be no doubt that the rising of many is a result of Jesus' liberating messianic ministry. Jesus himself expresses a sense of urgency in executing a divine plan for a comprehensive ministry (4:43). He is optimistic about the role of Peter as one who will catch human beings (5:10). Jesus' ministry empirically defines lepers, paralytics, demoniacs, toll collectors, and sinners as among those destined to rise.

Jesus' statement that disciples will be like their teacher (Luke 6:40) then provides a major control for channeling the reader's view of the rise of many in Israel. The reader is aware that since 6:17 Jesus is the teacher who is instructing his disciples. In that context he has been renegotiating norms, and so for the disciples to be like their teacher means a reversal of values. But then, for the time, being the progressive discovery stands in suspension over the question: In what way will the disciples be like this teacher?

Simeon's anticipation of Jesus as a revelation to the Gentiles takes on some new contours with the healing of the centurion's servant (Luke 7:1-10). There is still no direct mission to Gentiles because Jewish elders mediate between the centurion and Jesus. Nevertheless, the centurion and his slave are attached to the rising of many in Israel.

The reader's vision broadens with the healing of the Gerasene demoniac (Luke 8:26-39).[7] Jesus goes explicitly among Gentiles, and he heals a man who is an outcast even among them. The demoniac is so far outside the pale that he lives among tombs—a living man in the place of the dead. Such a person is associated with the rising of many in Israel—the reversal could hardly be more dramatic!

The parable of the sower establishes a criterion for further definition of the rising of many in Israel. The fruitful seed corresponds to those who heed the word (Luke 8:15). A few verses later, family members make a demand on Jesus. But Jesus redefines his familial commitments in terms of those who heed God's word according to the criterion of the parable

(8:19-21). Those destined to rise in Israel are now those who heed God's word. The same dynamic recurs in 11:27-28 where commitment to God's word is a higher form of blessedness than Jesus' relationship to his own mother.

The question of how disciples are like their teacher resumes with the sending of the twelve. Their mission parallels his not only in style but also in power and authority (Luke 9:1-6). The same goes for the sending of the seventy(-two) (10:1-12, 17-20). On the other hand, in between the two sendings, Jesus foretells his suffering (9:22). A reader who remembers Jesus' declaration that the disciple will be like the teacher might hazard a guess that the disciple will also emulate the teacher's suffering. Such a guess finds immediate confirmation in 9:23-24 where Jesus makes discipleship an issue of following him even to the point of the sacrifice of life. Thereafter, every allusion to the identity of Jesus as the suffering one implies an analogous destiny for his disciples (9:44; 13:33; 17:25; 18:32-33).

Luke 11:49 also ties the disciples' fate to that of Jesus. The saying is a completing analepsis because it refers to a saying of the wisdom of God in the past. That saying is in the future tense, but is it future with respect to God's past or with respect to Jesus' present? Because 11:50-51 has to do with prophets of the past, the saying is probably future with respect to a primeval voice of God, and so it is also an external completing analepsis. The future from the point of view of the primeval voice of God includes Jesus and his apostles. Thus, in the following episode in 12:4-12 Jesus makes explicit the fate of suffering for his followers (Fitzmyer 1985:950, Schweizer 1984:201, Tannehill 1986:244). A close parallel in 21:12-19 reinforces persecution as the expected destiny of Jesus' disciples.

Along with the prospect of suffering there are clues that disciples are under divine care. They are far more valuable than sparrows who nevertheless are not forgotten before God. God's providence is like keeping account of the number of hairs on each disciple's head (Luke 12:6-7). Further, the Holy Spirit will teach them what to say when they are on trial before persecutors (12:11-12). Jesus makes a similar promise in 21:12-18.

Here too there is a promise of divine care: "But not a hair of your head will perish" (21:18).

The obverse of the blessedness of heeding God's word is Jesus' warning against those who do not repent (Luke 13:3, 5). Similarly, the parable of the banquet portends the exclusion of those who consider themselves to be among the blessed and the unexpected inclusion of those who do not (14:15-24). The parable of the rich man and Lazarus dramatizes such a reversal (16:19-31).

The parable of the pounds reflects three aspects of Jesus' relationship to the Jewish populace (Luke 19:11-27): (1) On the one hand, according to the apparent Lucan allegory, Jesus associates with faithful followers in his kingdom (19:15-19). (2) There is an exhortation to fidelity and productivity among followers. (3) There is judgment against the enemies of Jesus (cf. L. T. Johnson 1982:139-59). The fall of many in Israel now means judgment for those who reject Jesus. The rise of many in Israel means association in the reign of Jesus.

One other text in Luke associates followers in Jesus' reign. At the last supper, Jesus passes on to the twelve the legacy of the kingdom (Luke 22:29-30). To sit on thrones judging the twelve tribes of Israel is the exclusive prerogative of the twelve (Jervell 1972:79-89). As such they rule over the many in Israel who are destined to rise.

Finally, Jesus dies, emphatically innocent (Tyson 1986:129-39), nevertheless condemned. The reader may anticipate a similar destiny for disciples who are like their teacher. But there is a redemptive footnote. At his death Jesus commits his life to divine care (Luke 23:46). Furthermore, the passion narrative is coupled with the resurrection.

Nevertheless, mystery circumscribes the abrupt transition from death to resurrection. Does Jesus rise by his own agency? Acts repeatedly resolves the question by declaring that God acts to raise Jesus from the dead (e.g., Acts 2:24; 3:15; 4:10; 13:30). Recalling the promises of divine care in Luke 12:6-12; 21:12-19, the reader may now understand that Jesus' disciples, who like their teacher commit their lives to God, can expect that God will also act to raise them from the dead. Such a reader will now understand Simeon's prediction of the *rising* of many in Israel in a carefully nuanced new way.

As Jesus departs in Luke 24, he leaves behind a promise. Presumably God is the source of the power in the promise (24:49). Acts 1:4-5 picks up the allusion to the promise and 1:8 to the power so that the promise becomes defined as the coming of the Holy Spirit. In Luke, Jesus is uniquely anointed with the Holy Spirit (Conzelmann 1961:179). But now he promises that his disciples will be endowed with the Spirit, a promise that Pentecost fulfills (Acts 2:1-4).

In addition, the promise reaches into the future for those who repent and are baptized. In Acts 2:38 Peter extends the promise to his Jewish audience, and in 8:17 it expands to include Samaritans. Now the reader understands the reference to Samaria in Acts 1:8 not merely geographically but also ethnically. On the other hand, the baptism of an Ethiopian eunuch presents some enigma (8:26-38). His ethnic and religious status are indeterminate, but not his inclusion.

In a closely related vein, the reader comes upon Paul's commission that he is to carry the name of Jesus before Gentiles as well as Jews, a prolepsis that for all the previous hints is a sudden unveiling of a mission to Gentiles (9:15). Moreover, divine intervention leads Peter to preach to Gentiles, and God pours out the gift of the Spirit on them (10:45).

Only at this point can the reader move to some resolution of Simeon's allusion to Jesus as a light for revelation to the Gentiles (Luke 2:32) and of the hint that Jesus is related to another Gentile centurion by faith (7:1-10). The revelation is not merely an open disclosure to Gentiles, but a means of including them in God's salvation. Briefly put, disciples, including Gentiles, are endowed with the Spirit *like their teacher.*

But on the heels of the coming of the Spirit, the disciples begin to be like their teacher in suffering. Sadducees and the high priestly party arrest Peter and John (Acts 4:3). The same opponents arrest all the apostles, beat them, and charge them not to speak in the name of Jesus (5:17, 40). Stephen's death manifests remarkable parallels to Jesus' (6:8-7:60). Persecution scatters the believers (8:1) and the Pauline persecution ravages the church (8:3). Then Paul himself becomes a messianist destined to suffer (9:16). Jews and Gentiles persecute Paul and Barnabas (13:50; 14:2, 5, 19). Paul continues to suffer first with Silas (16:19-24; 17:13) and then alone (18:12; 20:2). Threats foreshadow his final journey to Jerusalem (20:22-23; 21:4, 11, 13). Then, a mob attempts to kill Paul (21:27-22:29). Acts comes to an end with Paul suffering threats from the high priestly party and the Sadducees, zealous Jews who plot against him, and even the perils of the sea and a viper (23:1-10, 12-35; 24:1-9; 25:2-12; 27:13-28:6).[8]

Yet divine care accompanies these disciples in their suffering. The promises of God's providential care (Luke 12:6-12; 21:12-19) keep finding fulfillment. Peter and John impress the Sanhedrin with their testimony, and that is in line with the promise that Jesus or the Holy Spirit would respond appropriately to persecuted disciples (Acts 4:8-12, 19-20; cf. 5:29-32). An angel of the Lord opens the prison doors when the apostles are arrested (5:17-19). Even Gamaliel argues that divine providence will determine the validity of the messianist movement (5:34-39). An angel of the Lord releases Peter from prison so that he averts Herod Agrippa's machinations against him (12:3-11).

In addition, reiterated cases of deliverance from suffering reinforce God's providential care for Paul. Suffering within God's providence brackets his entire career (Adams 1979:16-20). Acts 9:15 predicts it proleptically as a part of his call, and his speech before Agrippa recalls it analeptically (26:17). In between Paul escapes plot after plot (e.g., 9:23-25; 14:19-20; 16:25-26). Amidst Paul's trials in Jerusalem, the Lord promises Paul that he will bear witness in Rome (23:11). Paul's responses during his trials recall the promises of Jesus that he or the Spirit would provide persecuted disciples with appropriate answers (Luke 12:12; 21:14-15). In Acts 26:17 Paul reports that at his call the risen Jesus promised him deliverance, and immediately he claims the fulfillment of the promise (26:22). Divine care, rather than suffering, has the last word.

In sum, when Jesus' declaration that disciples will be like their teacher routes the reader's response, biography evolves into ecclesiology. Modern interpretation of the ecclesiology of Luke-Acts has fallen under the sway of Hans Conzelmann and Ernst Haenchen. They both advance the thesis that Luke-Acts shows how the church maintains continuity with Israel while becoming a predominantly Gentile entity (Conzelmann 1961:95-136, 145-48, Haenchen 1971:94-102). With that, ecclesiology has taken on such dimensions as to overshadow the portrayal of Jesus. But in the progressive discovery of what is true in the narrative world, ecclesiology cannot, like a black widow, consume biography because disciples will be like their *teacher*. And therefore, the ecclesiology of Luke-Acts is christological.

But the christology of Luke-Acts, as Gerhard Lohfink puts it, is structured theocentrically (Lohfink 1975:85). That is, Jesus commits his life to God's care, and God acts to raise him from the dead. Thus, suffering does not forestall divine care. Following the paradigm of the resurrection, the power of God turns setbacks into triumphs. And therefore, the ecclesiology of Luke-Acts is also theocentric.

# 3

# RETROSPECTIVE RECOVERY: THE LOGIC OF THE STORY IN LUKE

S tory corresponds closely to the plot, provided the concept of plot includes motivations and consequences of action. Retrospective recovery of the story has to do with describing the logic of action: that is, how action derives from its initiation, moves toward its completion, and forms a unit that the reader can name (Brook 1984:287). Luke 5:12-14 recounts the healing of a leper. The healing derives from Jesus' encounter with the leper. The leper's plea for healing and Jesus' desire to heal motivate the action. The healing is a consequence of Jesus' touch and command. The incident forms a unit that the reader can name "healing." It then combines with others in sequences that derive from an initial point and form a coherent whole.

## MOVING TOWARD A GOAL

The coherent whole is a teleological pattern. That is, actions in narratives fit into causal networks out of which the reader constructs a thematic pattern moving toward a goal.[1] In Acts 22

Paul addresses a mob. But before the address he gestures with his hand. Paul's speaking is part of the action moving toward a goal and, therefore, is a part of the plot, whereas the hand gesture is ancillary and does not contribute to the thematic goal.

Post-modern literary theory objects to the idea of action fitting into a thematic pattern. Traditional plots assume a rational universe in which events are connected by cause and effect. In contrast, the post-modern world view presupposes that reality is random and chaotic, and literary works with this perspective rupture the causal ties among events so that the reader moves from one existential experience to another without ever arriving at an end (Docherty 1983:134, 202, Kort 1975:62). This is not to deny, however, that literature produced out of other world views organizes actions in plots that move toward a thematic goal. Further, in a curious way, because the modern concept of cause and effect does not include divine intervention, the rupture of causal ties may correspond to unexpected grace (cf. Docherty 1983:204).

The teleological goal is not merely a matter of content but also a matter of structure. Structurally gratifying plots exhibit particular relationships between the beginning and the end.

Victor Shklovsky describes four types of parallels between beginnings and endings that produce satisfactory plots: (1) The relationship among characters shifts to its opposite. (2) The plot moves from a prediction or fear to its realization. (3) The line of action develops from a problem to its solution. (4) The plot moves from a false accusation or misrepresentation to a rectification (Shklovsky 1965:170-77, cf. Culler 1975:223).

To a significant degree, the retrospectively recovered story in Luke-Acts unfolds from (2) predictions and their fulfillment. A case in point is Luke 1:31-35 where Gabriel makes predictions about Mary's child that the narrative moves to fulfill. It also moves from (4) misunderstanding to rectification. It vindicates Jesus over against his rejection by the people of Nazareth and over against the scandal of his crucifixion, and it exonerates Paul from accusations that he advocates apostasy from Judaism.

The development toward the thematic goal does not follow a direct linear path. Chapter 2 has already elaborated on

Gérard Genette's enlightening discussion of the anachronies of analepsis and prolepsis. Genette discusses additional discordance between the abstract chronology and the narrative order. Narratives also summarize events (ellipsis) and introduce sidelines that parallel the main narrative but break off without fruition (paralipsis) (Genette 1980:39-58, 107; cf. 52, n. 25). Jesus' instructions to Peter and John to prepare for the passover (Luke 22:7-13) are proleptic. The message from the two men to the women at the tomb, recalling Jesus' predictions of his passion, is analeptic (24:6-7). The story of Barnabas and his mission to Cyprus (Acts 15:39) is a paralipsis. And the notice that Paul was teaching in Corinth for a year and six months is an ellipsis (18:11).

Repetition is an additional deviation in linear development. There are two primary forms of repetition in Luke-Acts. One is narrating a number of times what occurred only once. Examples of this are Paul's christophany (Acts 9:3-9; 22:6-11; 26:12-18) and the conversion of Cornelius (10:1-11:18, 15:7-9). The second is narrating once what happened a number of times (iterative narrative) (Suleiman 1980:131, Genette 1980:115-16). A case in point is the report about Jesus in Luke 4:15: "And he taught in their synagogues . . . ."

Retrospective recovery of the story, however, goes beyond that which can be isolated analytically as action fitting into the development of a teleological pattern. It also includes behavior that causes action or is a consequence of it. With this qualification the story is a close equivalent to R. S. Crane's understanding of functional interrelatedness. Crane opposes abstracting plot. He argues rather for understanding plot as a part of a particular temporal synthesis of elements of action, character, and thought (1961:159-65). This functional interrelatedness corresponds to the notion that the behavior and thought of characters that motivate action and derive from it are parts of the retrospectively recovered story.

## READERS AND STRUCTURES

Retrospective recovery is the reader's task. For Roland Barthes, the goal of a literary work is to make the reader a producer of the text rather than a consumer of it. The reader constructs meaning out of the plurality of the signifiers of a text. This led Barthes to reject his earlier work in structuralism. He argued that texts are unique and resist reduction to a uniform structure. Further, there is ambiguity about texts which allows readers, as the producers of meaning, to impose upon them a variety of structures (Barthes 1974:3-6, cf. Greenwood 1985:41-42).

But in celebrating the uniqueness of texts Barthes overlooks the shared conventions underlying them. To take narrative as an example, there are some conventional assumptions that readers take with them in any interpretation of narrative.[2] Barthes may be accurate in advocating the impossibility of prescribing the essential shared characteristics of narrative. But it is possible to describe what many narratives have in common, and recognizing the universal qualities of narratives can help a reader discovery what is unique about an individual narrative.

Accordingly, structuralism is a productive method for studying action in its causal nexus when it is viewed as an activity of imposing structure onto a text in order to perceive it in a meaningful way. Because recognizing the plot depends on conventions underlying the text at a subconscious level, a structural analysis that focuses on that subliminal level can facilitate the reader's ability to link actions together into a more precise sequential and coherent order. But novices confronted with structuralism are often dismayed by its esoteric jargon and the world view it presupposes.

What is the world view undergirding structuralism? For centuries a Platonic view of reality held sway over biblical interpretation. From this perspective, authentic reality lay beyond what we grasp with our sense perceptions. In biblical studies this implied symbolic interpretation. The apparent sense of a text pointed to another essential meaning such as Augustine's allegory of the good Samaritan. That essential meaning, however, derived from the interpreter, and the allegorical method proved to be thoroughgoing subjectivism.

With the rise of rationalism and the scientific method, interpretation presumably became objective. As in other fields of investigation, biblical interpreters supposedly became disinterested observers who could analyze phenomena (the biblical text) and by rational abilities arrive at the truth.

But the implication that the observer could stand at a distance from the phenomenon under observation came under scrutiny from science itself. In trying to describe the motion of particles within the atom, Werner Heisenberg discovered that certain characteristics of the particles are interrelated. He concluded that it is impossible to know both the position and momentum of an electron at the same time. That is, analytical procedures may separate part of a system from its interrelations with other parts and distort the observation.

Further, science became aware that methods of observation influence the observations. For example, microscopes using ordinary light become useless for magnifying particles smaller than the wavelength of the light. A remedy is to use electromagnetic oscillations with shorter wavelengths such as X-rays. But X-rays are also high energy radiations which excite the minute particles under observation.

By the same token, from a holistic perspective, a human being can never be a disinterested observer of reality because human beings are a part of the system. We are bound in relationships to all of reality, and, therefore, there are uncertainties and indeterminacies in all our observations and reflections. But it is unsatisfactory to revert to the notorious arbitrariness of subjectivism. Thus, there is a modern propensity for a holistic perspective where the interpreter is understood to be a part of the reality which she or he wishes to understand.

Structuralism assumes that certain structuring elements constrain interpretation. The text cannot mean anything the interpreter wishes. On the other hand, the interpreter is the one who superimposes a structure onto the text in order to grasp a meaning. The imposed structure cannot be identified as *the* structure of the text, but only as one possible structure that resonates to a greater or lesser degree with the text.

One of the basic concepts of structuralism is that meaning is a matter of differentiation. One particular way of differentiating is by comparing binary opposites. We give meaning to "white" because we understand it in opposition to black, and because we differentiate it from everything that is not white. In narrative, we also differentiate departing from arriving or helping from opposing or domination from submission.

Structuralism views the text as a sign. The sign is made up of a signifier and a signified. How does a reader determine what the signifier signifies? Structuralism postulates that the reader is able to reconstruct the story (aspects of the signified) because it is founded on unconscious conventions (aspects of the signifier). This process is analogous to a reader's recognition of the meaning of a sentence without consciously cataloging the subject, verb, and other parts of speech. Thus emerges a distinction between the narrative surface and the underlying structure.

One surface structure may have more than one underlying structure. On the other hand, different surface structures may have the same underlying structure (Rimmon-Kenan 1983:10). The ambiguity of the sentence, "Time beats," depends on the reader imposing two distinct grammatical structures—time may function either as subject or verb (imperative), beats may be either verb or object. Theoretically, it is possible to put the same structures on the sentence: "Rain drops." Rain may be subject or verb (imperative), and drops may be either verb or object. In a comparable way, a reader may superimpose more than one structure on a given narrative or view distinct narratives as conforming to the same structure.

## THE NARRATIVE SCHEMA

A. J. Greimas and Joseph Courtés maintain that narrative invests in overcoming a situation of need (1982: "Narrative Schema," "Program, Narrative"). Claude Bremond objects that this allows the end of the action to determine how an action functions, and he proposes, rather, that narrative proceeds by continuous cycles of potential followed by success or failure (1970:248-76, cf. Rimmon-Kenan 1983:27, Greenwood 1985: 68). The story of the temptation of Jesus in Luke 4:1-13 establishes hunger as a situation of need (4:2). Rather than invest in overcoming the hunger, however, the narrative creates another potential—will Jesus submit to the devil or not?

However, Jonathan Culler has demonstrated that Bremond confuses the progressive discovery with the retrospective recovery. Bremond opposes allowing the consequence of the action to determine how the action functions. But that is precisely the way retrospective recovery operates. Progressive discovery develops from a prospective point of view. In suspense the reader anticipates the resolution of a mystery. But retrospective recovery is defined from the teleological consequences (Culler 1975:208-210). And it is the case that vast numbers of narratives do invest in overcoming a need.

Greimas and Courtés have described, therefore, a standard structure underlying wide-ranging varieties of plots in which there are (1) a situation of need, (2) a competence phase in which a character becomes obliged, willing, and able to meet the need, (3) a performance stage in which the need is met, and (4) a sanction phase in which there is recognition of the success or failure of the performance (1982: "Narrative Schema," cf. Boers 1985:61-62).[3]

Miracle stories easily demonstrate this four part schema. For example, in Luke 5:17-26, (1) the need phase identifies a paralyzed man. (2) The competence stage overcomes hindrances. A crowd separates the man from Jesus, and opponents reject Jesus' ability to forgive sins. (3) Jesus performs a healing and announces the forgiveness of sins. (4) The paralytic sanctions the healing—and implicitly the forgiveness of sins—by taking up his bed and walking. Further, the sanction is reinforced by the amazement that seized all.

This healing, however, is deceptively simple. Other narratives may be quite intricate. But complex narratives are combinations of elementary narratives—combinations resulting from the introduction of one narrative schema into another. Daniel and Aline Patte have classified the combination of elementary narratives in three categories—parallel, converging, and diverging (Patte and Patte 1978:33-36, 120-21, nn. 51-55).

(1) Parallel narratives juxtapose events without narrative development from one to the other. The imprisonment of John the Baptist by Herod, interrupting John's ministry of preparation (Luke 3:18:-20), is a case in point.

(2) Converging narratives integrate one elementary narrative into another as a part of the narrative development. For example, an elementary narrative may form the competence phase of the primary narrative. The coming of the Holy Spirit on Pentecost is the performance stage in an elementary narrative schema deriving from the need of the disciples for power, but it also constitutes the competence stage for the narrative schema generated by Jesus' mandate to the apostles to be witnesses (Luke 24:48-49; Acts 1:8; 2:1-4).

(3) A diverging narrative introduces a new elementary narrative as a development from the primary narrative but at another level. For instance, the sanction stage of the primary narrative may be a new elementary narrative. Zechariah's prophecy is part of the sanction phase in the birth of John the Baptist, but it contains predictions that create the need in another narrative schema for a prophet to prepare the way of the Lord (Luke 1:67-79).

In this connection, it is possible to critique a wide-spread interpretation of Zechariah's silence as his inability to bless the people in contrast with Jesus' blessing of his disciples at the end of Luke (so, e.g., Schweizer 1984:378, Fitzmyer 1985:1590, Parsons 1987:74-75). To portray Zechariah as a silent priest who cannot bless is to fail to follow the narrative schema where there is no narrative need for Zechariah to bless the people.

The narrative schema provides a particularly helpful way to analyze thematic patterns. Narratives invest in the process of overcoming a situation of need, or in structuralist terminology, a situation in which a subject is disjoined from a desirable object or conjoined with an undesirable object. In Luke 5:17-26, a man is conjoined with paralysis, and the narrative invests in disjoining him from this undesirable object. Conversely, the man is also disjoined from forgiveness, and the narrative invests in conjoining him with forgiveness as a desirable object.

Transformations take place in narratives when a subject comes into conjunction with a competence or value. Greimas and Courtés have termed these transformations narrative programs (1982: "Program, Narrative," "Acquisition," "Deprivation"). In Luke 5:17-26, the ultimate value for the paralytic is the ability to walk. But before that can happen, the man must be brought into close proximity to Jesus. There is, therefore, a narrative program in the competence phase that conjoins the paralytic with the presence of Jesus. In the performance stage another narrative program conjoins the paralytic with the ability to walk—an object of value.

In the diagram (cf. Boers 1985:65), narrative programs fit into each phase of the narrative schema as the transformations constituting need, competence, performance, or sanction.

| I<br>Need | II<br>Competence | III<br>Performance | IV<br>Sanction |
|---|---|---|---|
| A subject disjoined from a desirable object or conjoined with an undesirable object | A subject willing or obliged, and able (having the power) to overcome the need specified in #1 by a performance | The subject performing the action transforming the need specified in #1 into its opposite | Recognition of the success or failure of the performance or of the achievement of a desired value |

Further references to narrative schemata presume this diagram.

Further, narrative programs may be represented in a useful schematic shorthand: S1 (S2 ∩ Ov). This is part of a larger formula, $NP = F[S1 \rightarrow (S2 \cap Ov)]$.

The narrative program (NP) is a function (F) of transformation that results from one subject (S1) bringing about the conjunction (∩) of another subject (S2) with an object of value (Ov). The transformation may also be the disjunction (U) of an undesirable object (Ou), that is, S1 (S2 U Ou) (Greimas and Cortés 1982: "Program, Narrative").

Narratives do not always manifest every formula element: for example, Luke 1:4 lacks the subject who effected the conjunction of Theophilus with information about which he now needs certainty. Thus, in applying the formula "?" represents the subject (S1) bringing about a conjunction (S2 ∩ Ov) not manifested in the text. In addition, one personage in the surface narrative may correspond to both S1 and S2 as in the case where a character obtains an object of value for her/himself.

Greimas and Cortés termed the interrelationship of narrative programs the narrative trajectory (1982: "Narrative Trajectory"). The final transformation toward which the narrative is oriented is the main program. But a subsidiary program may be necessary for the main program to come to completion, and yet another for that subprogram to come to completion, etc. This means that transformations of subprograms may be required to facilitate the final transformation. In schematic form, the narrative trajectory may be represented as follows:

$$S1 \ (S2 \cap Ov)$$
$$|$$
$$S1a \ (S1 \cap Ov1)$$
$$|$$
$$S1b \ (S1a \cap Ov2)$$

etc.[4]

An example of such a trajectory (in Acts 2) is:

$$Disciples \ (Pentecost \ crowd \cap word) \ (2:5\text{-}11)$$
$$|$$
$$Jesus \ (Disciples \cap power \ of \ Spirit) \ (2:33)$$
$$|$$
$$God \ (Jesus \cap Promise \ of \ Holy \ Spirit) \ (2:33)$$

## PRINCIPAL AND POLEMICAL AXES

Earlier, I suggested that a basic assumption of structuralism is that meaning takes place by differentiating binary oppositions. This is true not only of individual terms, but also of narrative processes. Narrative develops by polarities. Oppositions are evident in narrative programs involving transformation when a subject comes into a conjunction with a competence or value. Competing programs, which threaten to thwart the competence and performance states in the narrative schema, stand in opposition to the primary programs. In fact, Greimas and Courtés claim that narrative organization is based on a polemic principle. That is, human beings conceive of their activity in terms of confrontations (1982: "Polemic," "Narrative Schema"). Thus, narratives juxtapose principal and polemical programs.

Traditional interpretation has directed major attention to thematic development but has shown little interest in the polemical counterpart. But this is to neglect an essential half of the story. There is an interplay between the principal and polemical axes that is essential to retrospective recovery of the story.[5]

Moreover, narratives establish antitheses early and develop them in consistent patterns so that polarities at the end are parallel to those at the beginning. Greimas and Courtés call this "homologation," that is a rigorous analogy on the pattern A : B :: A´ : B´ (1982: "Homologation"). Thus, the opposition between the principal (A) and polemical (B) axes at the beginning of Luke-Acts correspond to the principal (A´) and polemical (B´) axes at the end. In this connection, Jean Calloud has shown that the temptations in Luke 4:1-13 manifest the oppositions that organize the rest of the Gospel (Calloud 1976:73), or more inclusively, I argue, the rest of Luke-Acts.

In summary, determining narrative structure, as advocated here, requires that the interpreter (1) analyze the relationships among the narrative schemata, that is primary, parallel, converging, and diverging; (2) determine the phases in the narrative schema, that is, need, competence, performance, or sanction; (3) ascertain the transformations (narrative programs) that take place when a subject comes into conjunction with an object of value or into disjunction from an undesirable object; and (4) compare negative narrative programs in the polemical axis with positive narrative programs in the principal axis.

## LUKE 1-4

Luke-Acts begins on a level outside the story time, where an inscribed author addresses an inscribed reader directly but externally to the story. After the prologue (1:1-4) the narration shifts to another level with a covert narrator with an internal position (Uspensky 1973:147-49, Parsons 1987:97, 176-77).

(1) The prologue is concerned with overcoming the need of the uncertainty of Theophilus. From this perspective, the remainder of Luke-Acts is a converging narrative that provides the competence phase for communicating certainty to Theophilus.

(2) To determine the phases in the narrative schema, the interpreter looks for situations of need and their resolution. (A) The narrative is compiled in order to alleviate uncertainty on the part of Theophilus concerning the things about which he has been taught. (B) The inscribed author has become competent to accomplish this because he is a member of a community ("us," 1:1-2) that has received tradition from eyewitnesses and ministers of the word. He is made competent further by his own investigation (1:3). (C) The performance is the writing and reading of Luke-Acts. (D) There is no sanction stage, however. The sanction would require a positive response on the part of Theophilus, and such a response is not manifested in Luke-Acts.

(3) Narrative programs are the transformations that take place when a subject comes into conjunction with an object of value or disjunction with an undesirable object. In the need stage, Theophilus is conjoined with uncertainty, an undesirable object. In the competence phase, the inscribed author comes into conjunction with the tradition from eyewitnesses and ministers of the word and with the results of his own investigation. In the performance stage, the inscribed reader comes into conjunction with the narrative of Luke-Acts.

(4) When narrative programs are represented by substituting appropriately in the formula S1 (S2 ∩ Ov), they can be aligned into a principal axis or a polemical axis as follows.

| Principal Axis | Polemical Axis |
|---|---|
| Eyewitnesses and Ministers of the Word (Inscribed Author ∩ Tradition) | |
| Inscribed Author (Inscribed Author ∩ Investigation) | |
| Inscribed Author (Inscribed Reader ∩ Certainty) | ? (Inscribed Reader ∩ Uncertainty) |

At the end of the prologue there is little clue as to what organizes the oppositions. In 1973 Paul Minear advocated drawing up a checklist of doubt-generating forces in Luke-Acts (135-36). He anticipated the principle of homologation, namely, that the oppositions in the narrative programs correspond to principal and polemical axes throughout Luke-Acts. But tracing the principal and polemical axes goes a step beyond Minear's theme of doubt. The narrative manifests basic antitheses beyond the doubt of Theophilus—by way of anticipation, the divine and the satanic.

As Luke-Acts moves to the birth of John the Baptist, the need of a prophet to prepare a people for the Lord determines the primary narrative schema (Luke 1:17). A host of other needs that the narrative overcomes define subsidiary schemata. But they are subsidiary because they serve the competence phase of fulfilling the need of a prophet to prepare a people. For example, in one converging subsidiary schema, Gabriel's announcement creates a need for Zechariah and Elizabeth to have a child (1:13, cf. 1:7). Their age and Elizabeth's sterility are obstacles to the performance. Divine action overcomes the obstacles in the competence stage (1:25). Luke 1:57 straightforwardly announces the birth in the performance phase, and the communal rejoicing, circumcision, naming, and spreading of rumors constitute the sanction stage (1:58-66).

| (Primary Schema) Need | | Competence | Performance | Sanction |
|---|---|---|---|---|
| Prophet to prepare people (1:14-17) | | | Preaching (3:3, 7-17) | Baptisms (3:3-21) |

| (Converging Schema) Need | Competence | Performance | Sanction |
|---|---|---|---|
| Elderly Couple Childless (1:7) | Divine Intervention (1:13, 37, 58) | Birth (1:57) | Celebration (1:58, 65-66) |

Similarly, Zechariah's prophecy in Luke 1:68-79 is part of the sanction of the birth of John the Baptist. But it also makes predictions that create a narrative need of fulfillment (Talbert 1984:91-103).[6] The prophecy anticipates that John will be a prophet who will prepare the way of the Lord. With that anticipation, the subsidiary narrative converges with the primary one. And the performance that fills the need for Zechariah and Elizabeth to have a child then functions as a part of the competence phase of the prophet's preparation of a people.

The competence phase continues in Luke 3:2 with God's word coming to John. This leads directly to the performance stage in which John preaches a baptism of repentance for the forgiveness of sins (3:3, 7-17). There is then a peculiar type of sanction in that Herod the tetrarch imprisons John (3:19-20). A narrator's summary about all the people having been baptized then constitutes a further sanction, a sanction that is reiterated in 7:29; 20:6 and Acts 13:24-25 (cf. Acts 10:37).

The complex narrative schemata fit into a hierarchical pattern where the performance stage of one comprises the competence phase of another. Within that complexity, there are numerous narrative programs. To illustrate, in the subsidiary narrative schema where Zechariah's unbelief is the need to be overcome, Gabriel is conjoined with the divine presence and sent by God (God is concealed in the passive verb in Luke 1:19) as a part of the competence phase. In the primary narrative regarding a prophet to prepare the people, the word of God comes to John as a part of the competence stage.

In Luke 1:5-3:21a the polemical axis is manifested chiefly in three narrative programs. Zechariah is conjoined with unbelief (Luke 1:20). Herod the tetrarch is conjoined with evil things (3:19). In a negative narrative schema, the conjunction of Herod with evil things is a part of the competence phase in his imprisonment of John, and thus John is conjoined with imprisonment, an undesirable object. In schematic form, the narrative programs appear in opposition as follows.

| *Principal Axis* | *Polemical Axis* |
| --- | --- |
| ? (Gabriel ∩ Divine Presence) (1:19) | |
| God (Gabriel ∩ Message) (1:19) | |
| Gabriel (Zechariah ∩ Good News) (1:19) | ? (Zechariah ∩ Unbelief) (1:20) |
| God (John ∩ Word) (3:2) | |
| John (Herod ∩ Reproof) (3:19) | ? (Herod ∩ Evil Things) (3:19) |
| John (People ∩ Good News) (3:18) | Herod (John ∩ Prison) (3:20) |
| John (People ∩ Baptism) (3:21) | |

But because John's prophetic ministry is to prepare a people for the Lord, the narrative schema to which he belongs is subsidiary to yet another narrative schema regarding king and people. Gabriel's annunciation to Mary has established a primary need for a ruler over the house of Jacob (Luke 1:33).

Many interpreters take Mary's song (Luke 1:46b-55) as a prophetic prediction. Joseph Fitzmyer shows correctly that, from a form critical perspective, it is a hymn of praise rehearsing what has happened in the past rather than predicting what is to come. Nevertheless, Fitzmyer views the past tenses as corresponding to the author's retrospective point of view and thus understands the rehearsal of God's past deeds to be indications of the future career of Jesus (Fitzmyer 1981:358-61, cf. Lohfink 1975:26-27). Literarily, however, Mary's canticle is not a prophetic prediction that creates a narrative need of fulfillment.

The virginal conception and the birth of Jesus are part of the competence phase in establishing the reign of the king. This subsidiary schema follows the pattern of need, competence, performance, and sanction. Gabriel's announcement creates a need for conception and birth (Luke 1:31) (a need complicated by the absence of a husband [1:34]), and the power of God overshadowing Mary constitutes the competence stage (1:35). The birth of Jesus is the performance (2:7). The testimony of angels and shepherds is the sanction (2:10-17).

Gabriel's announcement creates another narrative need. He predicts that the child will be named Jesus and called holy, the Son of God (Luke 1:31, 32, 35). This creates a narrative need for identification. At the circumcision the child is duly named Jesus (2:21), but not until Jesus' baptism is he called Son of God (3:22). The voice from heaven is a part of the performance in the identification schema. The genealogy breaks from the narrative mode as an intrusion from the narrator who supplies this information directly to the implied reader. Nevertheless, it functions as a sanction for the identity of Jesus (3:23-38).

John the Baptist makes another prophetic prediction that creates a narrative need. In Luke 3:16 John the Baptist announces the coming of a mightier one who will baptize with the Holy Spirit and with fire, and who will gather the wheat into his granary, but who will burn the chaff with unquenchable fire. Later Jesus reiterates the motif by claiming that his purpose is to cast fire on the earth and produce division (12:49-53). Here "fire" carries two distinct connotations. Baptism with fire is metonymy for divine power in a positive sense, burning with fire in a negative sense.

Because Acts 1:5 and the tongues of fire and other events at Pentecost (Acts 2) recall the first part of the prediction of John the Baptist, then the ministry, death, resurrection, and ascension of Jesus can be seen as the competence phase in this narrative schema. According to Luke 3:9 John is already involved in pruning and burning the unfruitful branches from Israel. But the second half of John's prediction anticipates Jesus' ministry of gathering and sifting a people for God.

But before such a precipitous leap forward, the baptism and the genealogy function as a transition to the ministry of Jesus. The narrative needs with respect to king and people created by the anticipations in Luke 1-3 now begin to be correlated with competence, performance, and sanction stages. The baptism not only identifies Jesus but also is part of the competence phase for his role. The Holy Spirit descends upon him, and thereafter the narrator describes Jesus as full of the Holy Spirit (Luke 4:1).

Moreover, the temptations play a double role in narrative schemata, first as an additional sanction for Jesus' identity, and then as a part of the competence phase in qualifying him for his ministry. For the first time in Luke-Acts two characters, Jesus and the devil, contradict each other with opposing enterprises. Two of the temptations challenge the identity of Jesus as the Son of God by enticing him to submit to proofs contrived by the devil. In this regard, the underlying plot is a repetition. The same thing happens to the same character in distinct events. That helps to eliminate ambiguity and imposes constraints for a single "correct" reading (Suleiman 1980:120).

On the primary level the narrative juxtaposes Jesus' being led in the Spirit with his being tempted by the devil. On the one hand, the descent of the Spirit is linked with the identity of Jesus as Son of God in Luke 3:22. If the narrative is to sanction that identity, Jesus must continue to be in the Spirit rather than be led by the devil. On the other hand, for Jesus to be in the Spirit is to render him competent for his ministry.

In the first temptation, the devil attempts to displace the need for Jesus to be in the Spirit with hunger as the narrative need. That narrative schema aborts, however, because in the competing narrative schema, Jesus refuses to install hunger alone as the need to be fulfilled, and being led in the Spirit continues to occupy the place of narrative need. In the competence phase, Jesus cites scripture in order to reject hunger as the lack to be met, and so the devil is unable to dislodge him from being in the Spirit.

Jean Calloud argues that the refusal of the devil's program of action is more than a mere return to the point of departure, namely, Jesus' relationship to God as Son. Rather, according to Calloud, Jesus establishes a hierarchy of two orders—the word and bread. In this way, Calloud suggests, Jesus presents the word as a way of life superior to bread (1976:59-61).

But Calloud is working from the Matthean form of Jesus' response where the partial negation of bread as a way to life ("not by bread alone") is followed by the affirmation of the word of God as a way to life ("but by every word that comes from the mouth of God"). In the Lucan version, Jesus' claim that human beings shall not live by bread alone is but part of the competence phase in the primary narrative schema of being led in the Spirit. Hence in Luke Jesus' response does not establish the hierarchy of orders, word-bread; and Jesus does return to the point of departure, that is, being led in the Spirit.

The second temptation is a frontal assault. The devil attempts to get Jesus to worship him. In the competence stage, the devil offers in exchange all the kingdoms of the world. An underlying narrative program here has the devil claiming that another subject (concealed in the passive voice) has given him all this authority (Luke 4:6), and thus ironically admitting to an authority beyond his own (Calloud 1976:71-72). This narrative schema also aborts because the potential performance of Jesus being led by the devil goes unfulfilled. Once again in the competence phase of the competing schema, Jesus cites scripture, and in the implied performance continues to be led in the Spirit.

In the final temptation, in the competence stage of his narrative schema the devil places Jesus on the pinnacle of the temple, cites scripture, and urges Jesus to test promises in Psalm 91. As with hunger earlier, the devil is attempting to install the validity of this text as the narrative need. But in the competence stage of the competing schema Jesus counters with scripture, and the devil's schema again aborts. The temptations, therefore, sanction the identity of Jesus as Son of God and establish his competence for his ministry as one who is in the Spirit.

Underlying the narrative schemata are narrative programs in competing axes as follows.

| *Principal Axis* | *Polemical Axis* |
|---|---|
| Spirit (Zechariah ∩ Prediction) (1:71,74) | |
| Spirit (Simeon ∩ Prediction) (2:32, 34) | |
| Spirit (Mary ∩ Conception) (1:35) | |
| Mary (Son ∩ Birth) (2:7) | |
| Angel (Shepherds ∩ Message) (2:11-12) | |
| Mary & Joseph (Child ∩ Name) (2:21) | |
| ? (Jesus ∩ Baptism) (3:21) | |
| Heavenly Voice (Jesus ∩ Sonship) (3:22) | |
| God (Jesus ∩ Spirit) (3:22) | Devil (Jesus ∩ Temptation) (4:2) |
| Spirit (Jesus ∩ Leading [Spirit]) (4:1) | Devil (Jesus ∩ Leading [Devil]) (4:3, 7, 9) |
| Jesus (Jesus ∩ Leading [Spirit]) (4:4, 8, 12) | |
| ? (Jesus ∩ Scripture) (4:4, 8, 12) | ? (Devil ∩ Scripture) (4:10-11) |
| Jesus (Jesus ∩ Authority [Satanic]) (4:8) | ? (Devil ∩ Authority) (4:6) |

Whereas the prologue and the remainder of chapters 1-3 provide little clue as to the forces organizing the principal and polemical axes, the temptations manifest a basic antithesis between the divine and the satanic. The uncertainty of the inscribed reader (Luke 1:4), Zechariah's unbelief (1:20), Herod's evil deeds, and Herod's imprisonment of John (3:19-20) align in the polemical axis with the devil's temptations of Jesus. Hans

Conzelmann takes 4:13 quite literally and claims that with the end of the temptations the devil abandons Jesus until the resumption of the temptation motif in 22:3 (Conzelmann 1961: 28). However true that may be as far as temptation of Jesus is concerned, the continuing alignment of negative narrative programs with those in the devil's temptations shows, as Calloud suggests, that the satanic is the organizing force for the polemical axis throughout Luke-Acts.

Narrative programs in the polemical axis in the remainder of chapter 4 bear this out. In the incident in Nazareth, the people are filled with wrath, [? (people ∩ wrath) (4:28)], and they attempt to kill Jesus [people (Jesus ∩ death) (4:29)]. In the exorcism in Capernaum (4:31-36), Jesus disjoins a man from an undesirable object, a demon [Jesus (man ∪ demon) (4:35)], and the polemical counterpart is that the man is conjoined with an unclean demon in the need phase of the narrative schema [? (man ∩ demon) (4:33)].

But to understand the incidents in Nazareth and Capernaum merely as antitheses between Jesus and opponents is inadequate. Rather, in Nazareth Jesus claims an identity as one anointed with the Spirit of the Lord [God (Jesus ∩ Spirit) (4:18, 21)], and surprisingly in Capernaum the demon identifies Jesus as the Holy One of God. On one level, this continues the narrative schema developing from Gabriel's prediction to Mary that the child would be called "holy" (1:35). In fact, the demon in Capernaum is the first explicitly to call Jesus "holy." But on a second level, the utterance creates a narrative need for Jesus to silence the demon, and on this level the demon's naming of Jesus [demon (Jesus ∩ title) (4:34)] is a part of the negative polarity. The basic antithesis, therefore, is not between Jesus and opponents. Rather, the opposition to Jesus is a manifestation of a larger conflict between the divine and the satanic. The devil does not succeed in tempting Jesus but does succeed in organizing a potent antithesis to him.

The incident in Nazareth (Luke 4:16-30) involves a complex relationship between two narrative schemata. After reading from Isaiah, Jesus claims fulfillment of the text. The citation from

Isaiah then anticipates Jesus' kind of ministry and creates a narrative need for Jesus to fulfill such a ministry.

But there is a second narrative schema. Jesus not only predicts his ministry but also claims identity as Spirit-filled Messiah (the anointed one). The question of Jesus' identity has not escaped the notice of many interpreters, but most wish to continue to interpret the passage as a description of Jesus' ministry. And so when Jesus refers to Elijah and Elisha, most interpreters see an anticipation of the Gentile mission. But does this fit in with the two narrative schemata in Luke 4:16-30?

First, in relating himself to the citation from Isaiah, Jesus establishes a need phase in one narrative schema, and a large part of the remainder of Luke corresponds to performance and sanction stages in that narrative schema. But in the second place, in relating himself to the citation from Isaiah, Jesus claims an identity, and from 4:22b on the narrative is moving to counter an inadequate identification of Jesus as (merely) Joseph's son. In order to fulfill this narrative schema, yet another need phase is established by the proverb, "No prophet is acceptable in his own country" (4:24). According to this criterion, rejection of Jesus in his own country confirms that he is a prophet. The cases of Elijah and Elisha prove the proverb, and thus they serve as a part of the competence phase in the schema establishing the criterion. And in the performance stage, the people of Nazareth reject Jesus, thereby confirming, ironically, the prophetic identity of Jesus.

According to this analysis, the relationships of Elijah and Elisha with Gentiles establish that they are prophets who are not accepted in their own country, but their relationships with Gentiles have nothing to do with the kind of ministry Jesus will fulfill—Jesus carries out no Gentile mission. Neither do the incidents involving Elijah and Elisha anticipate the Gentile mission in Acts.[7]

To summarize, in the first four chapters of Luke a coalition of Gabriel, Zechariah, Simeon, John the Baptist, and Jesus offer anticipations that call for a king to reign over the house of Jacob, to deliver Abraham's descendants from their enemies, to baptize with the Holy Spirit and with fire, to gather and sift

God's people, and to carry out the Spirit-filled messianic and prophetic ministry outlined in 4:18-19.

## THE REMAINDER OF LUKE

Manifestly, this type of structural analysis is time-consuming and its results complex and bulky. Constraints of space, therefore, perhaps justify my abridging large portions of the remaining analysis of Luke-Acts. Not until the trial, death, resurrection, and ascension of Jesus can we speak of his enthronement as messianic king. John the Baptist's prediction of baptism with the Holy Spirit and with fire foreshadows Pentecost in Acts, and that development of the plot is also held in abeyance. But after Luke 4:30 most of the Gospel portrays Jesus gathering and sifting God's people, preaching good news to the poor, releasing captives, giving sight to the blind, and setting the oppressed at liberty—all against the background of the eschatological Jubilee year (cf. "the acceptable year of the Lord," 4:19).[8] In short, the remainder of Luke is primarily the competence and performance stages of the narrative schemata of the fulfillment of Jesus' messianic identity, his ministry of liberation, and the gathering and sifting of God's people.

Immediately following the incident in Nazareth, Jesus exorcises a demon in Capernaum (Luke 4:31-36). By his rebuke, Jesus proclaims release to one who is a captive and is oppressed. Similar episodes, marked by the redundancy of the same thing happening to different characters, continue the performance stage of the narrative need for Jesus to carry out a ministry corresponding to Luke 4:18-19. Jesus releases a leper from his disease (5:12-15), releases a paralytic from his oppression(5:17-26), heals a man with a withered hand (6:6-11), heals the centurion's servant (7:2-10), raises a man from the dead (7:11-17), forgives the sins of a woman who is a notorious sinner (7:37-50), cures a demoniac (8:26-33), heals a woman with a hemorrhage (8:42c-48), raises Jairus's daughter from the dead (8:41-56), exorcises a demon (9:37-43), cures a man who is mute (11:14), liberates a woman who is bent over (13:11-12), heals a man with dropsy (14:2-4), cleanses ten lepers (17:11-19), heals a blind man (18:35-43), heals the wounded slave of the high priest (22:50-52), and promises a suppliant thief paradise (23:40-43).

All of these actions are transformations that can be written schematically as narrative programs of disjunction from an undesirable object or, less frequently, conjunction with a desirable object—for example, Jesus (leper ∪ leprosy) (5:12-14) or Jesus (woman ∩ son) (7:11-17). Together they constitute the performance stage in the narrative schema developing from the need for Jesus to exercise his ministry of liberation.

The surface sequence is not linear. The phases may occur out of sequence. Along the way competence, sanction, and occasionally even need alternate with performance. As a case in point, Luke 7:18-23 may be understood both as a part of the performance phase in the narrative schema of the identity of Jesus and as a part of the sanction stage in the fulfillment of Jesus' ministry. In response to the inquiry of messengers from John the Baptist, Jesus' summary of his works is a part of the sanction phase of the narrative schema of his ministry.

Other parts of the sanction stage are the response of crowds, and in some cases the opposition of detractors. This last point is particularly true in the case of the accusation that Jesus casts out demons by the prince of demons. In Luke 11:15-26, even the opponents agree that Jesus casts out demons and, hence, are part of the sanction. But they contest the divine origin of his exorcisms. The ensuing controversy establishes that what Jesus does is a manifestation of divine rule, and, consequently, sanctions Jesus' exorcisms.

But Luke 7:18-23 obviously has to do also with the identity of Jesus. Is Jesus the one who is to come (a periphrasis for "Messiah") or not? Thus, in the narrative schema developing from the need to identify Jesus, Jesus' summary of the results of his ministry forms part of the performance stage.

Likewise the transfiguration obviously continues the performance stage in the identification of Jesus. Presumably, nothing less than a divine voice calls Jesus "My Son, my Chosen" (Luke 9:35). But the incident also picks up on the first passion prediction in 9:22. The first passion prediction creates a narrative need for Jesus to suffer and die. Moses and Elijah reinforce the narrative need by giving Jesus additional revelation about his passion. They call it his *exodos*, and then create a new narrative need by indicating that it will be fulfilled in Jerusalem. Significantly, Jesus begins his journey in 9:51 as a part of the competence phase in the narrative need to go to Jerusalem.[9] And the journey to Jerusalem is a converging narrative that constitutes the competence stage of Jesus' passion.

Besides providing the performance and sanction stages of the identification of Jesus, his healing ministry, and his passion, the Gospel of Luke also portrays Jesus proclaiming good news. In addition to the announcement in Luke 4:18-19, another anticipation from Jesus in 4:43 reinforces the narrative need of proclamation. There are narrator's summaries of Jesus' teaching and preaching (e.g., 4:31, 44). But the Gospel also portrays Jesus teaching and preaching in dramatic episodes.[10]

First, teaching is one of the functions of many of the conflict stories. To illustrate, in the controversy with the scribes and Pharisees over the healing of a man who has a withered hand (Luke 6:6-11), Jesus raises the question of the *halakah* regarding the sabbath. When he heals the man, Jesus illustrates dramatically that his *halakah* is superior. A similar case occurs in 13:10-17. Significantly, the narrator introduces this incident as "teaching," and here again the controversy over healing on the sabbath allows Jesus to demonstrate dramatically the superiority of his *halakah*. In a third redundancy, healing creates a controversy over the sabbath and enables Jesus to establish the superiority of his *halakah* (14:1-6) (Sanders 1985:153, 158-59, 170, 174-86). There are additional conflict stories in Jerusalem that Jesus uses as an occasion to teach (20:1-44).

Second, Jesus teaches the disciples privately. For example, he interprets the parable of the sower for his disciples (Luke 8:9-18). When Peter identifies Jesus as the Messiah (9:18-20), Jesus instructs the disciples about his suffering and the nature of discipleship (9:21-27). On another occasion Jesus responds to the disciples' request to teach them to pray (11:1-13, cf. 18:1-8). Finally, the risen Jesus instructs them how to understand the divine necessity for the Messiah to suffer, and to comprehend their own mission (24:27, 45-49; cf. Acts 1:3-8).

Third, the narrator presents Jesus proclaiming his message to multitudes. The most obvious of these is the so-called sermon on the plain (Luke 6:17-7:1). But Jesus makes briefer proclamations to the crowds in 7:24-35; 8:4-8; and 14:25-35. He also teaches specific groups such as the guests in the home of a ruler of the Pharisees in 14:1-24 and the Pharisees and scribes in 15:1-32. In Jerusalem, Jesus' typical activity is to teach the people (19:47; 21:37; 20:1-18; 20:45-21:36). Thus, Luke is rich in episodes that fulfill the performance and sanction stages of the narrative schema relating to Jesus' ministry of proclamation.

A major narrative need emerging from the predictions of Gabriel, Zechariah, and John the Baptist is for Jesus to gather the people of God. But according to Luke 3:17, the process of gathering involves sifting out the inauthentic.[11] Jesus' ministry is closely connected to the divine covenant with Abraham (1:73). But being a descendent of Abraham is no guarantee of inclusion. Therefore, John enjoins his hearers to bear fruits of repentance rather than to claim descent from Abraham. And the implied consequence for failure to repent is to be excluded. The double edges of Jesus' relationship with the people come to expression in the agricultural imagery of gathering wheat into a granary and burning the chaff.

In the narrative schema developing out of the need to gather and sift, John's preparation of the people lays the foundation in the competence stage (Luke 3:21). Then rumors spreading Jesus' fame and bringing crowds to him are also part of the competence phase (4:14-15, 37, 42; 5:1, etc.). The miraculous catch of fish in 5:2-11 is another part of the competence stage. The miracle establishes the occasion for Jesus to predict to Simon: "Henceforth you will be catching men" (5:10). A fishing metaphor has replaced the agricultural one in 3:17, but the point of gathering is quite the same.

In the episode of the miraculous catch of fish Simon, James, and John follow Jesus. Their following plays a double role in the narrative schema. It is the initiation of gathering and, therefore, belongs to the performance stage. But inasmuch as the disciples will also discharge a function in gathering the people of God, the initial following also conforms to the competence phase. The calling of Levi fits into the same type of double function—part of the gathering and part of the capacity to gather (5:27-28).

Another relevant part of the competence phase is the selection of the twelve from the number of Jesus' disciples (Luke 6:13-16). And their selection is a proleptic anticipation of Luke 22:30, where Jesus cements their significance for gathering the people of God by promising that they will sit on thrones judging the twelve tribes of Israel. In the meantime, Jesus gives the twelve authority over demonic opponents (9:1-6)—an additional component of the competence phase.

Similarly, Jesus empowers the seventy and adopts the agricultural metaphor of gathering by designating them laborers in the harvest (10:1-12, 17-20). A major part of the competence stage here is that Jesus claims to have witnessed Satan's demise (10:18). Represented in schematic form are the following narrative programs underlying the competence phase: Father (Jesus ∩ all things) (10:22), Jesus (twelve ∩ authority) (9:1), Jesus (seventy[-two] ∩ authority) (10:19), ? (Satan ∪ heaven) (10:18).

The story of Zacchaeus well illustrates performance in the narrative schema of gathering and sifting, echoing themes that recall the predictions of Zechariah and John the Baptist. Zacchaeus dramatizes repentance, but Jesus also spells out the relationship of Zacchaeus to Abraham (19:1-10). Thus he highlights the theme of the Abrahamic covenant together with the criterion of repentance for inclusion in the people of God.

For all of Jesus' fame and contact with the people, the Gospel of Luke ends with a gathering that is unpretentious at best. After the crucifixion Judas falls out of the number of the apostles, and the narrator describes the group that remains as the eleven and those with them. Acts 1:13-15 sets the number at 120. This number has a definite relationship to the twelve and overtones of the twelve tribes of Israel. Gerhard Lohfink suggests that the number corresponds to Jewish requirements for 10 men to constitute a synagogue (12 X 10 = 120) (Lohfink 1975:70-72). This is unlikely, however, because Acts 1:14-15 specifically includes women in the number (Conzelmann 1987: 10). The number more likely alludes to Ex 18:21 where Jethro advises Moses to appoint leaders to rule over the people in groups of thousands, hundreds, fifties, and *tens*. In any case, the earthly Jesus gathers a very modest number of followers, and the performance of the narrative need to gather and sift a people for God falls primarily upon the witnesses in Acts.

But first, at the end of Luke, the polemical axis develops full blown. In line with Gabriel's prediction that God would give Jesus the throne of David, a multitude of his disciples designate him messianic king (Luke 19:38). This draws the rebuke of some Pharisees but the affirmation of Jesus (19:39-40). Then as Jesus teaches in the temple, chief priests and scribes and the leaders of the people seek to destroy him (19:47) and question his authority (20:1-6).

At the time of the passover, Satan enters Judas, from which time Judas conspires with the chief priests and officers to betray Jesus (Luke 22:3-6). Satan also seduces Simon (22:31). Judas leads a crowd of opponents to arrest Jesus (22:52). The sanhedrin hears Jesus' testimony and accuses him before Pilate (22:66-23:5). Herod and his soldiers treat Jesus with contempt (23:11). Although Pilate proclaims Jesus' innocence three times, he ultimately sentences him to be crucified (23:4, 14-15, 22, 24). At the crucifixion rulers, soldiers, and a criminal mock him (23:35-37, 39) and in so doing oppose the identity of Jesus as the Messiah, the chosen one of God, and king of the Jews.

Alignment of characters within principal and polemic axes corresponds not only to the principle of homologation but also to Marianna Torgovnick's literary theory of circular closure. According to Torgovnick, there are two particular tactics for closure—circularity and parallelism. In circularity, the end recalls the beginning in language, situation, grouping of characters, or in combinations of these. In parallelism the language, situations, or grouping of characters recalls not merely the beginning but a series of points in the narrative (Torgovnick 1981:13).

Corresponding to the uncertainty of Theophilus with which Luke opens, Cleopas and his companion have eyes that are kept from recognizing the risen Jesus (Luke 24:16). Luke 4:18 anticipates a ministry of opening the eyes of the blind. Thus, there is a striking circular recall in the opening of the eyes of the two disciples in Emmaus (cf. Acts 9:18). Not only are their eyes opened so that they recognize Jesus, but also their hearts are made receptive to Jesus' interpretation of scripture (24:27, 31, 32). Finally, the eleven and those with them also correspond to Theophilus in that Jesus exposes their questionings, and they disbelieve and wonder even in their joy (24:38, 41). And so Jesus opens the minds of the eleven and those with them to understand the scriptures (24:45).

In the closing chapters antithethical narrative programs align in the principle and polemical axes as follows:

| *Principal Axis* | *Polemical Axis* |
|---|---|
| Disciples (Jesus ∩ Title [King]) (19:38) | Pharisees (Disciples ∩ Rebuke) (19:39) |
| Jesus (Disciples ∩ Affirmation) (19:40) | Chief Priests, Scribes, Leaders (Jesus ∩ Destruction) (19:47) |
| Father (Jesus ∩ Authority) (10:22) | Chief Priests, Scribes, Elders (Jesus ∪ Authority) (20:1-8) |
| Jesus (Jesus ∪ Trap) (20:19-26) | Spies (Jesus ∩ Trap) (20:19-26) |
| Jesus (Sadducees ∩ Error) (20:27-40) | Sadducees (Jesus ∩ Question) (20:27-40) |
| | ? (Judas ∩ Satan) (22:3) |
| | Satan (Judas ∩ Opponents) (22:4-6) |
| Pilate (Jesus ∩ Innocence) (23:4, 14-15, 22) | Satan (Simon ∩ Denial) (22:31-34, 54-62) |
| Second Criminal (Jesus ∩ Innocence) (23:41) | Judas (Authorities ∩ Jesus) (22:47-53) |
| Centurion (Jesus ∩ Innocence) (23:47) | Sanhedrin (Jesus ∩ Accusation) (22:66-23:2, 5) |
| | Herod, Soldiers (Jesus ∩ Contempt) (23:11) |
| | Pilate (Jesus ∩ Sentence) (23:24) |
| | Rulers, Soldiers, Criminal (Jesus ∪ Identity) (23:35-39) |
| ? (Cleopas & Companion ∩ Opened Eyes) (24:31) | ? (Cleopas & Companion ∩ Closed Eyes) (24:16) |
| ? (Cleopas & Companion ∩ Receptive Hearts) (24:32) | |
| Jesus (Eleven & Companions ∩ Understanding) (24:45) | ? (Eleven & Companions ∩ Questionings) (24:38, 41) |

## PRIMARY NARRATIVE SCHEMATA IN LUKE

To summarize, an analysis of the primary narrative schemata helps to highlight the retrospective recovery of the story and to delineate three primary developments toward teleological goals. (1) There is a movement toward the identity of Jesus. (2) Jesus fulfills a ministry of liberation anticipated from prophetic predictions and his own claims. (3) Jesus embarks on the task of gathering a people for God and engages his disciples for the fulfillment of the task.

Further, aligning narrative programs into principle and polemical axes manifests the antithetical character of the development of the narrative and shows that whatever the individual motivations for behavior may be, they correspond ultimately to the antipodes between God and Satan. Those who align with the inscribed author in Luke 1:1-4 and with Jesus in the rest of Luke also align with God. Those who align with Theophilus and with the opponents of Jesus align with Satan.

# 4

# RETROSPECTIVE RECOVERY: THE LOGIC OF THE STORY IN ACTS

The passages in Luke-Acts where the narrator intrudes by using the first person pronouns "I" and "we" convinced H. J. Cadbury that the prologue to Luke anticipates Acts. He argued that the author claims to have participated in or observed events closely (Luke 1:3). Because the author was not a participant in Luke, he must have claimed to have participated in events in Acts (1956-57:128-32). Therefore, the prologue to Luke testifies to the literary unity of Luke-Acts. But against Cadbury, Ernst Haenchen and Hans Conzelmann pointed out that the prologue refers to predecessors who had compiled similar narratives. Luke had antecedents, but Acts is apparently the first of its kind and is hardly anticipated in the prologue to Luke (Haenchen 1961:329-66, Conzelmann 1961:15, n. 1).

Another difficulty in assuming literary unity is the rough transition from Luke to Acts. In Luke the ascension presumably occurs near Bethany on the same day as the resurrection whereas in Acts it occurs on the Mount of Olives after forty days (Luke 24:50-51, Acts 1:3, 12). On the other hand, both documents are dedicated to Theophilus, and the prologue to Acts makes reference to "the first book" and summarizes Luke (Acts 1:1-2). Additionally, Acts reiterates themes and literary patterns found in the Gospel.[1]

But aside from these arguments, narrative schemata originating in Luke and bridging over into Acts provide forceful evidence for literary unity.

(1) Even with allusions to Jesus' kingship and kingdom in Luke, the narrative need for Jesus to rule over the house of Jacob for ever (1:32-33) finds little to correspond to performance and sanction stages in Luke itself.

(2) Closely related, although much of Luke fits the competence and performance stages of gathering and sifting a people for God, the sanction stage at the end of Luke shows that the gathering and sifting produces a meager harvest (24:33).

(3) Jesus' ministry, death, and resurrection constitute the competence phase in the narrative schema arising from John the Baptist's announcement of one who would baptize with Holy Spirit and with fire (3:16), but the performance and sanction stages penetrate into Acts.

The narrative schema of Jesus' identity does move adequately through competence, performance, and sanction stages in Luke. Similarly complete is the narrative schema unfolding from predictions about the nature of Jesus' ministry. Nevertheless, strands of both extend into Acts. The problem of identifying the one who was crucified as the Messiah, reflected by the disillusionment of the disciples in Luke 24:20-21 (cf. 24:38), leads to the explanation that it is a divine necessity in Acts 2:23 and 3:18 as well as in Luke 24:26-27. Moreover, the resurrection is a divine affirmation of Jesus' messiahship that vindicates him from the scandal of the crucifixion (Acts 2:24; 4:10-11; 10:39-40). And the narrative schema showing the nature of Jesus' ministry finds sanction in Peter's summary of it in his speech to Cornelius (10:38). This is to say that the narrative structure links the two volumes together literarily.

The narrative schema concerning the enthronement of Jesus as king ripens in Acts from seeds sown in Luke. To reiterate, Gabriel's announcement to Mary is a prophetic prediction, and it creates a narrative need for Jesus to reign on the throne of David (Luke 1:32-33). Although Jesus speaks of God's kingdom (e.g., 4:43; 6:20; 12:31, etc.), there is little development toward Jesus' enthronement until the Lucan parable of ten pounds (19:11-27).

Against the conventional interpretation of the parable as an allegory of the ascension and the delay of the parousia, Luke Timothy Johnson shows that the parable refers to the kingship of Jesus to be established with his arrival in Jerusalem (1982: 139-59). Already in Luke disciples designate Jesus king (19:38).

Also, Jesus claims that his Father has assigned him a kingdom (22:29). In his trial Jesus gives an enigmatic but affirmative answer to Pilate's question: "Are you the king of the Jews?" (23:3). In addition, some hint at enthronement arises from Jesus' assertion before the sanhedrin: "From now on the Son of man shall be seated at the right hand of the power of God" (22:69). Quite obviously the resurrection and ascension are parts of the performance phase in this narrative schema.

But it is the book of Acts that makes it obvious. Peter's speech at Pentecost explicates the relationship between Jesus' resurrection and exaltation and his enthronement as the Davidic king (Acts 2:30-36). This same text contributes to the sanction phase. In Luke 24:49 Jesus pledges to send the promise of his Father. In the narrative schema generated by that pledge, Pentecost belongs to the performance phase. But Peter declares also that the pouring out of the Spirit is an act of the risen and exalted Jesus who in turn has received the promise of the Holy Spirit from the Father (Acts 2:33). Thus, in the narrative schema of the kingship of Jesus, the pouring out of the Spirit sanctions the resurrection and exaltation as enthronement.

Acts 5:30-32 functions in a comparable manner. In face of the scandal of Jesus' rejection and crucifixion, Peter and the apostles again assert that the resurrection is God's affirmation of Jesus. Then they announce the exaltation and claim a double sanction for it. First, their own witness is a sanction; second, so is the gift of the Holy Spirit.

Stephen also confirms the enthronement of Jesus. Because Stephen is full of the Holy Spirit, he can see into heaven. When he looks into heaven, he announces that he sees the Son of man standing at the right hand of God (Acts 7:55-56). Significantly, this is the point at which Stephen so enrages his opponents that they lynch him. That is, Stephen's christology, rather than his attacks on his opponents, precipitates his death. At any rate, Stephen's heavenly vision is a sanction of the enthronement of Jesus.

A thin part of the sanction of Jesus' kingship is the accusation from opponents in Thessalonica that Paul and Silas act against Caesar in saying that Jesus is another king (Acts 17:8). The reliability of the characters making the accusation comes into play. But in Acts unreliable characters may unwittingly express the truth. And so this accusation alludes indirectly to the proclamation of Paul and Silas of the kingship of Jesus. But when Paul later denies that he has offended against Caesar (25:8), he shows that his proclamation of the kingship of Jesus carries quite a different sense from the accusation. The force of Acts 17:31 is comparable. Paul affirms that the resurrection is the sanction for Jesus' status as eschatological judge, which may be construed as a function of Jesus' kingship.

As far as sheer space is concerned, the most prominent narrative schema spanning Luke-Acts is the gathering and sifting of a people for God. Of course it shares an intimate bond with Jesus' kingship—Jesus is to reign over the house of Jacob. Within the context of God's promises to Israel, Simeon's canticle foreshadows a revelation to Gentiles but leaves unclear whether the salvation will include Gentiles or stand merely as a public disclosure to them (Luke 2:29-32) (Tiede 1988:26-27). But additionally, Simeon's oracle anticipates that Jesus will be the occasion for a division in Israel: "This child is set for the fall and rising of many in Israel" (2:34). John the Baptist explicitly distinguishes between descendants of Abraham and the genuine people of God (3:8-9) and predicts that the coming one will gather and sift the people of God (3:9, 17). Thus, Luke 1-3 creates a narrative need for Jesus to gather and sift the people of God with some implications for Gentiles that remain indeterminate for the time being.

When Jesus heals a centurion's slave, he contrasts the centurion's faith with the lack of faith in Israel (Luke 7:1-10). Jesus, therefore, thrusts the belief of a Gentile into prominence. Nevertheless, on only one occasion does Jesus travel into Gentile territory. He heals a demoniac in the country of the Gerasenes (8:26-39). Otherwise, Jesus carries out no Gentile mission even though he also heals a Samaritan leper whom he calls a foreigner (17:18) (Conzelmann 1961:49-50).

It is commonplace to see an allusion to the Gentile mission in the double invitation in the parable of the great banquet (Luke 14:21, 23) (Jeremias 1972:64, 69). This conclusion, however, derives from comparison with parallels in Matthew and the Gospel of Thomas, rather than from the narrative development in Luke. Within the narrative schema of gathering and sifting, Simeon's canticle foreshadows, in a nebulous fashion, the Gentile mission in the need phase, but the need is not actually established until Jesus' commission in 24:47. It gains force with another commission to the apostles to be witnesses to the end of the earth (Acts 1:8). And before the advent of the Gentile mission, a divine vision informs Ananias that Paul's mission is to include Gentiles (9:15).

The Gentile mission is part of a larger narrative need created by Jesus' mandate to his followers to preach repentance and forgiveness of sins. In connection with that mandate, Jesus anticipates a need for empowerment, but in so doing implies the absence of power (Luke 24:49). Acts 1 reinforces both situations of need. Jesus mandates that the Apostles are to be witnesses, and again, he anticipates empowerment which will overcome an implied lack of power (Acts 1:8). Pentecost is the competence phase of the mission and also contributes to the performance and sanction stages. The Spirit comes upon the company of believers and empowers them (competence). They speak in tongues that are universally understood (performance). Peter interprets the occasion, and 3,000 people believe (sanction).

The competence for the apostolic witness, however, does not rest entirely on the coming of the Spirit but also on the reconstitution of the twelve. In an indeterminate way the parable of the ten pounds associates the faithful servants of the king in the administration of his kingdom (Luke 19:17, 19) (L. T. Johnson 1982:153). Then in Luke 22:30 Jesus promises that the apostles will sit on thrones judging the twelve tribes of Israel.[2] Thus, there is a narrative need for the twelve to be associated in the reign of Jesus. But in the competence phase the defection of Judas from the twelve creates a need for the restoration of the number. Otherwise, the performance would abort.

To repeat by way of reminder, narrative develops by polarities. Competing programs, which threaten to thwart competence and performance stages in the narrative schema, stand in opposition to primary programs. The story of Judas corresponds in the negative both (1) to the reconstitution of the twelve and (2) to the formation of a community judged by the apostles.[3]

(1) The defection of Judas decimates the number of those destined to judge Israel, a lack which the narrative attempts to fill. Along the principal axis in the competence phase of the narrative schema, a divine appointment establishes Matthias in the place of Judas. Negative programs establish a polemical axis against the principal axis as follows:

| *Principal Axis* | *Polemical Axis* |
|---|---|
| ? (Matthias ∩ Shared Experience of the Twelve) (1:21-22) | ? (Judas ∩ Shared Experiences of the Twelve) (1:17) |
| God (Matthias ∩ Divine Necessity [Election]) (1:26) | God (Judas ∩ Divine Necessity [Removal from Office]) (1:16, 20) |
| God (Matthias ∩ Twelve) (1:26) | God (Judas ∪ Twelve) (1:16) |
| God (Matthias ∩ Place [*topos*] (1:25) | Judas (Judas ∩ Place [*topos*] (1:25) |
| God (Matthias ∩ *klêros*) (1:26) | Judas (Judas ∩ *klêros*) (1:17) |

Matthias associates with the twelve, Judas turns aside and goes his own way.

The analysis of the narrative schemata aside, the architectonic structure also evidences an antithesis between the destiny of Judas and the reconstitution of the twelve. Two citations from the Psalms form the focal point for a symmetrical construction of the second half of Acts 1. (A) Psalm 69:25 (LXX 68:26) explains the demise of Judas: "Let his habitation become desolate, and let there be no one to live in it" (Acts 1:20). (B) Psalm 109:8 (LXX 108:8) anticipates the reconstitution of the twelve: "His office let another take" (Acts 1:20). The account of Judas leads up to the citations from the Psalms, the election of Matthias follows. The Lucan theme of divine necessity introduces both sections (*edei*, 1:16; *dei*, 1:21). Judas forfeits the *klêros* (cf. 1:17), Matthias receives the *klêros* (1:26). Thus, the two cases of fulfillment of scripture form a diptych hinging on the citations in which the two matching parts stand in antithesis.

In keeping with the principle of homologation, the story of Judas and the reconstitution of the twelve also contains seeds of the future. In the remainder of Acts Jews who reject the gospel align with Judas in separating from the apostles. In fact, Acts 1:16 presents Judas not as an independent actor but as the leader (*hodêgos*) of the opponents who arrested Jesus. Thus within the antithetical tension established in the temptation of Jesus, Judas renews the polemical axis: he becomes the paradigm for Jews who separate from the community judged by the reconstituted twelve and who go their own way.

(2) Unrealized, along with the need for the twelve to judge Israel, is Jesus' mandate to the apostles to become witnesses. But the events on the day of Pentecost establish the apostles as witnesses and produce a community under their leadership. Again, the tension between the principal and polemical axes appears in a series of oppositions:

| Principal Axis | Polemical Axis |
| --- | --- |
| The Conjunction of the Nascent Christian Community (2:1) | The Disjunction of Judas from the Twelve (1:25) |
| God (House ∩ Sound) (2:2) | ? (Habitation ∩ Emptiness) (1:20) |
| God (Disciples ∩ Holy Spirit) (2:4) | ? (Some in the Crowd ∩ Mockery) (2:13) |
| Peter (Crowd ∩ Explanation) (2:14-36) | Opponents in Crowd (Crowd ∩ Competing Explanation) (2:13) |
| Repenters (Repenters ∪ Crooked Generation) (2:40) | Non-Repenters (Non-Repenters ∩ Generation) (2:23, 36, 40) |

As the Pentecost episode comes to an end, the narrator describes the community in relation to the apostles (Acts 2:42).

This sanctions the performance of the twelve on thrones. The twelve judge a community. Significantly, new believers stem from a crowd of Jews from all the diaspora and Jerusalem (2:5, 9-11).

Taking note that the crowd is made up of Jews and proselytes, some scholars have suggested that these Jews from all the world represent not diaspora Judaism but Gentiles (e.g., Jervell 1972:73, n. 37 [following O. Bauernfeind], cf. Dupont 1959-60:144). The connotations of a world-wide mission are obvious, but any idea that Jews represent Gentiles stems from infatuation with the Gentile mission that, on the basis of Acts 2, is unwarranted. The designation "Jews and proselytes" specifies the religious affiliation of the groups from all the nations (Haenchen 1971:171, cf. Zehnle 1971:122). The implication is that the believers in the crowd constitute a believing portion of the twelve tribes of Israel now judged by the reconstituted twelve.

One other brief but significant notice deserves attention here. According to Acts 6:7 a great crowd of priests became believers. They are important for the gathering of the people of Israel as officiants no longer associated with the temple as the central institution of the people (Lohfink 1975:53).

In ordinary terms, one would be hard pressed to construe the leadership of the apostles as fulfilling the promise that they would judge the twelve tribes. But the dispute among the apostles about greatness in Luke 22:24-27 qualifies Jesus' promise of twelve thrones for the apostles (22:30). In response to the dispute, Jesus contrasts leadership among the apostles with the lordship of Gentile kings and stipulates that greatness among the apostles means serving. The allusions to the leadership of the apostles in Acts 2:41-47; 4:32-37; 6:2 indicate that the apostles lead as just such servants.

A narrator's summary in Acts 4:32-35 portrays the apostles exercising the leadership of service in the community in the distribution of goods. The summary represents both performance and sanction stages. The attempt of Ananias and Sapphira to defraud the apostles follows (4:36-5:11). Not only do the apostles judge the community in a positive sense, Peter also sees through the actions of Ananias and Sapphira to their motives and implicitly implements their deaths. The demise of Ananias and Sapphira sanctions the fulfillment of Jesus' prediction that the twelve would judge the twelve tribes.

Only as the apostles derive their role in judging the twelve tribes from Jesus does Luke-Acts portray the gathering of a people for God under the kingship of Jesus. With the competence of the power from on high, the embryonic community proclaims the mighty works of God (Acts 2:6, 11). Part of the competence phase is that foreigners are able to hear the message in their own tongues. Then, the apostolic witness of Peter, standing with the eleven (2:14-40), belongs to the performance in two senses. It is part of the process of fulfilling the more immediate need for the apostles to be witnesses (Acts 1:8), but that is actually subordinate to the narrative schema of gathering and sifting. The conversion of 3,000 sanctions the performance both of the witness and of the gathering. The 3,000, however, are but a portion of the crowd who belong to "this crooked generation" (2:40). And so there is a performance of sifting, and the distinction between a repentant and unrepentant people sanctions the sifting as well.

Narrator's summaries in 5:14 and 6:1, 7 function as both performance and sanction stages in the narrative schema of gathering. But alongside is the schema of sifting. To digress, there are diverging narrative schemata in which the opponents generate narrative needs in the polemical axis. Thus, the high priestly party and the Sadducees have a narrative need to prevent the proclamation (5:17). But the polemical narrative need to stop the proclamation aborts in two steps. An angel of the Lord releases the apostles from prison and commands them to preach in the temple (5:19-20). Then Gamaliel's advice wins the day, and the apostles go free (5:33-42).

Another major performance and sanction of sifting comes with Stephen's ministry. Stephen's speech interprets Israel's history in such a way as to provide sanction for sifting his opponents (Acts 7:1-53). The speech rehearses cycles between God's acts of mercy and Israel's rebellion. The last cycle is the coming of the Righteous One whose death Stephen attributes to his audience. The audience then repeats the cycle by lynching

Stephen who is full of grace (Brawley 1987:121-22). The solidarity of Stephen's audience with the stiff-necked people of
Israel is a sanction of their sifting.

The narrative schemata of gathering and sifting continue in
a similar vein with the persecution of Acts 8:1-3. But the plot
twists around. The emphasis falls not on the opponents as
people to be sifted but on the gathering of a people for God.
That is, the persecution results in the extension of the proclamation (8:5-17, 26-40), an extension that is also a part of the
performance of the witness towards the end of the earth (1:8).

Until Acts 8:3; 9:1-2 the opponents who align with Judas in
the polemical axis are primarily the high priestly party, the
Sadducees, and Stephen's persecutors. Now, however, the
polemical axis shifts to Paul as an opponent. But a heavenly
light falls upon him, takes him out of alignment with Judas, and
propels him toward solidarity with the twelve tribes judged by
the reconstituted twelve. The voice of the risen Jesus creates a
narrative need for Paul to carry out a commission. In each of
the three accounts of Paul's call, emphasis falls on what he is to
do (9:6, 15; 22:10; 26:16). But the question of Paul's identity is
also prominent. He is identified as a chosen vessel (9:15), a
witness (22:15), and a servant and witness (26:16).

Each of these texts issue prophetic predictions and create a
narrative need for fulfillment. To be sure, Acts 22:4-16 and
26:12-18 are Paul's analeptic reflections on his past. But in
each case he confirms prophetic predictions about his mission
and his identity. Therefore, they are mixed analepsis and
prolepsis. In 9:17-18, in the competence phase, Paul regains his
sight (a recall of Jesus' ministry in Luke 4:18-19), receives
baptism, and (presumably) is filled with the Holy Spirit. Paul
then immediately enters the performance stage and begins to
fulfill his mission in Damascus (9:19b-22).

Interwoven with the beginning of the narrative schema
regarding Paul's mission and identity, there is a narrative
schema deriving from the need to bring the persecution to an
end. The narrative need is implicit in the question of the risen
Jesus: "Saul, Saul, why do you persecute me?" (Acts 9:4).
(Every question creates a narrative need if only in terms of

necessitating a response [Patte and Patte 1978:49-50].) The implementation is the transformation of Paul including the coming of the Spirit upon him. And Paul's proclamation to those who knew about his persecution sanctions the end of it (9:20-21).

Abruptly, the narrative tapestry picks up threads from Peter. Two healing incidents lead up to the story of Peter and Cornelius (Acts 9:32-43). The importance of the conversion of Cornelius in the narrative schema of gathering can hardly be overstated given that Acts states it over in three ways (10:1-48; 11:1-18; 15:7-11). On a primary level, this is a divine orchestration of earthly events. The divine activity comes first in the form of the interrelated double visions of Peter and Cornelius, but also quite forcefully in the gift of the Holy Spirit to the Gentiles.

The double visions correspond to two narrative needs—the belief of Cornelius, and Peter's recognition of the meaning of Cornelius's belief (Löning 1974:8). In the first narrative schema, Peter's reluctance must be overcome in the competence stage. Then his proclamation and the gift of the Holy Spirit fit into performance and sanction stages respectively.

Simultaneously, Peter participates in a narrative schema moving from perplexity about the meaning of his vision (Acts 10:17) to the understanding that God shows no partiality (10:34-35). His comprehension comes not with the manifestations of the Spirit but with Cornelius's recitation of his vision (10:24-35) (Löning 1974:14). But the manifestations of the Spirit do supply the warrant for the Jews who accompany Peter to accept the baptism of Gentiles (10:44-48). The Cornelius event meets the narrative need to convince Peter's detractors (11:1-18). It also is part of the competence phase of convincing the Jerusalem council of the propriety of the Gentile mission. And to follow the development of that schema, the decision of James then makes up the performance stage, and the decree the sanction stage (15:1-29).

But the Cornelius incident does not stand alone. Acts 11:19 reverts explicitly to the situation of 8:4. First, those scattered by the persecution that arose over Stephen carry out a new kind of mission among diaspora Jews (11:19). Second, some of them preach to Gentiles (Schneider 1982:88-89). This part of the performance stage in the Gentile mission finds sanction in a summary that many believe and in the exhortation of Barnabas (11:21-24).

Acts introduces Barnabas as one who sold a field and laid the proceeds at the feet of the apostles (Acts 4:36-37). He is, therefore, a member of the community of the twelve tribes of Israel judged by the reconstituted twelve apostles. In a derivative way, out of his relationship with the community under the apostles he sanctions the accession of diaspora Jews and Gentiles.[4]

The persecution of Herod Agrippa threatens the narrative schema of gathering a people for God. And so a narrative need to stop the harassment emerges (Acts 12:1-23). Jews who align with Herod join him in the polemical axis as a part of the competence phase in arresting Peter. But this negative narrative schema aborts because an angel releases Peter from prison. The ultimate performance developing from the narrative need to stop Herod's persecution is divine intervention resulting in the death of Herod (12:20-23), and the sanction is that he was eaten by worms and died. Thus, God vitiates the threat to gathering a people, and a narrator's summary of growth further sanctions the divine performance (12:24).

Acts 13:1-3 contributes to the narrative schema of Paul's identity and his ministry. The text identifies Paul, among others, as a prophet and teacher (13:1). To abridge radically, Paul then engages in the mission of gathering and sifting a people for God. He typically preaches in synagogues. Typically some believe, others disbelieve (e.g., Acts 13:43, 45; 14:1-2, etc.). And typically Paul and his companions go to the Gentiles.

According to the conventional wisdom, Paul's strategy represents the history of the early church in which Gentiles triumph over the Jews and supersede them as the people of God. When Paul announces twice that he is turning to the Gentiles (Acts 13:46; 18:6) and a third time proclaims that God's salvation has been sent to the Gentiles (28:28), many modern scholars think that Christianity cuts its ties with Judaism (e.g., Dibelius 1956:149-50, Haenchen 1971:101, 414, 417-18,

535, 724, 729-30, Cadbury 1933:348, Wilson 1973:138, 222-23, 232). I have tried to show elsewhere the inadequacy (1) of viewing Paul as a symbol for Christianity and (2) of envisioning Paul as the one through whom Christianity supersedes Judaism (Brawley 1987:29-41, 69-78). In Acts Paul remains Paul, and he remains committed to God's promise to Israel (26:6-7). Further, in Acts the Gentiles never supplant Israel. Gentiles now belongs to God in the same way that Israel does, but rather than displace Israel, they become an addition to Israel (Dahl 1957-58:326).

Analysis of the narrative structure strengthens these conclusions. The narrative need created by prophetic predictions about Paul's ministry anticipates that he will go to both Gentiles and Jews (Acts 9:15; 22:15, 21; 26:17-20). Case after case in Paul's typical mission fulfills the performance stage in this narrative schema. And the belief of both Jews and Gentiles sanctions the performance. In fact, his own summary of the matter in Acts 26:18 indicates that his mission to the Gentiles is in order that they might receive a *klêros* among the people of God, and that sanctions the performance of his ministry.

A prophetic prediction in Acts 19:21 creates a narrative need for Paul to travel to Macedonia, Achaia, Jerusalem, and Rome. Before this narrative schema can mature, a parallel narrative brings Paul under the accusation of Demetrius the silversmith in Ephesus (19:23-41). The accusation creates a narrative need for a defense. The town clerk offers a speech that thwarts a riot and so belongs to the competence phase in the performance of a defense. But no defense is given in this context. And with Acts 20, the narrative schema of Paul's travels resumes.

The visits to Macedonia and Achaia are, in the narrative schema, relatively uneventful. But prophetic predictions give added nuance to the narrative need with respect to the journey to Jerusalem. In the Miletus speech Paul recalls analeptically the plots of the Jews against him (20:18b-19), but also divulges that prophets have already informed him that imprisonment and affliction await him in Jerusalem (completing analepsis) (20:23) (Schneider 1982:295, cf. n. 26). Disciples in Tyre and Agabus in

Caesarea reiterate the warnings (21:3-4; 21:8-14). And so in addition to a journey to Jerusalem, there is now a narrative need for Paul to prevail over the danger.

The Miletus speech is a performance in the narrative need for a defense occasioned by the plots of the Jews. And so it is a defense of Paul's past. But because of the prophetic prediction in the speech (i.e., Acts 20:22-23), it is also a part of the performance in surmounting the dangers in Jerusalem (that is, it is mixed analepsis and prolepsis). I reiterate that the phases in narrative schemata do not necessarily follow a linear development. In this case the proleptic anticipation of dangers in Jerusalem gives to the Miletus speech the character of a performance of a defense before the full blown development of the accusations in the need stage.

When Paul arrives in Jerusalem, the problems from the Jews are two-fold. First, Jewish Christians are suspicious that he encourages diaspora Jews to commit apostasy (21:21). Second, Jews from Asia Minor accuse him of speaking against the people, the law, and the temple. Further, they accuse him of profaning the temple by bringing Gentiles into it (21:28). Paul's purification in the temple and his support of four men under a vow (21:23-26) is a performance that answers both charges. His behavior demonstrates his regard for Jewish institutions and establishes ahead of time the vacuity of the accusations of Asian Jews.

But a series of defense speeches fill out the performance stage in Paul's vindication. In Acts 22:3-21 Paul defends his conduct first as the behavior of a zealous Jew (22:3) and then as his response to God (22:14-21). The hearing before the sanhedrin in Acts 23:1-10 has to do with the same accusations. Not until Paul's trial before Felix does Tertullus renew the charges against Paul (24:5). But in his defense Paul adds a new wrinkle. Before both the Sanhedrin and Felix he introduces the resurrection (23:6; 24:15). Nevertheless, he also continues to appeal to his conduct as thoroughly Jewish (24:11-21). That remains his defense before Festus (25:8). When Festus explains the charges to Agrippa, he expresses them from Paul's point of view—the issue is that Paul asserts Jesus' resurrection (25:19).

Paul defends himself before Agrippa as thoroughly faithful to Judaism, but makes his proclamation of the resurrection a part of his fidelity to God and to Judaism.

Along the way woven into the narrative schema of Paul's defense there are threats to Paul's life that create a narrative need to overcome the danger. The mob aroused by the Asian Jews attempts to kill him (21:31). After Paul's speech to them, the same crowd advocates his death (22:22). As the focus of conflict between Pharisees and Sadducees, he is in danger of becoming a victim of their violence (23:10). In 23:12-15 more than forty Jews plot to ambush him. The chief priests and the leaders of the Jews plot a similar ambush in 25:2-3.

In each of these cases performances alleviate the dangers to Paul. Roman soldiers deliver Paul from the mob aroused by the Asian Jews (21:32-36; 22:24) and from the violence in the sanhedrin (23:10). Paul's nephew learns of the first plot against Paul, and again soldiers deliver Paul (23:16-33). Finally, Paul's appeal to Caesar negates the second plot of the chief priests and the Jewish leaders to ambush him (25:9-11).

Imbedded in these machinations there are hints of a narrative schema focusing on divine action to deliver Paul. Acts 19:21 creates a narrative need for Paul to travel to Rome. The text attributes the creation of that narrative need to the Spirit. A nocturnal audition from the Lord assures Paul of the divine necessity for him to bear witness in Rome (23:11). Acts 27:24 repeats the same kind of divine necessity for Paul to appear before Caesar. In the schema generated by that kind of divine necessity, the other schemata of Paul's defense and his deliverance from dangers correspond to the competence phase for the divine performance.

Paul's survival of a voyage and shipwreck are additional aspects of this schema of divine action to deliver Paul. In Acts 27:10 Paul makes a prediction about the dangers of the voyage, but the text gives no clues that it is divinely inspired. In fact, when Paul does attribute his prediction to an angel of God, he revises the prediction to specify that there will be no loss of life (27:23-26). The meal, an occasion for strengthening the sea-goers and for thanksgiving to God (27:33-38), and the desire of the centurion to save Paul (27:43) contribute to the competence phase in the divine schema.

One other danger threatens to frustrate the divine performance to bring Paul to Rome. On the island of Malta a viper bites Paul. The Maltese expect Paul to die. To be sure, there is no explicit statement that God delivers Paul from the viper bite, but the reaction of the Maltese is a sanction of a divine miracle the performance of which the text does not manifest (28:3-6).

Once Paul arrives in Rome, the narrative schema of his defense returns to prominence. He makes no mention of accusations, but his disclaimer of offending against the people or the customs of the forebears (Acts 28:17) shows that this defense continues to respond to the accusations of 21:21.

Cheek by jowl with the defense runs Paul's continuing part in the narrative schema of gathering and sifting. His address in Rome spawns another division (Acts 28:24). Just as the demise of Judas has been neglected as the *polemical* counterpart to the reconstitution of the twelve at the beginning of Acts, so the story of Paul and *believing* Jews has been neglected as the *principal* counterpart to unbelieving Jews at the end of Acts.[5] At this juncture Paul identifies the unbelieving Jews with hardened Israel addressed in Isa 6:9-10. Paul himself identifies with the hope of Israel (28:20; cf. 26:7). Paul and believing Jews align with the twelve tribes judged by the reconstituted twelve apostles. Unbelieving Jews fall in with Judas.

The narrative structure of Acts 28 displays these polarities. In the face of the need to vindicate himself, Paul communicates his defense to the Jews in Rome. But the sanction stage shows that the defense initially produces a hung jury (28:21-22). Therefore, the performance falls in abeyance.

Before the narrative ameliorates the need for a defense a new narrative converges. The Jewish leaders desire to hear Paul's views. The implicit need is for Paul to communicate to them the kingdom of God. Thus, there is now a dual need—the defense of Paul, which has been suspended, and the communication of the kingdom. When some Jews in Rome believe, they sanction the success of Paul's communication of the kingdom.[6]

At that point Acts launches a secondary converging narrative. The behavior among the Jews establishes a need for an explanation of their dispute and disbelief. The Holy Spirit's words to their fathers fulfills the competence stage. Paul's citation of those words and his comment that the salvation of God has been sent to Gentiles (Acts 28:28) constitute the performance stage.

These secondary narratives converge with the main narrative. That is, the communication of the kingdom of God to Jewish leaders in Rome and Paul's citation of Isa 6:9-10 merge with the suspended performance stage of Paul's defense. At the end of Acts Paul is preaching and teaching openly and unhindered (28:30-31). A clue that this sanctions the success of Paul's defense is that the focus shifts dramatically from unbelieving Jews and receptive Gentiles back to Paul.[7] Paul's apology is successful in that Jewish leaders in Rome no longer oppose him.

Thus, the citation from Isaiah 6 and Paul's comment about receptive Gentiles function in part as an apology. In particular they explain empirically why Paul turns to Gentiles (cf. Brawley 1987:74-78, 143). As in Luke 9:1-5; 10:8-11, receiving the kingdom of God means receiving its proclaimer.

Therefore, a polemical axis stands over against the principal axis. Paul identifies with the twelve tribes of Israel, which the apostles judge. His opponents manifest the fruition of the seeds of the Judas who turned aside from the twelve.

Narrative programs stand in antithesis as follows:

| Principal Axis | Polemical Axis |
| --- | --- |
| Romans (Jerusalem Jews ∩ Paul's Release) (28:18) | Jerusalem Jews (Romans ∩ Paul's Imprisonment) (28:19) |
| Jerusalem Jews (Roman Jews ∪ Accusations) (28:21) | Jerusalem Jews (Romans ∩ Accusations) (28:19) |
| Paul (Some Jewish Leaders in Rome ∩ Kingdom) (28:24) | Paul (Other Jewish Leaders in Rome ∪ Kingdom) (28:24) |
| Some Jewish Leaders in Rome (Some Jewish Leaders in Rome ∩ Belief) (28:24) | Other Jewish Leaders in Rome (Other Jewish Leaders in Rome ∪ Belief) (28:24) |

In keeping with the principle of homologation, the polarities at the end of Acts correspond to those at the beginning. At the beginning Judas turns aside from his heritage (*klêros*) with the twelve to go to his own place. But the election of Matthias reconstitutes the twelve, and the reconstituted twelve take their leadership over Israel. At the end of Acts Paul claims his heritage with the twelve tribes of Israel. But his Jewish opponents align with Judas and forfeit their *klêros*.[8]

The Gentile mission in Acts fits Shklovsky's category of plots that reverse relationships among characters. In the narrative schema of gathering and sifting a people for God, descent from Abraham loses its character as a criterion. God is able to raise up children to Abraham from stones (Luke 3:8). Repentance is the new criterion (Acts 11:18). And the new criterion shows that God shows no partiality (10:34-35). Thus, the mission reverses the exclusion of the Gentiles from the people of God and includes them.

Paul's relationships likewise invert. Initially, in league with the high priestly party he persecutes messianic Jews (Acts 9:1-2; 22:4-5; 26:10). But he then becomes a messianic Jew, and the high priestly party persecutes him (23:2; 24:1). Initially, Paul, like Judas, goes his own way against the community judged by the twelve. Eventually, he aligns with the community of the twelve tribes of Israel judged by the reconstituted twelve.

Luke-Acts also manifests Shklovsky's second category—development from a prediction or fear. Luke-Acts repeatedly fulfills prophecies (L. T. Johnson 1977:16-28).

Shklovsky's category of moving from misrepresentation to rectification also helps to describe the plot in Luke-Acts. The people of Nazareth evaluate Jesus (merely) as Joseph's son. But Luke-Acts invests heavily in establishing the identity of Jesus as Spirit-filled Messiah and prophet (Luke 4:16-30). Further, opponents accuse Jesus at his trial (23:2, 5). But Pilate, the penitent thief, the centurion, and the sorrowful crowd reinforce his innocence (Brawley 1987:140-41, cf. 141, n. 29). Moreover, Jesus's crucifixion is a scandal that potentially disconfirms his identity as Messiah. But the resurrection is God's affirmation of one who was killed by violent opponents (Acts 2:23-24; 3:14-15), and the potential disconfirmation turns into confirmation when the scriptures are properly understood (Luke 24: 20-21, 27, 45-46).

Acts also invests in overcoming misrepresentations of Paul. Paul comes under the suspicion of Jewish Christians who have heard rumors that Paul teaches diaspora Jews to commit apostasy. Further, Asian Jews accuse Paul of teaching against Judaism (21:20-21, 28). Against these accusations, Acts presents Paul as turning to the Gentiles not because he forsakes Judaism but (1) because God commissioned him to do so and (2) because Jews rejected his message (Brawley 1987:68-83). In addition, Acts portrays Paul as remaining thoroughly faithful to the hopes of Israel (24:14; 26:6-7; 28:20).

But the beginning and the end cannot finally correspond. In Luke-Acts external analepses and external prolepses rupture the limits of beginning and end. Analeptic recall of biblical prophets predating Luke-Acts establish narrative needs for fulfillment within Luke-Acts. And proleptic predictions within Luke-Acts create narrative needs for fulfillment beyond the end.

Isaianic passages create the narrative needs for John's ministry of preparation (Luke 3:4-6) and for Jesus' ministry of release and restoration (4:18-19). Isaiah 56:7 produces the narrative need for Jesus to reclaim the temple as a house of prayer (Luke 19:46). Psalm 118:22 establishes the narrative need for a rejected Jesus to be exalted (Luke 20:17, cf. Acts 4:11). A psalm installs the narrative need for the reconstitution of the twelve after the demise of Judas (Acts 1:20). Joel's prophecy of the last days generates the narrative need for the phenomena of Pentecost (Acts 2:17-21). David contributes to the narrative need for the resurrection of Jesus (Acts 2:25-28). Acts 13:47 founds the narrative need for Paul and Barnabas to go to the Gentiles on Isaiah 49:6. Acts 15:16-17 bases the narrative need for the accession of the Gentiles on Amos 9:11-12. And Acts 28:26-27 grounds the unbelief of recalcitrant Jews in Isa 6:9-10. Thus, Luke-Acts roots some narrative needs in analeptic antecedents external to its temporal limits.

On the other hand, some prolepses in Luke-Acts anticipate fulfillment beyond the end. Paramount among these is the parousia. Although Luke 17:24 does not explicitly refer to the parousia, the events surrounding the revelation of the Son of man ((Luke 17:30) point to a fulfillment beyond the end of Luke-Acts. In Luke 21:27 Jesus predicts the coming of the Son of man in a cloud, and that corresponds to the message at the ascension (Acts 1:10-11)—an external prolepsis. Similarly, Acts 3:21 ties the time of the consummation to prophetic predictions. Further, Acts 24:16 and 25 connect the future resurrection with the future judgment in consecutive contexts.

Acts 1:8 is a mixed prolepsis. A virtual consensus of scholars maintains that Acts 1:8 projects the geographical extension of God's salvation that is fulfilled within Acts. They assume that Rome corresponds to the "end of the earth" in Acts 1:8. To be sure, Acts portrays the inauguration of the witness to the end of the earth, but even with Paul's arrival in Rome, Acts anticipates a wider extension of God's salvation. Paul's final comment in Acts is that the Gentiles will listen to God's salvation (28:28). The future tense foreshadows a wider mission, and shows, therefore, that Acts 1:8 anticipates ultimate fulfillment beyond the temporal frame of the book (cf. Brawley 1987:22-41).

Overriding the entire story is a narrative schema that for modern plots is problematic—God's work. To touch some high spots, Zechariah is ministering before God when an angel of the Lord comes to him (Luke 1:8-9). God sends Gabriel to Mary (1:26). Mary interprets what happens to her as God's work (1:47-55). Zechariah interprets the birth of John the Baptist as God's doings (1:68-79). The Spirit inspires Simeon (2:25-26). The Holy Spirit comes upon Jesus and leads him henceforth (3:22; 4:1). The people interpret the raising of a dead man as God's visitation (7:16). Jesus claims that in his exorcisms the kingdom of God has come (11:20). Further, Acts understands that God was at work in Jesus (Acts 2:22, cf. 10:38). In retrospect, the crucifixion is a divine necessity (Luke 24:7, 26, 46).

In Acts the election of Matthias derives from divine initiative (Acts 1:24-26). The events at Pentecost stem from the empowerment of the Holy Spirit (2:1-4, 17-21). Acts understands the resurrection of Jesus as God's work (2:24 and passim). The gathering and sifting of a people for God is divine work (2:47). The insistent witness of the apostles is obedience to God (4:19-

20; 5:20, 29). God directs the opening of the mission to Gentiles (10:1-11:18). God is at work in the ministry of Paul and Barnabas (14:27). Paul's miracles are divine activity (19:11).

But the hermeneutical implications are quite problematic. To recall the beginning of the previous chapter, the modern concept of cause and effect excludes divine intervention. One could plead that divine grace corresponds to the rupture of causal ties in the post-modern world view. But then one would have to deny the coherence of the story in Luke-Acts because the post-modern perspective is that reality is random and chaotic. It is impossible to have it both ways. To revert to a pre-scientific world view that fills in the gaps with divine intervention is hardly acceptable to the vast majority of modern people. Perhaps, however, narrative offers an alternative.

Overarching Luke-Acts is a divine story. Within that divine story, there are human stories that move toward a teleological purpose. Accordingly, divine action does not consist of external interventions into history. Rather, divine action is coexistent with history. I think that this is also incompatible with the modern world view of scientific cause and effect and with the post-modern world view of random chaos. But that may be precisely the point. By presenting a theocentric story, Luke-Acts confronts us with another world view that challenges our own.

# 5

# CHARACTERIZATION: GOD AND JESUS

What produces characters in literary works? Modern literary criticism has moved away from the notion that an author produces characters toward the view that the reader constructs them out of clues in the text.[1] Roland Barthes termed these clues "semes." Semes are the basic units of signs, and this terminology corresponds to Barthes's conviction that characters are essentially signs made up of such elementary units. A character is, therefore, a product of combinations—combinations of semes (Barthes 1974:67, cf. Culler 1975:203). Texts beget characters when semes such as emotions, personal traits, thoughts, and actions repeatedly unite under a proper name. The combination of semes makes the character a signifier, a carrier of meaning. Ultimately, however, the character is the signified, that is, the meaning the reader constructs (cf. Barthes 1974:191).

Although characters are combinations, they are not conglomerates. Rather, the reader combines the semes into coherent wholes (Culler 1975:236-37). The premise that the character is a unified whole has come under scrutiny from a post-modern perspective. With the death of the consistent, stable, and static self, and with the birth of the existential subject moving from one existential experience to another, post-modernism considers character as an coherent whole a notorious fiction (Docherty 1983:129, 242).

Nevertheless, cogent reasons remain for understanding character as a coherent construct. In the first place, it is anachronistic to superimpose post-modern perspectives on literature that arises from a different world view. But in the second place, characters exist as integral wholes because the reader synthesizes them according to conventional genres (Chatman 1978:124). To illustrate how conventional the genres are, Northrop Frye traces three types back to Aristotle: the character trying to rise in the world, the self-deprecating character, and the typical or random victim (1957:39-41). Standard models such as these guide the reader in constructing characters. Moreover, far beyond the textual clues, the reader fills in gaps and molds characters after images of people, and in this fashion, inconsistencies and contradictions notwithstanding, characters still correspond to the impression of human beings who are not completely discontinuous and fragmented (Rimmon-Kenan 1983:33, Hochman 1985:7).

Literary criticism inherits from Aristotle a debate about the relationship between character and action. Aristotle advocated the primacy of plot over actor (*Poetics* 7.12-18). But the mutuality of the two has virtually won a consensus in accord with the dictum of Henry James: "What is character but the determination of incident? What is incident but the illustration of character?" (1961:302, cf. Crane 1961:165, Chatman 1978:109-110, Martin 1986:116). Holdovers persist where structuralism reduces characters to functionaries of action.[2] Some holdovers also persist where interpreters of Luke-Acts argue that salvation history dominates the personages (e.g., Conzelmann 1961, Haenchen 1971, Gaventa 1988:152).

The theoretical debates of literary critics aside, David Gowler argues that both the prologue to Luke and the prologue to Acts indicate that characters are subordinated to action (ch. 2, n. 74; cf. n. 24). He implies that the mention of "things" in Luke 1:3, 4 and the reference to ". . . all that Jesus began to *do* and *teach*" (Acts 1:1, emphasis added) subordinates the personages. But three retrospective reviews in Luke-Acts summarize previous material in terms of both personage and action. The two disciples on the road to Emmaus explain the happenings in Jerusalem as things concerning *Jesus*, and then they refer to deeds, words, and events (Luke 24:19-24). In spite of Gowler's emphasis on doing and teaching in Acts 1:1, the narrator actually summarizes the first book by saying that it dealt with ". . . all that *Jesus* began to do and teach" (emphasis added). Peter's speech to Cornelius refers to the *preaching* of good news by *Jesus* and to the anointing of *Jesus* (Acts 10:36, 38). Thus references of the text to itself witness to the blending of the personage of Jesus and the action.

Retrospective reviews also demonstrate Paul's prominence in relation to the action. At Miletus Paul recapitulates the action of his ministry. But his primary reference is to himself (Acts 20:18-35). Similarly, in his defense speeches, Paul ties an apology for himself to his actions (22:1-21; 23:6; 24:10-21; 26:4-23; 28:17-20). Thus, when the narrative alludes to itself internally, it interweaves character and incident.

Moreover, to separate action from character is to split Luke-Acts artificially. Action is never bald action but emerges from actors, impacts on actors, and to a large extent characterizes actors (Docherty 1983:7). Therefore, far from subordinating character, action is an integral part of forming character.

Although complex, the procedures for reading a character boil down to the interplay of information, action, personal traits, and evaluation. Complexity arises in that information may come from the narrator, from the primary character, or from another character; or it may be inferred. Similarly, action may be described by the narrator, reflected by characters, or inferred. Personal traits may be given in the narrator's direct description, claimed by characters for themselves, attributed by characters to others, or inferred (Berlin 1983:33-42, Alter 1981:116). Further, the reliability of the narrator or character cuts across the axes of information, action, personal traits, and evaluation. For example, false witnesses accuse Stephen of speaking against the temple and of predicting that Jesus will destroy the temple and change the customs of Moses (Acts 6:13-14). Is that a reliable characterization of Stephen?

Reliability is related to the degree of certainty. Depending on the reliability of the narrator or character, the reader may muddle around in uncertain inferences or make judgments with a high degree of certainty. According to Robert Alter's hierarchy of the degree of certainty, action alone leaves the reader in the realm of inference, direct speech from characters allows the reader to judge their claims, interior speech leads to relative certainty, and a reliable narrator's explicit statements imply the highest level of certainty (1981:117). One emendation on Alter's hierarchy, however, is that divine speech occupies the highest level of reliability.

Theoretically, therefore, divine speech and the narrator's clear assertions control weighing of claims and inference from actions. In practice, however, inferences from the action and statements from God, the narrator, and the characters are so inextricable as to make discussion in tidy categories unwieldy. Further, character builds up largely through thematization, that is, by repetition and correlation of information, action, traits, and evaluation (Barthes 1974:92-93, Iser 1978:94). Thus, reading character hangs on tracing lines of relationship among redundancies that correct, redirect, and reinforce one another.

In Luke-Acts there are but four major characters—God, Jesus, Peter, and Paul. My proposal to treat God as a character may require justification. Fred Burnett has warned against the temptation to read God in Matthew by Christian and Jewish theological codes as if God exists outside the story (1988:7). His warning is equally applicable to Luke-Acts. God stands within the Lucan literary world. But is God a character? Ian Watt maintains, correctly, that character can be individualized only if set in a particular time and place (Watt 1961:68). And, again with reference to Matthew, Burnett claims that God has no physical appearance, biography, or street address (1988:9).

Whatever may be the case with Matthew, in Luke-Acts God does have a biography and street address—not literally but equivalently. There is no biography from birth to death, but God does have a past, present, and future. God does not reside in the temple or any other structure made by human hands (Acts 7:48; 17:24). But God does occupy a particular location, namely, heaven. This is the point of Stephen's reference to the temple. God does not dwell in a structure built by human beings but occupies a divine creation. Then, as if to confirm the point, Stephen looks into heaven and sees Jesus at the right hand of God (7:49, 55-56).

To be sure, Luke-Acts does not give God a physical description. Paul specifically denies that God is like artistic and imaginative human creations (Acts 17:29). Nevertheless, God has a voice (Luke 3:22; 9:35) and sees (Acts 7:34). Luke-Acts speaks anthropomorphically about God's hand or arm (Luke 1:51, 66; 23:46; Acts 7:50; 11:21; 13:11, 17). And at the baptism of Jesus the Holy Spirit descends in bodily form (Luke 3:22).

Further, God is a character because semes repeatedly traverse the same proper name or cluster of names (the criterion of Barthes 1974:67). God is a character whom the reader constructs out of the intersection of information, action, traits, and evaluation. In addition, the construct will likely assume an anthropological shape according to the reader's image of human beings.

## GOD

In his influential *The Theology of St. Luke* Hans Conzelmann describes God essentially in terms of the relationship between the Father and the Son (1961:170-84). Virtually all the characterization of God does have implications for the relationship between God and Jesus, but there are aspects that stand independently.

Epithets and direct descriptions offer the simplest access to the divine characterization in Luke-Acts, but they are not so simple. They frequently belong to clusters of redundancy, and they reveal more than the features to which they point immediately. Part of the cumulative nature of the characterization is that epithets and direct descriptions arise from the narrator, reliable characters, unreliable characters, and even from God, and these shifts in point of view add depth to the character (Booth 1961:16-17, Berlin 1983:7, Harvey 1965:52-55).

"God" is a common identifying term cutting across various perspectives. Unreliable characters, such as the Samaritans who say that Simon is the power of God which is called Great (Acts 8:10), use the same term (*theos*) as the narrator, reliable characters, and even God (e.g., 7:32). Lord appears quite frequently as a divine appellation but only from the narrator or reliable characters or as a divine self-reference (e.g., 15:17).

The cases of unreliable characters require special comment. The Lycaonians call Barnabas Zeus and Paul Hermes (Acts 14:12). In Athens Paul alludes to an inscription to an unknown god (17:23). Jews in Corinth accuse Paul of worshiping God contrary to the law (18:13). In Ephesus Demetrius and the town clerk affirm the deity of Artemis (19:26-27, 37). And the natives of Malta aver that *hê dikê* (justice personified as a deity) has executed justice upon Paul and then say that Paul himself is a god (28:4, 6)).

But in each case the ideological point of view of the narrative disconfirms what the characters claim. In Lystra Paul and Barnabas claim that they are human beings like their admirers. There is no comparable protest when the Maltese proclaim Paul a god, but the text has established norms necessary for the reader to judge that they are unreliable. Paul contests the inscription in Athens and argues that God is not unknown but close and knowable. Paul's speeches in Lystra and in Athens also establish norms that contradict the claim of pagans for the divinity of Zeus and Hermes, or of Artemis, or of *hê dikê*. Paul says to the Lycaonians: "You should turn from these vain things to a living God who made the heaven and the earth and the sea and all that is in them" (14:15). And he tells the Athenians: "We ought not to think that the Deity is like gold, or silver, or stone, a representation by the art and imagination of human beings" (17:29). And contrary to the accusation of Jews in Corinth, Paul later claims that he worships God completely in accord with the law (24:14). Thus, unreliable characters provide a foil for a more precise characterization of God (Harvey 1965: 63).

The narrator and reliable characters also frequently refer to the Spirit or the Holy Spirit (God can speak of "my Spirit"). Gabriel (Luke 1:32, 35), Jesus (6:35), the Gerasene demoniac (8:28), the slave girl with a spirit of divination (Acts 16:17) refer to God as Most High (*hupsistos*). Demoniacs constitute a special case. At first glance they appear to be unreliable, but the narrator informs the reader directly that their knowledge of Jesus' identity is genuine (Luke 4:41), and thus they must also be reliable insofar as their knowledge of God's identity is correct.

To broaden the scope, the complexity of epithets and direct descriptions hangs not only on their redundancy but also on functions of the redundant clusters. In Luke-Acts there are four primary functions beyond direct portrayal: prolepsis, analepsis, evaluation, and relation.[3] They anticipate action, recall action, sanction or disapprove personages, and clarify the relationships among characters.

In a notable example, Mary designates God "my Savior" (Luke 1:47). In the first place, the epithet is analeptic. The title recalls what God has done. In chapter 3 I argue that the Magnificat is not a prophetic prediction generating a narrative need, and I contest Joseph Fitzmyer's claim that it anticipates the future career of Jesus (1981:361, see above p. 72). But now I wish to contend that the epithet is proleptic not in the sense of the career of Jesus but in the sense of the anticipation of manifestations of the power of God. In subsuming God's past actions, the title Savior also recalls Gabriel's characterization of God as omnipotent: "For with God nothing *will be* impossible" (Luke 1:37, emphasis added). The title is part of a redundant cluster anticipating the disclosure of divine salvific power.

A trajectory with reverberations of God's power runs throughout Luke-Acts. After the temptation, the power of the Spirit is upon Jesus (4:14) and enables him to heal (5:17). At his trial Jesus predicts that the Son of man will be seated at the right hand of the power of God (22:69). The risen Jesus promises his disciples that they will receive divine power (24:49; Acts 1:8). Acts 10:38 recalls that the power of God was with Jesus enabling him to heal. Signs and wonders of Paul and the apostles are manifestations of divine power (e.g., 14:3). Further, according to Gamaliel (the narrator's characterization of him as esteemed by all the people establishes him as a reliable character), God's *boulē* or *ergon* is something that the sanhedrin is unable to frustrate (5:38-39). Actually, it would not be far wrong to attribute virtually everything that is positive according to the norms established by Luke-Acts to God's power. But certainly the primary manifestation of divine power is that God raises Jesus from the dead.

The characterization of God as creator is analeptic, proleptic, and evaluative. In a prayer the community of believers recalls God's past creative acts (Acts 4:24). But the characterization as creator is also evaluative in that it identifies the God of believers and makes a distinction from any other deity. Stephen's allusion to the creation, citing Isa 66:1-2, is analeptic in that it recalls the creative act but also in that it recalls the prophet's words (Acts 7:49-50). In particular, however, it is evaluative in establishing God's domain beyond the temple. Before a pagan audience Paul uses the creation evaluatively to distinguish the true God from pagan deities (Acts 14:15). Similarly, Paul's address on the Areopagus differentiates the true God from the unknown (17:24). But there are also proleptic connotations. In 4:24 God the creator is tied with the empowerment of the community for speaking God's word with boldness. In 14:15 and 17:24 distinguishing God from pagan deities anticipates a new relationship of pagans with God.

The association of God with promises has strong analeptic and proleptic overtones. Promises recall not only commitments in the past but also commitments to be fulfilled in the future. Mary's allusion to God's promises to Abraham attaches the promises to Abraham's posterity forever (Luke 1:55). Zechariah's recall of the covenant with Abraham issues in hope for future deliverance (1:72-75). In Acts 3:25 Peter remembers the Abrahamic covenant with the purpose of encouraging his hearers to turn from their wickedness. Stephen calls up the covenant with Abraham analeptically as a memory of God's grace in the past (7:5, 17).

Peter recollects the Davidic covenant as an analepsis whose proleptic dimension has come to pass in Jesus' resurrection (Acts 2:30). Nevertheless, there is still an element of prolepsis in that the exaltation of Jesus to the Davidic throne anticipates the future divine conquest of Jesus' enemies (2:34). There is also a strong evaluative implication. On the one hand, the divine

promise is a sanction for Jesus. On the other, the partial fulfillment of the promise sanctions God as one who fulfills promises.
Paul appeals to similar promises in Antioch of Pisidia. Jesus is
the fulfillment of the Davidic promise (13:23), and the realization of the promise characterizes God as one who fulfills promises (cf. 13:32-33).

The promise from God for empowerment that Jesus communicates to the disciples is proleptic in Luke 24:49. Acts 1:4
evokes the same promise analeptically, but its effects are still
proleptic. But as a part of Peter's explanation of the phenomena at Pentecost, the promise is analeptic (2:33). Here there is
another case of mutual sanction. The divine promise sanctions
the phenomena of Pentecost, but the phenomena of Pentecost
sanction God as faithful to the promise.

A major function of epithets and direct descriptions is to
clarify relationships among the characters. Although the divine
appellation "Holy Spirit" may serve as nothing more than a
convenient designation of God, it frequently occurs in situations
where God is particularly related to human beings. The Holy
Spirit is the agent of divine revelation or the inspiration for
prophecy (Luke 2:26-27; Acts 21:11, cf. 28:25). Jesus promises
that the Holy Spirit will teach persecuted believers what to say
(12:12). The coming of the Holy Spirit upon the nascent community marks its empowerment for mission (Acts 2:4, 17-18).
When Peter and John are arrested, Peter, filled with the Holy
Spirit, addresses the sanhedrin and so fulfills Jesus' promise in
Luke 12:12. Stephen is filled with the Holy Spirit (Acts 6:5, 10).
The Holy Spirit comes upon Cornelius and his household and
is the confirmation that they stand in a favorable relationship
with God (10:34, 44; 11:16-17; 15:8). The Spirit directs Peter
and Paul in the course of their ministries (11:12; 19:21; 20:22).
And the Holy Spirit establishes overseers for the care of the
church (20:28).

From a contrary perspective, resisting the Spirit is one of the
ways Luke-Acts indicates an unfavorable relationship between
God and human beings. Jesus equates apostasy with blasphemy
against the Holy Spirit (Luke 12:12). For Peter, the ruse of
Ananias and Sapphira is lying to the Holy Spirit (Acts 5:3, 9). In

brief, the title Holy Spirit clarifies relationships positive and negative between God and human beings.

In addition, Jesus has a special relationship with the Holy Spirit. The Holy Spirit descends upon him at his baptism (Luke 3:22), he is led in the Spirit (4:1), and he is Spirit-anointed (4:18). His anointing with the Spirit is connected with his access to divine power (Acts 10:38). Jesus is uniquely endowed, and although the Spirit inspires Elizabeth, Zechariah, and Simeon, Jesus is the only bearer of the Spirit for the period of his ministry up until Pentecost (Conzelmann 1961:179-84).

Other divine designations that reveal relationships relate God to the patriarchs, to the people, or to Israel. The title "Lord" makes little sense without a people who respond to God's sovereignty. But the text frequently makes that relationship explicit. Gabriel informs Zechariah that his son John will turn many of the people of Israel to the Lord their God (Luke 1:16). Zechariah then identifies God as the Lord God of Israel in his prophecy (1:68). Both Jesus and Stephen allude to Exod 3:6 to identify the Lord as the God of Abraham, Isaac, and Jacob (Luke 20:37; Acts 7:32). Peter identifies the one who raised Jesus as the God of Abraham, Isaac, and Jacob and as the God of our fathers (3:13). Paul similarly identifies the God who raised Jesus as the God of this people Israel (13:17). Ananias informs Paul that his commission comes from ". . . the God of our fathers" (22:14). And Paul himself claims to worship ". . . the God of our fathers" (24:14).

Frequently when the epithet "Father" applies to God, the divine relationship with Jesus is at stake. This fits in with the thematization of Father-Son that Gabriel initiates when he predicts that Jesus will be called the Son of God (Luke 1:32, 35). It is Jesus' own address for God in prayer (11:2; 22:42; 23:34; cf. 10:21) and in the cry at his death (23:46). It is also Jesus' way of expressing his unique relationship to God, and so he can refer to God uniquely as "my Father" (10:22; 24:49; but cf. Acts 1:4).

But the title Father is also one of the ways Jesus speaks of the relationship of the people to God. And in this regard repetitions of Jesus' reference to ". . . the promise of *my* Father"

(Luke 24:49) manifest a fascinating development. In narrative the narrator can direct repetitions at the reader, or characters can direct them toward other characters (Savaran 1988:11, cf. Sternberg 1987:365-440). In the case at hand, characters advance the repetitions. In the first repetition Jesus recalls his command to the apostles. But intriguingly, this time he refers to the promise of *the* Father (Acts 1:4). Peter makes another allusion to the same promise in his speech at Pentecost, and he also speaks of "the Father" (2:33). The force of the repetitions is a subtle shift away from the uniqueness of Jesus' relationship to God, indicated by the possessive pronoun "my," to a more inclusive relationship. The hearers in both cases can only understand that God is also their Father.

This shift is part of a thematic development in Luke. In the sermon of the plain Jesus exhorts his hearers to "be merciful, even as your Father is merciful" (6:36). In teaching about prayer, Jesus promises that the heavenly Father will give the Holy Spirit to those who ask (11:13). The God of providential care for Jesus' disciples is "your Father" (12:30; cf. 12:32). People who attain the age to come and the resurrection are "children (*huioi*) of God" (20:36).

Fred Burnett argues that the characterization of God as Father in Matthew is anti-semitic because it makes God uniquely the Father of Jesus and his followers and excludes the Jews (1988). I will not engage Burnett on the evidence in Matthew, but I will use his thesis to launch my own argument that this is not the case in Luke-Acts.

In the first place, Jesus addresses his sermon on the plain to a great multitude of people from all Judea and Jerusalem and from the seacoast of Tyre and Sidon. It is these to whom Jesus directs the exhortation: "Be merciful, even as *your* Father is merciful" (Luke 6:36, emphasis added). Further, the parallelism of Luke 10:21 shows that the God whom Jesus addresses as Father is Lord of heaven and earth. The one whom Jesus addresses as Father is also the one to whom he appeals for forgiveness for his opponents (23:34). In addition, on the Areopagus Paul cites a pagan poet, with approval, to claim that *all human beings* are God's offspring (Acts 17:28). Thus, the image of God as Father is inclusive rather than exclusive. On the other hand, to balance the evidence, to know the Father is exclusively for those to whom the Son gives revelation (Luke 10:22).

To make a transition, part of the previous discussion attempts to show how epithets and direct descriptions may function beyond their immediate meaning to clarify relationships. But the inverse also holds. Relationships among characters also characterize.

The early chapters of Luke portray God in special relationships with the pious Zechariah, Elizabeth, Mary, Joseph, Simeon, and Anna and with a particular bias for people of low estate. God also manifests goodness toward all people (Acts 14:17) and kindness and mercy even toward the ungrateful and selfish (Luke 6:35; 18:13). God has a peculiar historical relationship with Israel marked by promises, redemptive acts, and judgment, but that does not preclude that God shows no partiality (Acts 10:34). God has angels under dispatch. There is a struggle between God and the powers of evil, but curiously the demons know the relationship between God and Jesus. John the Baptist is an agent of God. In a particular way, God is at work in Jesus (Luke 7:16; 8:39; 11:20; Acts 10:36). The identity is so close that to receive Jesus is to receive the one who sent him (Luke 9:48), to reject Jesus is to reject God who sent him (Luke 10:16), and to deny Jesus is to blaspheme the Holy Spirit (12:10). But God is also at work in the apostles, Peter, Stephen, Barnabas, and Paul.

If relationships characterize, then the designation of Ananias as God's high priest (Acts 23:4) also characterizes God. But this raises a difficult question of reliability. Paul's statement that he did not know that Ananias was the high priest is incongruous with his challenge to Ananias, "Are you sitting to judge me according to the law?" (23:3).

Theodor Zahn tried to resolve the incongruity by considering Paul's claim that he did not know the high priest irony (Zahn 1919:762-63, cf. nn. 52, 53, cf. Haenchen 1971:640). But Exod 22:28 can serve to illustrate Paul's fidelity to the law only if it is taken seriously as a reference to Ananias. A solution is at hand, however. In the norms established by Luke-Acts Ananias is unworthy to be high priest as his violation of the law in this text and his accusation against Paul in Acts 24:1 show. In keeping with these norms, Paul never does recognize Ananias as God's high priest. His citation of Exod 22:28 constitutes a deliberate variation (Sternberg 1987:419) of titles for Ananias, and in the repetition there is a subtle but dramatic modification. As the perspective changes from the supporters of Ananias to Paul, Paul shifts the terminology and speaks of a *ruler* of the people. Worthy or unworthy, he is a ruler of the people. Paul, therefore, can remain faithful to the law and still give a caustic twist to Ananias's alleged status as *God's* high priest.[4]

Not only do relationships with characters reflect on God but also relationships with objects or circumstances, especially those with metonymic or metaphorical overtones (Harvey 1965:35-38). The narrator presumes a correlation between God and the law (Luke 1:6; 2:22, 24, 39). Jesus advocates obedience to the law (10:28) and affirms its abiding validity (16:17). On the other hand, the law is impotent for salvation and holds no sway over Gentiles. Still it is the appropriate way of life for Jews and Jewish Christians (Wilson 1983:27-102, 114-15). The narrator makes a similar presumption of a divine relationship with the temple (1:9), but the perspectives of Jesus and Stephen provide critical insight into the relationship. It is a place of prayer, teaching, and worship (2:37; 19:46, 47; 24:53; Acts 3:1; cf. 24:11). But it is not God's dwelling place (7:48; 17:24), and Jesus predicts its demise (Luke 21:6).

Luke-Acts repeatedly associates God with the word. It can be metonymy for a divine message, such as the preaching of John the Baptist (Luke 3:2-17), or the proclamation of Jesus (5:1; 8:11). In Acts it is predominantly the Christian message (Fitzmyer 1981:565), but can also be a synecdoche for the life of the community of believers (e.g., Acts 12:24). Luke-Acts also associates God with the divine plan (*boulē*) or work (*ergon*) (Luke 7:30; Acts 2:23; 5:38-39, etc.). Paul Schubert has shown how the speeches of Acts clarify what the plan of God is (cf. Acts 20:27), that is, the working out of divine purposes in history from the creation to the consummation (1968:235-61).

Closely connected, Luke-Acts reflects a reiterated relationship between God and the kingdom of God. Sverre Aalen has challenged the prevailing consensus that the kingdom of God means God's ruling activity. He argues instead for a locative nuance comparable to "house," although by house he means the organic community of the household (1961-62:215-40). He focuses on the meaning of God's kingdom for the historical Jesus rather than on its function in Luke-Acts, and his thesis neglects that certain events are experiences of God's kingdom (e.g., Luke 11:20; cf. 10:9) (cf. Perrin 1976:67, Friedrich 1965: 710). Nevertheless, he contributes intuitively to understanding the communal nature of the kingdom of God in Luke-Acts.

In Luke-Acts God's kingdom is divine lordship over God's people (cf. Luke 1:16-17). Further, God assigns the kingdom to Jesus so that Jesus is God's vice-regent, and Jesus, in turn, associates the twelve as judges in his rule (22:29-30). Therefore, the relationship between God and the kingdom as an object turns out to be nothing other than the relationship between God and the people of God. But also, in contrast to Aalen's locative nuance, God's ruling activity involves subduing the enemies of the exalted Jesus (Acts 2:34-35).

In addition, Luke-Acts links the Holy Spirit with a dove, with fire, and with glossolalia. The association of the Spirit with a dove is enigmatic except that it clearly reflects the peculiar relationship between Jesus and the Spirit (Luke 3:22). John the Baptist correlates a baptism with the Holy Spirit with a baptism with fire (3:16). Although the traditional understanding of the parallelism as synonymous—that is, conferring the fire of the Holy Spirit—may be anachronistic on the level of the historical John, in all probability Luke-Acts alludes proleptically to the events of Pentecost (Fitzmyer 1981:473-74). Literary repetitions bear this out. When Jesus recalls John's prediction (Acts 1:5), and when Peter later recalls these words of Jesus (11:16), they both refer to the baptism with the Holy Spirit, and they both omit any mention of baptism with fire. The events of Pentecost, however, dramatize the baptism with fire. Jesus and Peter fail to mention baptism with fire because their reference to baptism with the Holy Spirit is the equivalent. Repeated cases of glossolalia are clear manifestations of the Holy Spirit and confirm the peculiar relationship of believers with the Holy Spirit.

Already I have indicated the evaluative function of epithets. But evaluation may also come as reflections from the narrator or from other characters. Although the narrator presupposes that God is irreproachable, interaction among characters provides some evaluative characterization of God. Some unknown agents have called Elizabeth barren (Luke 1:36). This combines with Zechariah's doubt to imply a negative evaluation of God's power. And so in contrast to Elizabeth's alleged sterility, Gabriel characterizes God as omnipotent: "For with God nothing will be impossible" (1:37). In a comparable case, when Jesus' auditors ask him who can be saved in face of the obstacle of wealth, Jesus implies that the query conceals doubt of divine power, and he asserts: "What is impossible with human beings is possible with God" (18:27). Interaction between Jesus and the rich ruler provides opportunity for Jesus to esteem God alone as good (18:19).

Evaluations of God also come in the form of evaluative responses from characters. One of the most notable cases is the very ending of Luke. Jesus' disciples are continually blessing God (Luke 24:53). That response has overtones for evaluating the entire Gospel of Luke primarily as a story of what God has done. The conversion of Cornelius provokes another prominent cluster of evaluative responses. The amazement of the six Jews from Joppa (Acts 10:45), the response of the apostles and Judeans to Peter's report (11:18), and the acceptance of Peter's report at the Jerusalem council (15:14, 22, 28) confirm Peter's conclusion that God shows no partiality. The people in Jerusalem who glorify God when they hear Paul's report of the Gentile mission play a similar evaluative role for the Gentile mission as God's work (21:19-20).

Earlier, I claimed that action is a means of characterization. All actions characterize, but they do so especially when they are typical or "characteristic," that is, when they are redundant. Redundancy means that similar actions occur in a variety of contexts (Harvey 1965:32-33). In a variety of contexts God repeatedly fills people with the Holy Spirit. The action of the

Spirit is frequently, though not invariably, connected with revelation, both direct (e.g., Luke 1:67; 2:15; 2:26) and through scripture (Acts 1:16; 4:25). The contexts vary: God's revelation to Abraham (Acts 7:2), the foresight of David (2:31; 4:25), Jesus' work of revealing the Father (Luke 10:21-22), the revelation of Paul's commission (Acts 9:15), Peter's solution of the riddle of a double vision (10:28, 34-35), and general revelation to pagans (14:17). God repeatedly sends emissaries including Moses (Acts 7:35), angels (Luke 1:19, 26), Jesus (10:16), and Paul and Barnabas (Acts 13:4). Further, God acts redemptively for both Israel and the Gentiles (Luke 1:54-55; Acts 7:25; 13:17-23), forgives (Luke 23:34; cf. 15:7, 10; Acts 7:60; 15:9), and saves (2:21). The belief of Gentiles is what God has done among the Gentiles (10:1-11:18; 13:47; 14:27; 15:7,12, 16; cf. the divine passive in 28:28).

Preeminently, however, God acts with respect to Jesus. God anoints Jesus for his ministry (Luke 4:18, cf. 3:22; Acts 10:38) and acts through him to heal (5:17) and to cast out demons (11:20). Through such acts God attests Jesus (2:22). But especially God raises Jesus, exalts him, and makes him Messiah and Lord (2:32, 33; 3:15, 26; 4:10; 5:30-31; 10:40; 13:30-34, etc.).

God not only acts but acts toward an intended future, an index of motivation (Docherty 1983:201) and a forceful clue toward integrating the character into a coherent whole. The intended future means salvation from the enemies of God's people and inclusion in God's kingdom (Luke 1:71; 13:29; Acts 2:34). Another cluster of repetitions portrays the intended future as peace (Luke 1:79; 2:14; Acts 10:36). But there are enemies from whom to be saved, and there is wickedness from which to turn, and so the intended future also includes judgment (Luke 3:17; 13:28; Acts 10:42; 17:31).

Interior emotions convey highly reliable characterizations. And occasionally Luke-Acts offers the reader glimpses of God's interior attitudes. In divine speech God says with respect to Jesus: ". . . with thee I am well pleased" (Luke 3:22). Paul recalls God's own words about David: "I have found in David the son of Jesse a man after my own heart . . . " (Acts 13:22). Stephen cites God's reaction to the suffering of the people in

Egypt: "I have surely seen the ill-treatment of my people that are in Egypt and heard their groaning" (Acts 7:34). Though the evidence is slight, God is pleased with those who obey the divine will and grieved at the suffering of the oppressed.

According to E. M. Forster readers quickly recognize a "flat" character as one who remains unchanged by circumstances (1954:105-106). By this criterion, God would be a flat character in Luke-Acts, because God is superior to changing circumstances.[5] But also according to Forster, the test of a "round" or developed character is the capacity to surprise (1954:118).

Although Forster means the unpredictable nature of life, his criterion effectively distinguishes the complex character of God. God frustrates expectations of other characters and undoubtedly of readers (Iser 1974:37). Unexpectedly God works through an aged priestly couple, Zechariah and Elizabeth, whereas the high priestly party characteristically is at enmity with God. God favors a virgin of low estate to be the mother of the Messiah and repudiates the mighty (Luke 1:26-55). Immediately after naming world and regional rulers, the narrator says wryly that the word of God came to John the son of Zechariah in the wilderness (3:2). The anointing of Jesus with God's Spirit comes as a surprise to the people of Nazareth (4:16-30). Jesus portrays God as joyful over repentant sinners (15:7, 10) and claims that God justifies a toll collector who pleads for divine mercy rather than a meticulous Pharisee (18:9-14). As the one with whom God is pleased, Jesus ironically becomes the victim of crucifixion according to divine necessity. With equal irony the crucified one receives divine attestation by the unexpected resurrection. The kingdom is not restored to Israel according to expectations, but incongruously the non-nationalistic twelve judge Israel. The God of Israel's forebears extends divine salvation to Gentiles without circumcision.

To inquire into the character of God is an effort to fix that character. But it remains elusive. For one thing, it is complex, and even the complexity that I have described is dreadfully incomplete. For another, with all the complexity there are gaps that render God's character indeterminate. Thus, all efforts to epitomize the character of God in Luke-Acts will be frustrated.

Ironically, the fact that the God of Luke-Acts is incalculable is another facet of the character of God.

## JESUS

Luke-Acts attributes the existence of Jesus to divine action (the virginal conception) and yet forcefully establishes his existence also in the historical realm. Parentage and genealogy authenticate Jesus as a real person in a real world (cf. Docherty 1983: 62-63). A decree from Augustus during the tenure of Quirinius as governor of Syria situates Jesus' birth chronologically. Similarly, the synchronization in Luke 3:1-2, the implication that Jesus followed closely on the heels of John the Baptist, and the age of Jesus when he began his ministry (3:23) locate his ministry chronologically.

Luke-Acts also locates Jesus in space.[6] Born in Bethlehem, his hometown is Nazareth (Luke 4:16). Pilate alludes to him as a Galilean (23:6). Although he repeatedly shows up in Capernaum, Luke-Acts portrays him as an itinerant. Even after his resurrection, he travels with two disciples on the road to Emmaus. With the ascension Acts locates Jesus in heaven (Acts 1:11). Peter alludes to his continuing habitation there (3:21), and Stephen sees Jesus in heaven at the right hand of God (7:55-56).

Luke-Acts paints no physical portrait of Jesus. The nearest equivalent is some typical gestures. He lifts up his eyes as a sign of concern for people (Luke 6:20) or reverence for God (9:16), but also as a sign of reproach (18:23; 22:61). He repeatedly breaks bread in a pattern that indicates sharing but also has eucharistic overtones (9:16; 22:19; 24:30). Jesus touches in compassion and with the power of healing (5:13; 7:14; 8:54; 22:51), and he lifts up his hands in the posture of blessing (24:50). On the Mount of Transfiguration his countenance is altered and his apparel becomes dazzling white (9:29). Once Jesus' clothing is described when Herod Antipas dresses him in a shining robe (23:11). Otherwise, the narrative ignores the physical appearance of Jesus.

Jesus' ancestry also insinuates his status (cf. Berlin 1983:36). But the clues are enigmatic. On the one hand, Joseph and Mary

belong to a low social class (cf. Luke 1:48). A thematic development fits Jesus into such a class. He has nowhere to lay his
head (9:58), and women of means support him and the twelve
(8:1-3). On the other hand, Joseph is a descendant of David.
Some of the ancestors in Jesus' genealogy are otherwise unknown, but many of them are prominent in Israel's history.
Further, a thematic development also fits Jesus into the royal
line of David (1:32; 18:38, 39; Acts 2:30-36).

In a closely connected development, Jesus' disciples call him
a king (Luke 19:38). At his trial before Pilate his opponents
accuse him of claiming to be a king (23:2). They are unreliable
characters because (1) both Pilate and Herod find Jesus innocent of political charges, (2) the opponents allege that Jesus
forbids tribute to Caesar when in fact Jesus volleyed the tribute
question back to his adversaries (20:21-26), and (3) Jesus'
followers, rather than he, say that he is a king. Opponents then
mock him as the king of the Jews, and he dies with an inscription over him: "This is the king of the Jews" (23:37-38).

A similar theme emerges from accusations against Paul in
Thessalonica that he proclaims Jesus another king over against
Caesar (Acts 17:7). Paul's direct denial of offending against
Caesar shows that too is unreliable (25:8).

In short, the title "king" as such is correct, but Luke-Acts
establishes the norms for its proper understanding by playing
the meaning for reliable characters off against the meaning for
unreliable ones (Iser 1974:48).

The characterization of Jesus by epithet and direct description is complicated. The name "Jesus" itself comes from Gabriel, and later it is associated with divine power (Acts 3:16;
19:13). Gabriel also predicts that Jesus will be called "holy"
and "Son of God." These epithets are both evaluative and
relational. They distinguish the special nature of Jesus and
affirm his relationship with God. Broadening the perspective
adds depth to this characterization. God addresses Jesus as "my
Son" (Luke 3:22; 9:35). Paul proclaims that Jesus is the Son of
God (Acts 9:20; cf. 20:28). Demons specify that Jesus is both
holy and Son of God (Luke 4:34, 41; 8:28). Peter and Paul
apply a reference to the Holy One in scripture to Jesus (Acts

2:27; 13:35), and Peter makes it a part of his own language (3:14).

The title "Lord," the most frequent title for Jesus in Luke-Acts, is applied to Jesus from a wide variety of perspectives—from an angel (Luke 2:11), suppliants (e.g., 5:12), disciples (e.g., 5:8), the narrator (e.g., 10:1), scripture (Acts 2:34-36), and Jesus himself (Luke 6:5; 19:31). Its nuances vary from polite address ("sir") to a confessional formula (e.g., Acts 16:31) (S. Johnson 1962:151).

Whatever the nuance, the title never appears on the lips of opponents, with the exception of Paul, who, because he is in the process of becoming an overthrown enemy (Gaventa 1985: 439-49, 1986:52-95), is not an exception. This feature points to at least four relational connotations of the epithet.

(1) God raises and exalts Jesus to make him Lord, and thus his lordship implies his relationship to God, a relationship of co-regency (Foerster 1965:1089, Fitzmyer 1981:202-203). The identity is so close that occasionally references to the Lord are ambiguous as to whether they refer to God or to Jesus (e.g., Acts 7:60; 11:21; 16:32).

(2) Jesus exercises lordship over those whom he and his disciples have gathered as the people of God. The lordship of the risen and exalted Jesus analeptically recalls Gabriel's prediction that Jesus would reign over the house of Jacob (cf. Luke 1:33). For Luke-Acts this means that Jesus is Israel's Lord (Foerster 1965:1094). But there are proleptic connotations external to Luke-Acts because Gabriel predicts that Jesus will reign over the house of Jacob forever.

(3) Among followers of Jesus, the term implies a relationship of humility before Jesus and of dependence upon the power of Jesus (Dawsey 1986:11).

(4) Jesus' lordship establishes his authority over all (Acts 10:36). The Greek word for "all" is ambiguous. It can mean "all things" or "all people." But in the context the universality of God's salvation is a strong clue that it refers to all people, that is, it specifically includes Gentiles (cf. 10:35) (Haenchen 1971:352, Conzelmann 1987:83).

Over against lordship, Luke-Acts counterpoises Jesus' identity as God's servant (*pais*)—an epithet appearing twice on the lips of Peter and twice on the lips of the early messianists (Acts 3:13, 26; 4:27, 30) (Cullmann 1963:74). This terminology echoes the LXX and implies that Jesus stands in a relationship with God like David, another servant of God (4:25) who did God's will (13:22). In an analogous way, Jesus submits to God's will (Luke 22:42). And so Jesus' identity as servant of God tempers his status as Lord.

Although unrelated linguistically to the epithet *pais*, Jesus' identification of himself as one who serves (*ho diakonôn*, Luke 22:27) also qualifies his lordship. In settling a dispute among the twelve, Jesus redefines greatness not in terms of lording it over others but in terms of serving others, and he gives himself as an example as one who waits on tables.

The epithet "Messiah" (*christos*) likewise undergoes redefinition with strong evaluative implications. In conjunction with Gabriel's prediction that God would give Jesus the throne of David (Luke 1:32), the angelic message of the birth of the Messiah (2:11) is charged with political inferences. Those inferences remain viable in the expectation of the apostles that the risen Jesus would restore the kingdom to Israel (Acts 1:6). But a thematic development corrects them.

(1) Messengers from John the Baptist inquire of Jesus: "Are you the one who is to come?" (Luke 7:19). Jesus responds in terms of his deeds of healing and preaching without any nationalistic allusions. (2) When Peter designates Jesus the Messiah, Jesus talks of suffering, death, and resurrection (9:20-22). (3) The disillusioned disciples on the road to Emmaus show that the crucifixion of Jesus carries the potential of disconfirming his messianic identity. In response, Jesus explains that the suffering of the Messiah is a divine necessity (24:26; cf. 24:46). (4) The thematic development also bleeds over into Acts where Paul proves the necessity of the Messiah to suffer (Acts 17:3).

Thus, Luke-Acts transforms a potential disconfirmation of Jesus messiahship into its confirmation and redefines messiahship in non-nationalistic terms.

Nevertheless, Jesus has a distinct relationship with Israel as its Savior. An angel announces to shepherds: ". . . for to you (*humin*) is born this day in the city of David a Savior . . ." (Luke 2:11). Two additional references in Acts clarify that Jesus is Israel's Savior (Acts 5:31; 13:23). The epithet also implies a relationship with God because Jesus' identity as Savior depends on God's act of raising and exalting him (5:31). Quite obviously, as a designation for the infant Jesus the term is proleptic. But for Paul it is analeptic in that he recalls what God has already accomplished. Although the term applies to the risen and exalted Jesus, the thematic development places little emphasis on salvation in the eschatological judgment but makes it a present reality.

Quite to the contrary "Son of man" has present connotations but is also strongly eschatological. Compared with other epithets the diversity of perspective is extremely narrow. With one exception (Acts 7:56), this title comes to the reader only from Jesus as a self-designation. It occurs in analeptic contexts (Luke 7:34) and it points to a prolepsis internal to Luke-Acts when Jesus uses it in connection with predictions of his betrayal, suffering, death, and resurrection (e.g., 9:22, 44).[7] But it also has proleptic implications external to Luke-Acts when Jesus anticipates the parousia (e.g., 18:8). In the parousia the Son of man is an awesome figure of judgment (e.g., 11:30) but also an assuring figure of redemption (e.g., 21:27-28).

The interrelated titles teacher and master are primarily relational. They both occur in direct address as an acknowledgment of Jesus' leadership. Only disciples call Jesus "master," but antagonists and followers alike can refer to him as "teacher" (Luke 7:40; 9:38). The spies in 20:21 are unreliable characters who address Jesus insincerely; nevertheless, they unwittingly characterize Jesus correctly as a teacher. But even antagonists appear to place themselves in a relationship with Jesus where they are listeners who seek an opinion.[8] Once Jesus calls himself the teacher (22:11). In this case the relational nuance ceases, and the label analeptically subsumes his career.

The designation prophet also conveys implications of a relationship of hearing and heeding. This is precisely the meaning Peter attaches to his claim that Jesus is the prophet like Moses (Acts 3:22). But that also carries overtones of Jesus' relationship with God because God has raised up the prophet. Closely connected, in the transfiguration the voice from the cloud gives a direct command: "Listen to him" (Luke 9:35). Jesus' allusion to himself as a prophet (13:33) proleptically anticipates his solidarity with the prophet-martyrs of Jerusalem. On two other occasions the identification of Jesus as a prophet is analeptic. (1) The crowd at Nain calls Jesus a great prophet recalling his raising of a dead man but also evaluating him in terms of his relationship with God who is at work through him (7:16). (2) The two disciples on the road to Emmaus couple Jesus' identity as a prophet with his deeds and words (24:19).

The title "Righteous One" is forcefully evaluative. Peter juxtaposes Jesus as the Holy and Righteous One to a murderer (Barabbas) (Acts 3:14). Stephen juxtaposes the Righteous One to those who killed the prophets and to those who killed Jesus (7:52). In the second account of Paul's commissioning, Ananias identifies Jesus with the same epithet after reiterated references to Paul's persecution of Jesus (22:14). These all pick up the same term as the centurion who declares Jesus innocent at his crucifixion.

In 1986 Robert Karris argued that the centurion's remark means "righteous" rather than "innocent" (65-74). But against Karris, the centurion's comment is a part of a symmetrical frame around the death of Jesus. Notably, three times Pilate declares that Jesus is innocent (Luke 23:4, 14-15, 22). Three times antagonists mock Jesus (23:35, 36-37, 39). And three times allies of Jesus declare him innocent—the suppliant criminal, the centurion, and the multitude who return home beating their breasts (23:41, 47, 48). Thus, the echoes of the centurion's commentary and the juxtaposition of the Righteous One to murderers and persecutors confer potent evaluative shades to the term as an indication of Jesus' innocence.

Twice the epithet "leader" (archêgos) applies to Jesus. But the functions are quite distinct. In one case, Peter calls Jesus the "author of life" in juxtaposition to his death (Acts 3:15). The juxtaposition makes it evaluative but also strongly analeptic because it refers to Jesus as the first to be raised from the dead (cf. 26:23) (Haenchen 1971:206, Conzelmann 1987:28). Others presumably will follow—implicitly an external prolepsis. In another situation, Peter again juxtaposes the title "leader" to the crucifixion (5:31). In this instance, the term reflects God's affirmation of Jesus over against his death at the hands of opponents. But it also represents Jesus' relationship with Israel as its leader.

Beyond epithets and direct descriptions, the narrator and other characters give their characterizing evaluations of Jesus. The narrator views Jesus as favored and approved by God as a child and youth (Luke 2:40, 52). John the Baptist alludes to Jesus as his superior (3:16). Repeatedly the crowds function as a chorus to affirm Jesus, and their amazement, fear, wonder, astonishment, and joy all convey a positive evaluation.

But also groups of opponents respond repeatedly with suspicion, anger, and murmuring. Further, unreliable characters give evaluations that conflict with norms established by Luke-Acts. The people of Nazareth identify Jesus inadequately as (merely) Joseph's son (4:22). Some Pharisees and teachers of the law accuse Jesus of blasphemy (5:21). Others imply that Jesus breaks the law (6:2; 14:3). The people at large suggest that Jesus is John the Baptist *redivivus*, or Elijah, or another of the prophets (9:7-8, 19). Adversaries characterize Jesus as a glutton and drunkard (7:34). Simon the Pharisee thinks that Jesus is not a prophet (7:39). Antagonists contend that Jesus is in league with Beelzebul (11:15). Jesus refuses to accept the rich ruler's evaluation of him as "good" (18:18). Accusers and mockers at the trial and crucifixion give negative evaluations of Jesus (23:2, 5, 35-39). Even Stephen's accusers give an indirect unreliable characterization of Jesus (Acts 6:14).

Unreliable evaluations, however, present a dilemma. Are they unreliable because the perpetrators are opponents or because they are incorrect? Even unreliable characters may unwittingly express at least a degree of the truth. Therefore, the reader ultimately has to weigh and judge the degree of accuracy (Alter 1981:117). Thus, evaluations from unreliable personae, even if negative, aid the reader in fixing the character of Jesus (Iser 1974:48).

This process is particularly evident in three instances where unreliable characters portray Jesus as inferior in knowledge.

(1) In interior monologue Simon the Pharisee presumes that Jesus does not know that the woman who touches him is a sinner and therefore denies his prophetic nature (Luke 7:39). The implication that Jesus is inferior in knowledge places Jesus in a presumed ironic role (Frye 1957:34). But in actuality Jesus demonstrates that his knowledge is superior to Simon's. He knows that the woman is a forgiven sinner. Simon is the victim of an irony that confirms Jesus' prophetic identity all the more.

(2) At his trial opponents beat the blindfolded Jesus and command him, "Prophesy! Who is it that struck you?" But the irony turns on those who mock Jesus. They do not know it, but they are fulfilling Jesus' prophecy in 18:32: "[The Son of man] will be mocked and shamefully treated and spit upon."

(3) On the road to Emmaus Cleopas treats the risen Jesus as the only one who does not know what has happened in Jerusalem and presumes to tell him (24:18-24). In fact Jesus is the only one who does know. And so Jesus turns Cleopas and his companion on their ears and instructs them. The irony and their burning hearts accent the risen Jesus as the interpreter of the scriptures who reverses the scandal of a crucified Messiah (24:32).[9]

Although there may be no sharp delineation between evaluations by other personages and Jesus' relationships with them, his associations also individuate him. God chooses (Luke 9:35), empowers (5:17), and sends Jesus (9:48; 10:16). In return, Jesus serves only God (4:8; 23:46). But in derivative fashion Jesus chooses (5:1-11; 6:12-16, cf. Acts 9:15), empowers (5:1-11; 9:1), and sends disciples (9:2; 10:1). He demands that they obey and follow (5:27; 9:23; 14:27, 33). Similarly, Jesus reassigns to the twelve the kingdom assigned to him by the Father (22:29). Thus, Jesus plays a role as an intermediary between God and his disciples. In an apropos manner, God is at work in Jesus (e.g., 7:16; Acts 2:22), and human beings appeal to him for mercy (Luke 17:13; 18:38), believe in him

(Acts 11:17), receive baptism in his name (2:38; 19:5), and pray to him (7:59).

Jesus evokes generally positive relationships from crowds (6:17; 12:11; 18:35; 19:37),and he reciprocates (9:11). But he maintains a particular relationship with disciples. From among them he chooses twelve apostles (6:13) and sends out seventy(-two) emissaries (10:1). Notably, women are among his disciples (cf. Acts 1:14), and in cultural reversals women support him and the twelve (Luke 8:3) and are witnesses to his death, burial, and empty tomb (23:49; 23:55-24:11; 24:22). The twelve form a group of insiders with whom Jesus shares the last supper (22:14). Out of their number Peter, James, and John are particular confidants (8:51; 9:28), but James and John fail to understand Jesus' ministry (9:54-55), and Peter denies him (22:54-62).

Moreover, sinners and disreputable people form a part of Jesus' entourage, and he identifies them as the appropriate concern of his ministry (Luke 5:27, 32; 19:1-10). That brings on criticism from Pharisees, scribes, and murmuring crowds. But Pharisees and scribes are not stereotypical opponents because they also appear as inquirers, as people who warn Jesus of danger from Herod, and as Jesus' hosts. The high priestly coterie forms the primary opposition at Jesus' trial and death. But there can be positive relationships with local Jewish elders (7:3). In 13:14 a ruler of the synagogue opposes Jesus, but in 8:40-42, 49-56 another ruler of the synagogue entreats Jesus to heal his daughter.

Jesus contends with his opponents, and he bests them in debates. Moreover, he issues dire warnings against his foes (e.g., 11:50; 12:5; 13:35; 23:28-31). But he also teaches love for enemies (6:27), and he asks God to forgive those who execute him (23:34).[10]

One pattern in Jesus' relationship with adversaries that is reinforced by repetition is his ability to discern their thoughts (6:8; 11:17; 20:23, cf. 5:22; 7:40). Moreover, Jesus also discerns the thoughts of his disciples but only when they function at least partly as antagonists—when they dispute among themselves about who is the greatest (9:46) and when they are startled and frightened by a resurrection appearance (24:38). A particular case is Jesus' prescience of his betrayal by Judas (22:21). Thus, there is a thematization of Jesus' ability to discern the motives of opponents.

Jesus' family relationships are enigmatic. On the one hand, as a youth Jesus lives in subjection to Joseph and Mary. But at twelve years of age he professes commitment to another father (Luke 2:49). Subsequently, he continues to assert his dedication to God above family. He redefines kinship by renouncing family commitments and allying himself with those who hear and do God's word (8:19-21). Closely related, Jesus rejects madonna and child as the image of blessedness and substitutes hearing and doing God's word (11:27-28). After the resurrection, Mary and Jesus' brothers are part of the embryonic community of believers (Acts 1:14). Implicitly, familial ranks invert—the family venerates Jesus rather than Jesus honoring the family.

A contextual knowledge of Jesus' character also depends on his relationship with objects and conditions, particularly those with metaphorical significance (Harvey 1965:35-38).

Jesus produces a spectacular catch of fish (Luke 5:4-10)—a miracle that demonstrates his dominance over the environment. But the fish have a metaphorical significance related to Jesus' mission of gathering a people for God. The stilling of the storm (8:22-25) likewise portrays Jesus as dominant over his environment, and in that regard it fits in with other miracles. But it uncharacteristically does not fit the preview and review of Jesus' ministry in 4:18-19 and 7:22.

Additionally, on other occasions Jesus is susceptible to the environment. He is hungry (4:2). He does not accept his crucifixion on his own volition (22:42), and so he is susceptible to suffering. At his crucifixion rulers scoff: "He saved others; let him save himself . . ." (23:35). They are unreliable characters, but in the typical Lucan sense they unwittingly speak truth. Jesus cannot save himself (Tannehill 1986:198). But the catch is that he has already declared that those who would save their own lives will lose them (9:24) (Danker 1988:376). Further, it is not Jesus who manifests power in the crucifixion and resurrection but the God to whom Jesus commits his life (23:46).

Jesus maintains positive relationships with the synagogue, the law, and the temple. The narrator characterizes Jesus' presence in the synagogue on the sabbath as customary (e.g., Luke 4:16). Although Jesus exhibits autonomy from conventional interpretations of the law (e.g., 6:5), he observes it and condemns disobedience (cf. 16:17). He makes a claim on the temple as a place of prayer (19:45-46) and makes it a center for teaching. But he refuses to join those who admire it, and he forecasts its destruction (21:5-6).

Baptism with water marks a decisive point at the beginning of Jesus' career. Its meaning is clarified in that it coincides with the descent of the Spirit and God's affirmation of Jesus as "my beloved Son" (3:21-22). Correspondingly, the cup and the bread are metonyms at the end of Jesus' career. The cup alludes to Jesus' death (22:42), and in combination with the broken bread, anticipates the crucifixion.

But the cup and the bread are also closely integrated with the expectation of the kingdom of God (22:16, 18). Further, the second cup marks the establishment of a new covenant (22:20). Significantly, the cup is poured out "for you," and although in the immediate context "you" refers to the apostles, the future celebration of the meal in remembrance of Jesus (22:19) makes the "you" inclusive, and therefore, Jesus' death establishes a new covenant that corresponds to the Mosaic covenant as a community founding event (Tannehill 1986:285, n. 15). Acts 20:28 corroborates that the death of Jesus establishes the community (Zehnle 1969:440).

Jesus makes three metaphorical references to himself—"physician" (Luke 4:23; 5:31), "bridegroom" (5:34), and "stone" (20:17). Bo Reicke has argued that Jesus identifies himself as a physician—an identity that is harmonious with his healing ministry (1973:49-50). But Jesus himself provides a commentary on the title in 4:23 that proves it to be a parabolic analogy of his relationship to the people of Nazareth. Similarly, the physician for the sick in 5:31 is analogous to Jesus' relationship to sinners. The bridegroom is also clearly an analogy of Jesus' relationship with his disciples. Luke 20:17 leaves the metaphorical sense of the stone up in the air since the citation from Ps 118:22-23 forms part of Jesus' query to his audience. But Acts 4:11 leaves no doubt that it is a scriptural allusion to the double nature of Jesus' relationship with detractors and with God. Opponents reject him, God affirms him.

A contextual knowledge of the character also depends on actions in a variety of contexts. Both narrator's summaries and dramatic episodes portray Jesus typically as a teacher and preacher. There are also two characteristic ways Jesus speaks. The narrator notes repeatedly that Jesus speaks in parables. The narrator also notes that Jesus speaks in an authoritative manner— a manner further dramatized by the formula on the mouth of Jesus: "I tell you." Additionally, Jesus' arguments are generally arguments from authority (Dawsey 1986:39). Jesus repeatedly makes predictions—notably of his death and resurrection and of the destruction of Jerusalem. Remarkable coincidences between his predictions and their realization imply reliability even for predictions to be fulfilled beyond the end of Luke-Acts. Closely related, Jesus makes promises (e.g., Luke 22:29-30, 69; 23:29-30; 24:49; Acts 1:5) that have high probability of fulfillment, including promises of judgment (e.g., Luke 23:29-30).

Exorcisms are likewise dramatized and summarized, and in Luke 11:19-20 Jesus mentions his exorcisms himself. Summaries and dramatized incidents also present Jesus as a healer, although his role as a healer is not always clearly differentiated from his role as an exorcist. Jesus himself gives an iterative summary of exorcisms and healings in 13:32. Notably, at his arrest Jesus heals the slave of the high priest who is associated with his opponents (22:51). Then in Acts Jesus becomes an agent for healing (Acts 3:16; 4:10, 30). In two dramatic episodes Jesus raises the dead (Luke 7:11-17; 8:40-42, 49-56), and after the first episode Jesus himself claims that dead people (plural) are being raised (7:22).

Teaching, preaching, predicting, promising, and performing exorcisms and healings not only reflect the nature of Jesus' ministry, but also are strongly relational. This is what Jesus does with and for people. In addition, he forgives (Luke 5:20), and in Acts he becomes an agent for forgiveness (Acts 10:43; 13:38).

He also reveals God (Luke 10:22) and interprets scripture (20:42; 24:27, 45).

Additionally, in different contexts Jesus commissions others for mission (Luke 9:2; 10:1). In Acts 1:8 Jesus commissions the apostles specifically to be witnesses to the end of the earth. Closely related, in Luke 24:46-47 Jesus gives a mandate for the universal preaching of repentance and forgiveness of sins. Because this commission is formulated in the passive voice, it leaves open the identity of its agents, and, therefore, it is a comprehensive mandate. It is comprehensive enough to include Paul, who nevertheless claims that Jesus specifically commissioned him (Acts 22:21; 26:17).

Occasionally Luke-Acts offers the reader glimpses into Jesus' interior. Several references blend together into the thematization of Jesus' compassion.

A leper pleads for healing, "Lord, if you want to, you can make me clean." In his response, Jesus says, "I do want to" (Luke 5:12-13). Comparing this text to its Marcan parallel, Eduard Schweizer contends that 5:12-13 makes no reference to Jesus' emotions (1984:110, cf. Fitzmyer 1981:574). In Mark the narrator relates Jesus' compassion. In Luke the perspective shifts entirely to Jesus himself, and, against Schweizer, the interchange between Jesus and the leper does indicate Jesus' desire to heal.

In the case of the raising of the widow's son, the narrator informs the reader of Jesus' compassion (7:13). In a monologue addressed to Jerusalem Jesus laments his unfulfilled desire to gather Jerusalem's children (13:34). In a closely related incident the narrator reports that Jesus wept over the city (19:41), and then Jesus expresses his desire for Jerusalem's peace in an elliptical condition where "It would be pleasing to me" is to be understood ("It would be pleasing to me if you knew the things that make for peace" 19:42, Blass, Debrunner, Funk 1961:§ 482).

Luke 22:15 and 22:44 open two additional windows to Jesus' interior. Both cases unfold under the ominous cloud of approaching death. In the first Jesus expresses his intense desire to eat the passover with the apostles. The grammatical construction allows the possibility of inferring that Jesus did not actually eat the passover (Lohmeyer 1937:194). But such an interpretation arises largely from an effort to harmonize Luke with John where the last supper is not a passover. More likely, Jesus' ernest desire to eat the passover indicates a premonition that it will be his last (Danker 1988:345). Such foreboding sentiment gains intensity when Jesus prays for God to remove the cup of death (22:42). Equally significant, Jesus expresses the subordination of his will to God's.

The intended future provides clues for determining motivation (Docherty 1983:201). From a number of perspectives, it is double-pronged. Simeon predicts that Jesus will be a light for Gentiles and glory for Israel. But he also predicts that Jesus will be the occasion for the fall of many in Israel (Luke 2:32-34). Angels anticipate that Jesus will bring peace on earth, but with a reservation: ". . . for those with whom God is pleased" (2:14). Jesus forecasts his ministry largely in terms of releasing people from oppression (4:18-19). He confers the peace of forgiveness (7:50) and of healing (8:48), both of which imply reestablishment in society (cf. Acts 10:36), and he promises a messianic banquet that will include people from east, west, north, and south (Luke 13:29). But the other prong is that Jesus also disrupts social order (Luke 12:51). Ultimately Jesus predicts judgment over against peace (e.g., 11:32; 19:44) and exclusion as well as inclusion in the messianic banquet (13:28).

James Dawsey claims to document a discrepancy between the voices of the narrator and Jesus. According to him, the narrator portrays public support for Jesus as overwhelming; Jesus declares that those who will be saved will be few. The narrator extends the eschaton into the future; Jesus predicts it as imminent. The narrator softens the scandal of Jesus' suffering by attributing it to the ignorance of the people; Jesus attributes it to Satan and the collusion of Jewish leaders (Dawsey 1986: 73-102, 110, 123-24, 147-56). But Dawsey improperly separates the narrator's voice from Jesus, because there are no clues that the narrator misunderstands the words of Jesus (Tannehill 1986:7, n.4). The two voices, therefore, are ultimately complementary, and the distinct emphases expressed in third person narration and in direct speech from Jesus are components of the multi-faceted character of Jesus.

Such complexities form a part of the profile of a Jesus who frustrates expectations (Iser 1974:37). The reader discovers the necessity of revising the developing character of Jesus when threats of judgment plow into promises of peace. Or with Gabriel's prediction that Jesus will reign over the house of Jacob forever, the reader is unprepared for the conflict between Jesus and Jewish leaders. Or with assurances from the narrator that Jesus was obedient to his parents, Jesus' redefinition of familial relationships comes as a surprise. Or with the establishment of Jesus as the Holy One, his relationships with sinners catch the reader unaware.

For one destined to be a Davidic king, a wandering itinerancy with no place to lay his head seems strangely inconsistent. So often designated teacher, he sometimes refuses to give the answer or make an indicated decision (Luke 12:13-14; 20:21-25). And for the Messiah to suffer and to die as one who cannot save himself is a startling development. But the quality to elude classification is also a part of the depth of the character of Jesus.

# 6

# CHARACTERIZATION: PETER AND PAUL

## PETER

Though prominent in Luke, Simon Peter remains a minor character until Acts. Peter's place in Luke-Acts, it has been argued, derives from the author's interest in salvation history, and so Peter exits from Acts without a trace when he fulfills his function in that history (Schneider 1980:282). But his character develops far beyond requirements for his function. For example, the narrator describes Peter's arrest, imprisonment, and release with minute detail—an angel touches Peter's side and tells him to put on his sandals (Acts 12:3-17).

Notwithstanding Peter's initially low profile, the first reference to him assumes his identity (Luke 4:38). He is a known quantity by which the narrator can anchor the location of Jesus and the identity of a sick woman. According to the context stretching back to Luke 4:31-37, Simon's house is in Capernaum, a location from which he carries out his occupation as a fisherman on the lake of Gennesaret (i.e., the Sea of Galilee, 5:1).[1] The reader thus gets a geographical and a sociological[2] fix on Peter. But neither is very stable. Peter rises in his world to become one of the twelve who sit on thrones judging the tribes of Israel. He also accompanies Jesus as an itinerant. He can be located as precisely as if he had a street address (Acts 10:6, 32). But characteristically he moves from place to place.

In contrast to Matthew and John, Luke-Acts does not suggest Simon's ancestry by a patronym. But indirectly Luke 4:38 identifies him as married. Further, Luke-Acts locates him among other relationships. He has a brother named Andrew (6:14), and James and John are his fishing partners (5:10).

Though rare, epithets and direct depictions of Peter surface from diverse perspectives—from the narrator, Jesus, other characters, and Peter himself. By means of references to a few gestures the narrator hints at a rudimentary physical descrip-tion—Peter falls down at Jesus' knees (Luke 5:8), stands con-spicuously (Acts 1:15; 2:14; 15:7), gazes with captivating inten-sity (3:4), kneels in prayer (9:40), gives Tabitha his hand (9:41), and gestures with his hand for silence (12:17).

Especially noteworthy, Peter makes several characterizing references to himself. After the miraculous catch of fish, he assumes that Jesus has special status. In comparison, Peter deprecates himself as a sinner (*hamartôlos*) (Luke 5:8). But is that a reliable characterization? Other uses of *hamartôlos* in Luke indicate that Peter here includes himself among people who did not observe the law in detail (cf. Danker 1988:88-89, Rengstorf 1964:324-27). The perception of opponents in Acts that Peter and John are uneducated and common reinforces the impression (Acts 4:13). But Peter does not easily let that imprint stick. In a vision, he claims repeatedly that he has never eaten anything common or unclean (Acts 10:14; 11:8). Further, he is a customary worshiper in the temple (Acts 3:1; cf. Luke 24:53; Acts 2:46), and he alludes to the law of Moses as a yoke to which implicitly he and his forebears have submitted (15:10). Calling himself a sinner, therefore, creates a contrast with Jesus but does not identify Peter as one who did not observe Torah.

Further, designations for Simon disclose a development in his perception of himself. As a sinner he views himself unfit for association with Jesus. But Jesus immediately provides a correc-tive. In a metaphorical play on the miraculous catch of fish, Jesus names Simon one who catches human beings (Luke 5:10)—a label that is a prediction, although the future begins immediately. Further, it fits into the thematization of gathering and sifting a people for God in a double sense. (1) Peter and James and John immediately follow Jesus and become a part of the gathering. (2) Jesus commissions Peter for a particular role in gathering and sifting because Jesus singles out only Peter as one who will catch human beings (Schneider 1976:204).

Accordingly, by the time of Acts Peter's self-designations have undergone a dramatic shift. He now sees himself not as unworthy to associate with Jesus but as closely associated with Jesus. In Acts 1:8 Jesus designates the apostles "witnesses." The remainder of Acts 1 further defines that identity. In 1:17 Peter alludes to a ministry. This is an analeptic reference to the ministry of the twelve with the earthly Jesus. But it also proleptically anticipates an extension into the future that demands restoration of the twelve. Peter spells out explicitly that this ministry requires a witness from the time of the baptism of John (analeptic) who will become a (proleptic) witness to the resurrection (1:22, 25). From then on Peter associates himself repeatedly with these witnesses (2:32; 5:32; 10:39-41).

Peter experiences a further closely related development. As a law abiding, kosher Jew and customary worshiper in the temple, Peter initiates the Gentile mission, in relation to which he undergoes a transformation. He considers himself to be on the same level as Gentile believers. Twice he compares Gentile believers with Jewish believers (Acts 10:47; 11:15). But, true to his conviction, he also inverts the comparison. He regards Jews, not as the paradigm of salvation for Gentiles, but quite the reverse—Gentiles are the paradigm of salvation for Jews (15:11). Therefore, Peter develops from considering himself to be distinguished from Gentiles to viewing himself as on a par with them.

In the Cornelius episode Peter is self-deprecating in a way that both foreshadows his egalitarianism and also elevates his status. He counters Cornelius's obeisance by commanding: "Stand up; I too am a man" (Acts 10:26). The narrator first uses Cornelius's obeisance to heighten Peter's heroic status. But Peter's self-designation anticipates the equality of human beings from the divine perspective (10:34).

In one particular set of references to himself Peter is unreliable. When he follows Jesus to the high priest's house, some anonymous functionaries identify him as associated with Jesus (Luke 22:55-60). Peter replies with insistent denials. But Jesus' prediction in 22:34, Peter's recall, and his bitter sorrow establish norms for the reader to judge Peter as unreliable and the anonymous functionaries as trustworthy.

After the resurrection, the narrator registers the perception of opponents that Peter and John are bold, uneducated, and common (Acts 4:13). The boldness is implicitly derived from God, and, by way of contrast, before the resurrection of Jesus, Peter is grouped among people who are afraid (Luke 9:34 and presumably 8:25; 9:45). The notice that Peter and John are uneducated and common, however, implies the opposite—because they have been with Jesus they do not act like uneducated commoners.

A highly significant part of Simon's characterization is the name Jesus gives him (6:14). "Peter" has proleptic, evaluative, and relational connotations. It is a descriptive analogy. It implicitly compares Simon to "rock." In the context Luke 6:48 provides the clearest clue to a metaphorical significance. Heeding the words of Jesus is like rock as a steadfast foundation for a house. Thus, Jesus' name for Simon points toward his function and evaluates him as one who heeds Jesus' words.[3] But Simon has to grow into the name (Docherty 1983:56), as his denial of Jesus, his fear, and his lack of understanding show.

The relational nuance, however, goes far beyond the metaphorical significance of the name, because the phraseological plane also reflects Simon's relationship to Jesus (Uspensky 1973:15, 17-26). The narrator notes in Luke 6:14 that Jesus gave Simon the name Peter. Consequently, when the narrative refers to Peter, it reflects Jesus' relationship with him even though one of the references occurs before Jesus conferred the name (5:8). In Luke 22:31 Jesus addresses Peter ominously with a double vocative: "Simon, Simon, . . . ." This is more than an indicator of a pre-Lucan source (so Fitzmyer 1985:1421, 1424). Rather, it stands as a dire warning of Peter's potential apostasy in face of his impending satanic trial to such an extent that

Jesus reverts to a perspective outside the particular relationship. In addition, the only time other participants in Luke refer to Peter, they call him "Simon" (24:34)—reflecting their own point of view rather than Jesus'.

These perspectives persist in Acts where in direct address only the Lord uses the name—and that in a vision (Acts 10:13; 11:7). In a companion vision, a messenger of God, who is also addressed as "Lord," commands Cornelius to send for "Simon who is called Peter" (10:5, cf. 10:18, 32; 11:13). The narrator still employs the name Peter. But Acts 15:14 contains a transliteration of the Aramaic "Simeon" thereby reflecting the point of view of James and the Jerusalem assembly. Thus the phraseology indicates that the name Peter, even when used by the narrator, reflects a special relationship to Jesus.

Peter reciprocates. He addresses Jesus as "master" (*epistates*). Only Peter, John, the disciples as a chorus, and ten suppliant lepers address Jesus with this title. Thus Peter's phraseology also implies his special relationship with Jesus.

In one oblique reference, some mockers accuse the disciples, and indirectly Peter, of being intoxicated (Acts 2:13). This explanation is unreliable, as Peter's rebuttal shows. Rather, the charge of inebriation with wine allows for a clearer characterization of Peter as among those inebriated with the Holy Spirit.

Apart from the relational connotations of epithets, the reader also has access to Peter's character through his relationship with others. His relationship to God is sparsely but significantly indicated. He is certainly among those filled with the Holy Spirit on Pentecost (Acts 2:4; 4:8; cf. 4:31; 5:32; 11:17; 15:8). He places himself among those who are obedient to God (4:19-20; 5:29), and considers himself chosen by God as a witness to Jesus among the Gentiles (10:41; 15:7). The narrator repeatedly associates Peter with prayer, thereby implying a relationship with God (1:14, 24; 3:1; 4:31; 10:9). Further, given two literarily redundant, miraculous, prison releases (5:19; 12:6-11), the reader infers that Peter is under divine providence.

Luke-Acts implies Peter's relationship with Jesus by drawing increasingly tighter circles among people surrounding Jesus.

First, Peter is one among a group of disciples. Second, he is one of the twelve. Third, along with James and John he is a part of an inner circle. Fourth, he stands out individually as the most prominent of the apostles. Thus, Peter occupies a unique place in relation to Jesus.

But Peter's relationship to Jesus is unsteady. On the one hand, he identifies Jesus as God's Messiah (Luke 9:20). On the other, his reliability comes into question when he speaks at the transfiguration without knowing what he said (9:33). Further, he is implicitly among those who do not understand Jesus' prediction of his passion (9:45). And in the passion narrative Peter denies Jesus (22:54-62). That denial, however, also is ambiguous. On one side, it is a satanic trial that Peter fails (22:33). On the other, Jesus' prayer assures that Peter's faith will not fail (22:32) (Schneider 1976:202-203, 1980:281-82), and Jesus commissions Peter to strengthen his brothers and sisters.[4] But then Peter's response that he is ready to go with Jesus to prison or death is unreliable.

The ambiguity continues with the resurrection. The women who visit the tomb inform the eleven and their companions what had happened (Luke 24:9-10). According to 24:11, however, the apostles do not believe the women. Nevertheless, Schneider argues that Peter is not among the skeptics. Accepting the textually disputed twelfth verse, he reasons that Peter did believe the women, and so went to the grave to see (1976: 203). Further, Schneider makes Peter's position dependent upon his alleged status as the first witness of a resurrection appearance (24:34) (1980:280). Luke 24:24 alludes to a visit to the tomb, presumably by some men, and gives some warrant for accepting 24:12 as genuine (Metzger 1971:184, Dillon 1978:59-67). But even if it is an original part of the text, Peter's amazement stops short of belief.[5]

Moreover, apart from information in 1 Corinthians 15 that Peter was the first to receive a resurrection appearance, there is no justification for supposing that Luke 24:34 documents him as the first. Granted, in Luke 24:34 the reader anticipates that the two disciples from Emmaus will inform the eleven that the risen Jesus has appeared to them. But in a reversal, the eleven inform the two from Emmaus that the Lord has risen and has appeared to Simon. But the sequence of the text implies that the two disciples on the road to Emmaus were the first to receive an appearance, and that after the risen Jesus parted from them, he appeared to Simon. Thus, Peter stands in a unique but ambiguous relationship with Jesus—sincerely committed but quite fallible.

The increasingly tighter circles of those around Jesus also indicate Peter's relationships to others, particularly to the twelve. That he is the most prominent is beyond debate, but not his alleged role as their spokesperson (Schneider 1980:280, Cullmann 1962:25). To be sure, the narrator grants Peter priority as the first follower of Jesus to have his story told (Luke 5:1-11). The narrator also names Peter first in two lists of the twelve (6:14-16; Acts 1:13-14). Moreover, his designation of Jesus as God's Messiah (Luke 9:20), his inquiry in 12:41, and his declaration in 18:28 reflect his prominence but not his position among the twelve. In fact, in none of these cases does the text restrict the group of disciples to the twelve. In Acts 5:29 Peter is singled out as voicing what the apostles all express as a chorus. But he is no more a spokesperson for the twelve than John in Luke 9:49 or James and John in 9:54. He is the most prominent among the twelve but not preeminent.

Conflict and opposition contribute particularly distinguishing marks to Peter's character. In Acts 4:8-22 Peter takes on the Sanhedrin, but especially the high priestly party and the Sadducees. The opponents are annoyed by the proclamation of the resurrection and untouched by the healing of a lame man. Against them Peter draws a forceful correlation between a good deed of healing and God's act to raise Jesus. The opponents, deficient in both compassion and theology, highlight these qualities in Peter. The same opponents answer the bell for a second round in 5:17-32. But against the complaints, Peter and the apostles stand out in relief as obedient witnesses to God.

Peter also encounters opposition within the Christian community. Some detractors object to his relationships with Gentiles (Acts 11:3). Initially Peter shares the reluctance of the circumcision party. But in contrast to them he has particular divine guidance that calls on him not to contradict what God is doing. Thus, in ceasing to be a Jewish exclusivist Peter is obeying God (Plunkett 1985:465-79). Incidentally, when he gives appropriate explanations, his detractors also cease to be Jewish exclusivists (11:18; 15:7-29).

Peter's actions are essential features of his character. Preaching, teaching, and healing are prominent reiterated acts. Schneider places strong emphasis on Peter as the initiator of Christian preaching and the founding witness to Christ (1980: 280-82, 1976:204). But this neglects some details.

(1) Behind Peter's sermons in Acts lies the empowerment and commission from Jesus in Luke to the twelve to preach and heal (Luke 9:1-6). Pentecost is not, therefore, the initiation of the preaching ministry of Peter or the twelve.

(2) Neither is Peter the initiator of the Christian mission after Pentecost. Upon receiving the empowerment of the Spirit, the believers, including women (Acts 1:14; 3:1, 17-18), proclaim the mighty works of God (2:11).

Rather than being the first Christian preaching, therefore, Peter's sermon responds to reactions to the first Christian preaching.

Similarly, Peter's participation in a healing ministry in Acts has antecedents in the iterative summary of the preaching and healing of the twelve in Luke 9:6. But in Acts Peter also heals in dramatic episodes (Acts 3:1-10; 9:32-41). Peter diverts attention from himself in a self-deprecating manner in the healing of the lame man in 3:1-10, and he explains the healing as a manifestation of divine power. But the narrator elevates Peter to heroic levels by noting that even Peter's shadow possesses healing powers (5:15).

Peter's functions in the administration of the early Christian community round out his actions. In narrator's summaries (Acts 2:42; 4:35) and in the episode in 6:3-6 he is implicitly part of the leadership. At the first conversion of Gentiles, he is in a position to command that they be baptized (10:48). The most dramatic case of Peter's supervision of the community is his unveiling of the duplicity of Ananias and Sapphira. Here he stands out individually in the administration of the funds to be distributed to the needy. Beyond mere human administration Peter manifests an ability to discern the inner motivation of Ananias and Sapphira, and implicitly he is the agent for cutting off these inauthentic disciples from the people of God (cf. 3:23) (L. T. Johnson 1977:206-210). In a comparable case involving possessions, Peter curses Simon with the threat of death as a part of his function to legitimate Samaritan believers (8:20).

But Peter is also under the authority of the community. Peter and John travel to Samaria as emissaries of the apostles in Jerusalem (Acts 8:14). Further, even though Peter commands that Gentile believers be baptized, he must defend his decision (11:1-18). And the apostles and elders have the authority to review his decision (15:6-29). Therefore, Peter occupies a place in the administration of the community that recalls Jesus' prediction that the twelve would sit on thrones judging the twelve tribes of Israel (Luke 22:29-30). Again, he is prominent but not preeminent.

In short, Peter is full of ambiguity and defies categorization. Some of the ambivalence may be due to the scarcely noticeable detail that Luke-Acts traces Peter's career over a long period of time (Acts 15:7) in which he undergoes considerable change. His sociological status changes as much as his geographical location. He moves from relatively low status as a Galilean fisherman to sit on a throne judging the twelve tribes of Israel. He can call himself a sinner, and yet he can claim that he has always kept kosher. As a faithful Jew who remains obedient to God, he shifts from a Jewish exclusivist to a universalist.

But the ambiguity is also a part of his character. Unfit for association with Jesus, he is his closest confidant. He is both afraid and bold, sincerely committed and fallible, self-deprecating and heroic. He is the most prominent among the twelve but subject to them. As a complex character who exceeds the requirements of the plot, he is a full-fledged character (Berlin 1983:23-24, cf. Harvey 1965:88). Out of the semes the reader constructs a composite. But that composite is unsteady, partly because the reader can always reconfigure the semes, but also partly because it is the nature of Peter's character that he defies categorization.

## PAUL

If character builds up primarily by means of redundancies that correct, redirect, and reinforce one another, a redundancy with high potential for Paul's characterization is the triple narration of his conversion. Intrigued with discrepancies among the versions, some scholars isolate them atomistically and view them as creating patterns of interference.[6] But even if some incongruities give the reader pause, the shifts in point of view and context enrich the texture of Paul's character.

Beverly Roberts Gaventa has advanced discussion of the three accounts toward an integrated literary view (1986:52-95). According to her, Luke adapts each to its context. Thus, first, where the church is moving from a Jewish to a Gentile world, Paul is an enemy from the periphery of Judaism who is overthrown (Acts 9); then, where Paul faces accusations, he is a faithful Jew (Acts 22); and, finally, in the continuing context of a personal defense, Paul is faithful and obedient to his call (Acts 26). Nevertheless, Gaventa stops short of an integrated interpretation because she maintains that Luke uses one story in distinct ways. From a holistic perspective, the three accounts correct, develop, and reinforce each other. Thus, if Paul appears to be on the extremities of Judaism in Acts 9, Acts 22 and 26 undermine and amend the impression.

Paul's threefold announcement of turning to the Gentiles (Acts 13:46; 18:6; 28:28) offers another pregnant case of redundancy. Martin Dibelius takes the three references as a cumulative cluster but sees them as referring to Luke's rejection of the Jews rather than to the course of Paul's ministry (1956:149-50). David Lewycky has recently made a substantial case that acceptance and rejection of messianism by both Jews and Gentiles prior to Paul's announcement preclude Luke's rejection of the Jews (1985).[7] I reiterate my argument, published elsewhere, that the three references explain pragmatically why Paul turns to Gentiles, and, additionally, that the first two announcements establish patterns that undermine the impression of a final rejection of the Jews in 28:28 (Brawley 1987:69-78).

In Acts epithets and direct descriptions of Paul also belong to clusters of redundancy. As a significant case in point, the divine word to Ananias naming Paul a chosen vessel (Acts 9:15) impacts the action of the remainder of Acts. The saying immediately expands into an explicit prolepsis of action forecasting Paul's suffering and ministry.

Moreover, this text links up with Paul's two accounts of his conversion. In Acts 22:15 Ananias interprets the event as a divine appointment of Paul as a witness. In 26:16 the risen Jesus designates him a servant and witness. The latter two cases catch up the action analeptically by recalling Paul's ministry.

In Philippi a girl with a spirit of divination identifies Paul and Silas as servants of God (Acts 16:17). Her cry proleptically interprets the title to mean that Paul and Silas will proclaim the way of salvation. But it is also relational in that it ties Paul and Silas to the servants of the word in the early Jerusalem community (2:18; 4:29).

Apart from summaries that evaluate Paul by associating him with God (e.g., Acts 19:11), the narrator does not evaluate Paul directly but reports evaluations by other characters.[8] When Paul exorcises the evil spirit from the slave girl (16:18), her owners call Paul and Silas "Jews" (pejorative) and accuse them of inciting violations of Roman law. Jews in Thessalonica and Corinth raise similar allegations (17:6-7; 18:13). Against these unreliable characters Paul appears clearly differentiated as law abiding. Their indictments also anticipate accusations in Jerusalem where Paul again appeals to his Roman citizenship to demonstrate that he is law abiding (21:28, 39; 22:25-29). This line of development links up with Paul's explicit claim in 25:8 that he has not offended against Caesar. Thus, Paul's Roman citizenship functions beyond establishing status to evaluate him as law abiding.

In another case, philosophers in Athens refer to Paul as "this babbler" ("this" is pejorative). Others call him a preacher of foreign deities (17:18). These characterizations are juxtaposed to Paul's speech in such a way that dramatic irony is at work (Booth 1974:63). Far from being a babbler, Paul delivers a coherent speech, and rather than proclaiming a *foreign* deity, he proclaims the God who is *close* to the Athenians but unknown (17:22-28).

A similar case occurs in Acts 24:5 where Tertullus labels Paul a pestilent fellow, an agitator, and a ringleader of the sect of the Nazarenes. Tertullus stands out in relief against the context as a spokesperson for unreliable characters.[9] Further, Paul denies his accusations (24:10-21). Nevertheless, the epithets catch up the action by recalling Paul's career.

A complex situation arises when Festus evaluates Paul as "mad" (*mainomai*) and, in the same breath, so to speak, congratulates him on his great learning (Acts 26:24). Is Festus reliable? In 25:9 the narrator impugns Festus's motives for suggesting that Paul should be tried in Jerusalem. On the other hand, Paul insinuates that there is a connection between his education and his zeal *against* the church (22:3-4). Further, Paul clearly establishes before Festus and Agrippa that he was "mad" (*emmainomai*, 26:11) when he persecuted the church, a madness that God transformed into its opposite. That is, Festus inverts Paul's ideological perspective. Thus, the norms of Luke-Acts lead the reader to weigh Festus's evaluation as basically unreliable but somewhat reliable in acknowledging Paul's learning.

Over against the negative evaluation of others, Paul makes two direct claims that he is innocent (Acts 18:6; 20:26). Both claims are evaluative and portray Paul as faithful to his commission. But the first also proleptically anticipates the extension of his mission to Gentiles, and the second analeptically recalls his ministry among Gentiles and Jews.

Epithets also establish Paul's relationships. At his conversion, Ananias names him brother (9:17; cf. 22:13). Synagogue rulers in Pisidian Antioch call Paul and Barnabas brothers (13:15). James refers to Paul as brother in 20:21. Although the term can designate Gentiles (15:1, 23), as a relational epithet it always ties Paul to Jews (cf. 14:2; 15:7, 13). It then functions in reverse. Paul identifies with Jews by calling them brothers (13:26, 38; 22:1; 23:6; 28:17). In addition, Paul repeatedly calls himself a Jew (21:39; 22:3), twice claims to be a Pharisee (23:6;

26:5), and alludes to "our fathers" (24:4; 26:6) or "my nation" (26:4; 28:19).

Another cumulative device that adds depth to Paul's character is shifting the point of view (Booth 1961:16-17, Berlin 1983:7, Harvey 1965:52-55). Paul arrives on the scene from the narrator's perspective. Quickly the narrator opens Paul's interior attitudes by informing the reader that he consents to Stephen's death (Acts 8:1). This anticipates ravaging the church (8:3) and breathing threats and murder against the disciples (9:1). It also anticipates the reversal in Paul's conversion. At his conversion, negative characterization shifts to other characters. Ananias describes Paul as working evil against the saints (9:13). A chorus echoes Ananias's suspicions (9:26). Thus, the variation in point of view adds ambiguity to Paul's character. But the criterion for the reader's judgment is set by yet another point of view—a divine word declares that Paul is God's chosen vessel (9:15).[10]

On two other occasions the narrator opens Paul's interior emotions. The girl with the spirit of divination annoys Paul (16:18); idols in Athens provoke him (17:16). These cases link up with two related actions. Paul harshly opposes Elymas (13:10), and he reviles the high priest Ananias (23:3). These examples give the impression that in spite of his conversion Paul remains fiery and combative.[11]

In a closely related vein, the narrator repeatedly portrays Paul as speaking boldly (e.g., Acts 9:27; 13:46; 26:26; 28:31). The narrator's view corresponds to a divine word urging Paul not to be afraid to speak (18:9). This text echoes in the divine word in 23:11. Thus, divine providence confirms Paul's boldness, and, in turn, Paul's boldness confirms the fulfillment of his divine commission (cf. 26:22).

Shifting the point of view to Paul further verifies his boldness. He tells the Ephesians at Miletus that he did not shrink from testifying (20:20, 27). This ties in with his assertion before Agrippa that he was not disobedient to the divine commission (26:19). Along with that he claims God's promise of deliverance as a part of his commission. In addition, Paul's courage in the storm and shipwreck in Acts 27 is interwoven with divine providence to validate his fidelity to his mission further. Thus, Paul's courageous testimony is both evaluative and analeptic. It warrants and recalls his ministry.

Paul's character takes on additional depth because he acts in a variety of contexts (Harvey 1965:32-33). In Acts Paul is an itinerant, although there are periods of stability (9:30; 11:25, 26; 18:11; 19:8-10). Nevertheless, a reader can hardly avoid the impression that Paul is a vagabond. In fact, in 20:24 Paul summarizes his own career as a *dromos*. But he travels clearly under the guidance of the Spirit.[12]

Part of the context is the relationship between Paul and objects and conditions with metonymic or metaphorical overtones (Harvey 1965:35-38). Three particular objects link Paul to persecution of messianists: the *garments* of those who stone Stephen are laid at his feet (7:58; 22:20); he receives *letters* from the high priest empowering him to arrest Christians (9:1-2; 22:5; cf. 26:10); and he casts a *pebble* (i.e., he votes) against the saints (26:10). The garments associate Paul with Stephen's opponents. The letters identify Paul with the high priest and elders and also make him their functionary. The pebble is a metaphorical reminder of stoning as a form of execution. Thus, these objects align Paul strongly with persecution against the saints.

When Paul changes sides, he shakes out his garments as a sign of both the guilt of recalcitrant Jews and his own innocence (18:6). His garments now differentiate him from unbelieving Jews.

A similar shift occurs in the metonymy of chains. As a metonym for imprisonment, chains represent Paul's radical reversal. As a persecutor he binds and imprisons men and women of the way (Acts 8:3; 9:2; 22:4; 26:10) and ironically forecasts his own destiny. He becomes a part of the way and is bound with chains (21:33) from which he desires to be free (26:29) but which he interprets as a sign of the hope of Israel (28:20). The chains, then, are profound metaphors of Paul's reversal.

In addition, blindness, baptism, and food mark Paul's abrupt transformation. Paul's blindness implies punishment for persecuting the way.[13] But it also constitutes part of the christophany as a sign of divine action. Paul's recovery of sight corresponds to the coming of the Holy Spirit, and so the blindness attests a divine encounter. But beyond that, the blindness also has a metaphorical function. The christophany transforms Paul from one who sees inauthentically into one who sees authentically (cf. Luke 24:31; Acts 28:27).[14]

Baptism integrates Paul into the community and recalls Jesus' prediction that the apostles would be baptized with the Holy Spirit in contrast to John's baptism (Acts 1:5). That, in turn, links up with Pentecost (2:1-4). And so Paul's baptism relates him to Jesus, implies the coming of the Holy Spirit, differentiates him from the followers of John the Baptist (cf. 19:2-7), and serves to legitimate his conversion.

Food likewise has a metaphorical function at Paul's conversion. As a synecdoche for hospitality, it signals his integration into the community (Acts 9:19). Food is a sign of community among believers but also of their relationship with God (2:42, 46). Lines of development extend to Peter's table fellowship with Gentiles (11:3), to Paul's involvement in famine relief for Jerusalem (11:28-30), to the apostolic decree (15:20, 29; cf. 21:25), to the conversion of the Philippian jailer (16:34), and to the restoration of Eutychus (20:11).

Possessions also function metaphorically as a part of Paul's context (see L. T. Johnson 1977:30-36, 217-20). Paul's occupation as a tentmaker (Acts 18:3) links up with 20:33-35 to inform the reader retrospectively that he has supported himself and has used his labor to aid the weak. Thus, the text portrays Paul as free from covetousness and as benevolent toward others.

Another subtle connection between possessions and Paul's legitimation emerges when James suggests that Paul purify himself and pay the expenses for four men under a vow (Acts 21:23-24). Paul agrees as a part of a strategy to disabuse Jewish Christians of their opinion that he teaches Jews of the diaspora to forsake Moses. Thus, Paul's willingness to pay the expenses of the four attests his solidarity with Jewish Christians.

But Paul's habitual relationship with the word characterizes him more definitively that any other metonymic relationship.

When Paul and Barnabas arrive in Salamis, the narrator epito-
mizes their action as proclaiming the word of God (Acts 13:5,
iterative imperfect). Thereafter, narrator's summaries repeat the
portrayal.[15] The action likewise shows Paul taking up the word
in speeches (e.g., 13:6-41; 14:15-17; 17:22-31). In addition,
within his speeches he refers to his activity as a ministry of the
word (13:26, 46; 15:36).

In fact, Paul's ministry of the word is the last impression that
the narrator leaves with the reader. Acts ends with what Gérard
Genette calls a characterizing ellipsis (1980:87-109). In 28:30-31
the relative time for actual narration approaches zero while the
story time has a duration of two years. Paul's characteristic
activity for those two years is preaching and teaching. Thus, the
action, Paul's claims, and the narrator's information dovetail
into characterization of Paul as a proclaimer of the word.

To make a transition to the relationship between the narrator and the character (Harvey 1965:73, Sternberg 1985:130), it
is not always so. The narrator's claims can conflict with Paul's.

The narrator uses the Lycaonians' opinion that Paul and
Barnabas are divine to infer that they are heroes. But then in
direct speech Paul is self-deprecating: "We also are men of like
nature with you" (Acts 14:15). In a similar case the narrator
records the opinion of the Maltese that Paul is a god (28:6). In
contrast, in another direct speech Paul describes himself as
serving the Lord in humility (20:19). A discrepancy also occurs
in what is attributed to the Spirit by the narrator. The narrator
regards Paul's resolve to go to Jerusalem as inspired by the
Spirit (19:21) but also says that through the Spirit disciples in
Tyre tell Paul not to go to Jerusalem (21:4). Further, Paul's
remark before Felix that his accusers share his hope in the
resurrection (24:15) stands at variance with the narrator's
association of Ananias with the Sadducees who deny the resurrection (23:8; cf. 4:2; Luke 20:27). Although the reader cannot
be certain that the narrator recognizes Ananias as a Sadducee,
the incident in Acts 23:1-10 contains strong clues that he does.
Finally, the narrator's version of Paul's conversion (9:3-7)
deviates in several well-known details from Paul's own accounts
(22:6-11; 26:12-18).

But the voices of Paul and the narrator do not clash radically. Rather, the dissonance creates a comprehensive patchwork. For one thing, the famous "we" passages in Acts make the narrator a thick intimate of Paul. For others, the discrepancies in the accounts of Paul's conversion enable the reader to hold together the view that Paul's companions can confirm the incident with the view that the christophany is uniquely Paul's (Conzelmann 1987:71). In a comparable way, Acts 24:15 enables the reader to integrate Paul's identity with Judaism and his conflict with particular Jews. Similarly, the discrepant views on Paul's journey to Jerusalem link up with 20:23 and 21:11, 14 to heighten the danger, to emphasize Paul's courageous resolve, and to communicate a sense of divine guidance. Likewise, by relating the impression of pagan choruses that Paul is divine, the narrator is able to paint him in heroic proportions while Paul himself remains humble.

Part of the shaping of Paul is the way he repeatedly frustrates the reader's expectations (Iser 1974:37). Since Paul makes his entrance as a persecutor, the reader is unprepared to discover that he is God's chosen vessel (9:15). Familiar norms are further stretched when this zealous Jew carries the Lord's name to Gentiles as well as Jews. But then he associates only with Jews in Damascus, Jerusalem, and Antioch. By the time of the incident in Pisidian Antioch Paul's relations with Jews surpass cordial, and his message claims the heritage of Israel. Thus, his sudden announcement of a turn to Gentiles startles the reader (13:46). But then the surprise reverses; he goes to Jews in Iconium. After Paul's advocacy for uncircumcised Gentile believers leads up to the Jerusalem council, he astonishingly accommodates to Jews by circumcising Timothy (16:1-3). Then, going to Jews becomes habitual (17:2), so that another brusque announcement of turning to the Gentiles catches the reader by surprise (18:6).

Yet, interaction with Jews continues. Back in Jerusalem, Paul's attempt to purify himself and to support four men under a vow demonstrates his fidelity to Judaism. His defense speeches repeatedly declare his solidarity with Judaism. Then, unexpectedly, at the end of Acts Paul declares that God's salvation has been sent to the Gentiles. Which side is Paul on? In short, when the reader expects him to stand firm with the Jews, he announces his mission to Gentiles. When the reader anticipates his passing over to Gentiles, he remains ensconced among Jews.

Paul is an unpredictable, zealous Jew from the heart of Judaism who remains faithful to the hope of Israel by becoming a benevolent messianist. As such he aligns with the twelve tribes of Israel judged by the reconstituted twelve apostles. Within this larger picture, God calls him to a specific divine task as a servant and witness to Gentiles as well as Jews. In fulfilling his commission he becomes an itinerant as the Spirit leads him. But when he carries out his ministry of word and deed, he encounters misunderstanding and opposition. Against resistant Jews, he announces the extension of God's salvation to Gentiles. Yet he accommodates for the sake of the Jews and manifests solidarity with Jewish Christians. Against adversaries, he also defends himself as law abiding, obedient to God, faithful to his commission, and true to the heritage of Israel.

Some notable scholars have read Paul as a symbol of Christianity (Dibelius 1956:149, 160, Haenchen 1971:328, 691, Löning 1973).[16] According to them, attacks against Paul and his defenses in response turn out to be, therefore, attacks on and defenses of Christianity. One of the keys to the resolution of whether Paul is a symbol of Christianity or not is the referent of his character. If a character is self-referential, then the character is literal. But if the reference is to something beyond the self, then the character is symbolic (Hochman 1985:119).

Paul's highly repetitious references to himself, especially in the Miletus address and the defense speeches, point to a literal character. In addition, Acts individuates Paul as a persecutor of Christians, a Pharisee educated under Gamaliel, a tentmaker, and a Roman citizen (cf. Jervell 1972:154, 161-63)[17]—characteristics that have no symbolic counterpart in Christianity as a whole. He faces some typical opponents, but others confront him uniquely (e.g., Acts 21:21, 28; 24:5).

Recently Jacob Jervell argued that the Miletus address presents Paul as a symbol of the whole Christian movement in that he provides the legacy for the church (1986:382-83). In the

Miletus speech, however, Paul does not appoint overseers to guarantee the legacy of the church; he assumes them (Acts 20:28). Nor does he commit the church to them; he calls them to remember him, and he entrusts them to God (20:31-32). To be sure, in the Miletus address Paul is concerned with the integrity of the whole counsel of God. A close reading shows, however, that the legacy is nothing other than Paul himself. Paul contends ultimately not for the counsel of God but for himself as the one who boldly declared it (20:20, 27). Rather than making Paul the means by which Christianity passes on its legacy, the Miletus address vindicates him.

But Paul does become paradigmatic as a Jew who converts to messianism and associates Gentiles with the hope of Israel. Gaventa maintains that Paul is not a paradigmatic model for conversion (1986:92).[18] The sole converted persecutor, he is transformed by an unequaled christophany and uniquely commissioned. In Acts conversion typically occurs as a response to proclamation rather than to something like Paul's dramatic christophany.

On the other hand, in his dialogue with Agrippa, Paul establishes himself as a paradigmatic convert in terms of results if not means. Paul tells the king, ". . . I would to God that not only you but also all who hear me this day might become such as I am—except for these chains" (Acts 26:29).

Although the validity of the prophets dominates the immediate context, in the larger context Paul has related his transformation, commission, and obedience. Further, the reader has two options. One is to view the scene at a distance assuming that Paul's audience consists only of those originally present. The other is to identify with the scene as one who (over)hears and, thus, subtly fits into the category of "all." In one case, Paul takes on paradigmatic status for the conversion of his audience. In the other, he becomes a paradigm of conversion also for the reader.

But gaps sap the power of the paradigm. Remorse and guilt are lacking. Although Paul confesses complicity in the death of Stephen and the persecution of messianists (Acts 22:19-20; 26:9-11), he voices no compunctions of conscience. His actions subsequent to his conversion leave no doubt about its reality. But tears of forgiveness (Luke 7:38, 44), blows on the chest (18:13; 23:48), and a heart cut to the quick (Acts 2:37) are conspicuously absent. On the contrary, when the persecution comes back around, it vindicates rather than excoriates Paul. Thus, Paul is a paradigm for switching sides more than for the personal dynamics of conversion.

Paul remains ambiguous enough to frustrate formulaic classification (Harvey 1965:188). Some aspects of his personage dominate others, but transformations, shifting contexts, and divergent viewpoints see to it that the variety persists. For example, the apostles legitimate Paul (Acts 9:27), but the christophany and the vision of Ananias have already legitimated him.[19] In addition, the Holy Spirit legitimates Paul through the congregation at Antioch. And after the Jerusalem council Paul is an independent missionary guided by the Spirit. Thus, Paul is and is not subordinate to the apostles.[20] Or Paul bounces back and forth between extending the proclamation of God's salvation to Gentiles outside the pale and identifying with Jews and Jewish Christians. Paul is not a faithful Jew or a missionary to the Gentiles but something of both.

The indeterminacy of the literary portrait challenges efforts to reduce Paul to an epitome. Abstractions—whether as persecutor, teacher, prophet, preacher, convert, missionary, faithful Jew, pioneer to Gentiles, thaumaturge, servant, witness, or accused—either singly or collectively—draw his character to a limited extent only. The Lucan Paul is the synthesis of information, action, traits, and evaluation. Therefore, he eludes analysis, including, of course, this one. The Lucan Paul inhabits a literary world. When he steps out, he is no longer the Lucan Paul but our approximation, more or less accurate. Complexity makes the portrait of Paul in Acts nothing less than a mosaic. But to orient our perspective, the Lucan Paul is but a part of an even larger picture in Luke-Acts and in the biblical story.

# 7

# SHARED
# PRESUMPTIONS
# AND THE
# UNFORMULATED
# TEXT

Discourse presupposes that human beings share techniques of communication that we call language. Beyond that, a presumed stock of knowledge underlies communication. An allusion to Shakespeare's *Romeo and Juliet* need not further identify the author or summarize the play. Rather, it assumes a stock of knowledge that is embedded in our culture, and this vulgate constitutes a bank upon which a literary work may draw.

Roland Barthes, in a mildly cryptic way, terms the textual voice that rests on presumed knowledge "the cultural code" but also suggests that this voice is tacitly proverbial (1974:18, 100). Wolfgang Iser labels a similar but less cryptic concept the "repertoire" of the text (1978:69). The repertoire means literary allusions and social and historical norms. Jonathan Culler protests explicitly against Barthes and implicitly against Iser that the cultural code is unsatisfactory. He argues that not merely the cultural allusions but everything that draws on a shared view of reality, that is, verisimilitude, comprises the referential voice (Culler 1975:203).

Iser covers much of Culler's ground with his understanding of the unformulated text. Rather than giving full expression to its ideas, a text depends on what is presumed but left unsaid.

Gaps leave recovery of the unformulated text up to the reader. In addition, negation or revision of norms often leave the recall of the norms up to the reader (Iser 1978:225-29). To give a case in point, the healing of the centurion's slave in Luke 7:1-10 presupposes slavery and the structure of command in the Roman military. It leaves the centurion's Gentile identity unformulated. And Jesus' comparison of the centurion's faith to Israel's negates the unexpressed norm that Israel is the people of faith.

To illustrate further, the parable of the unjust judge in Luke 18:1-8 presupposes a judicial system without specifying whether it is Jewish or Roman. The parable of the Pharisee and the toll collector (18:9-14) assumes that the temple is a place of prayer and leaves the status of Pharisees and toll collectors unformulated. Acts 2:1 introduces the day of Pentecost and presumes the implied reader's acquaintance with the feast. In fact, the text is but the proverbial iceberg compared with what remains unexpressed.

Therefore, Culler is quite correct in his critique of Barthes's cultural code. Nevertheless, seldom does the unformulated text demand attention unless it is obscure, subtle, or decisive. A train schedule that lists an arrival at 8:00 a.m. requires no explanation of the convention of telling time. The convention is so routine as to remain submerged beneath the threshold of awareness. On the other hand, biblical literature frequently demands attention to ordinary minutiae because the presumed stock of knowledge is remote from ours.

When Luke 23:44 describes darkness at the crucifixion from the sixth to the ninth hour, the convention of telling time does not correspond to what underlies our train schedules. Joseph Fitzmyer translates: "It was already about noon, and darkness began to hang over the whole land until three in the afternoon" (1985:1512). His translation recognizes a convention for numbering the hours from dawn and restates it in terms of our convention. Therefore, to take this text on its own terms is to comprehend the unformulated text.

The notion that texts take on an autonomy independent from the historical and cultural circumstances out of which they arose has gained some ascendancy in recent years. Interest has shifted from historical dimensions to literary dimensions of texts (Gros Louis 1982:14-15). But the distance between the assumptions of antiquity and our own imposes historical constraints on the interpretation of literature from antiquity. Of course, it is possible for a reader to pick up a modern translation of the Bible and read it as an autonomous text set free from the circumstances of its origin. But such a reader is not an informed reader. In contrast, every interpreter who reads Luke-Acts in its original language is engaged in a historical task. How is it possible to determine that *doxa* in Luke 9:32 means "radiance" rather than "expectation" as it does in Homer except in relation to the changes in historical and cultural circumstances over some seven or eight centuries? If the autonomy of the text killed the historical dimension, the unformulated text brought it back.

Methodologically, therefore, we do not always begin or end with the text. For example, Luke-Acts makes abundant allusions to scriptures. The text may designate references with a formula such as: "It is written." Beyond that there are varying degrees of subtle allusions—allusions that we may not recognize unless we also read the scriptures, particularly the Septuagint.

Frequently there are clues in the text that help to clarify an obscurity elsewhere. To take a case in point, in Luke the limelight falls repeatedly on Jesus' identity as a prophet. Is he one among the prophets as public opinion implies (9:19)? In Acts 3:22 Peter relates Jesus to Deut 18:15, 18 so that the reader knows that Jesus is not merely a prophet but the prophet like Moses. In contrast, quite often obscurities remain veiled within the world of the text. In such a case an interpreter may scan the larger literary and historical environment of antiquity. Explicit parallels and widely distributed knowledge and conventions help to decipher the unformulated text.

To return to the convention of telling time, Pliny (*Natural History* II.79.188) shows that there were multiple modes of counting hours in antiquity. According to him, Babylonians count the period between two sunrises, Athenians between two sunsets, Umbrians from midday to midday, the common people everywhere from dawn to dark, and Roman priests and authorities from midnight to midnight. What convention is operative in Luke-Acts? Within the textual world, the ninth hour as the hour of prayer in Acts 3:1 corresponds to the Jewish time of prayer coinciding with the evening Tamid sacrifice (Haenchen 1971: 198). Therefore, Luke-Acts presupposes counting twelve daylight hours beginning at dawn.

In some sense unformulated referents lie behind every word. Fortunately, the conventions shared by Luke-Acts and modern readers are sufficient to render explication of every presumption unnecessary. Still, in addition to the following discussion, a thorough analysis of the unformulated text would include popular medicine, magic, soothsaying, the Roman military, the Olympian gods and their priesthood, Epicurean and Stoic philosophy, judicial and political systems, every biblical citation and allusion, Jewish eschatological expectations, commandments, purity laws, feasts, marriage customs, the nature and meaning of table fellowship, the functions and significance of the temple, and the social status of women, shepherds, priests, Sadducees, Pharisees, and toll collectors. Even then the discussion would be incomplete. In fact, the unformulated text is so extensive as to mandate that the following discussion be illustrative rather than exhaustive.

## THE UNFORMULATED TEXT AND GENRE

The earlier discussion of progressive discovery of what is true in the narrative world anticipated a further discussion of genre as a part of the unformulated text (p. 38). The raising and the resolution of the question of genre is a part of progressive discovery. But the unformulated text has a great deal to do with how the question is resolved.

Readers bring to a text not only knowledge of literary content but also of literary conventions. Literary works mix the old and the new. The new distinguishes individuality among texts. It is creativity. But readers can distinguish what is creative only if they also know conventional paradigms. In this sense a new literary work is possible only when readers can draw on familiar literary genres. Creativity is a departure from conventional expectations. But the conventional expectations must be present in order for the reader to detect the innovation (Iser 1974:xii-xiii, 34, 183, 288, 1978:18, Kermode 1967:19-24, Damrosch 1987:2).

The prologue to Luke expresses this friction between the old and the new. It classifies the work as a *diêgêsis* among many (Luke 1:1). That is, it portrays the work as an example of a common stock. A *diêgêsis* is a genre sufficiently fixed for Hermogenes to define it as a longer narrative incorporating multiple incidents in contrast to a *diêgêma*, which deals with one incident (*Progymnasmata* 2).[1] But then the preface indicates that there is something innovative about this work that will bring certainty to Theophilus (1:4). The prologue claims, therefore, to possess a character that distinguishes it from the many.

Even with the definition of Hermogenes, however, modern readers likely will have difficulty determining the genre. What conventional expectations establish the old over against which the new emerges? Moses Hadas and Morton Smith have studied aretalogies in antiquity as a species of biography that set forth the miraculous deeds of an impressive person for moral instruction. Smith then argues that the Gospels are nearest to aretalogies than to any other ancient non-Christian works (Hadas and Smith 1965, Smith 1971:174-99). One weakness of this position is that no complete text of any aretalogy has survived, and so Hadas and Smith postulate an artificial genre. Another is that it treats miracle stories atomistically as the basic element of the Gospels and thus ignores the larger narrative framework into which they fit. A third is that it also overlooks paradigms in the Hebrew scriptures.

Charles Talbert suggests that strong parallels link Luke-Acts to Greco-Roman biographies that are coupled with narratives about successors (1974:125-35, 1977:95, 107-108, 134, 1988: 53-73). There are two primary drawbacks: Successor biographies are rare and narrowly distributed, and Talbert's concentration on Greco-Roman biography also neglects backgrounds in the Hebrew scriptures. David Barr and Judith Wentling avoid these pitfalls in their proposal that Luke-Acts mixes biographical (focus on persons) with historical (focus on deeds) interests and has a strong affinity with prophetic biographies in the Hebrew Bible (1984:63-88).

In spite of acknowledging some resemblance between Luke and ancient biographies (focus on a person), David Aune argues that in Luke-Acts the spotlight on events rather than persons aligns it more closely with ancient history (1987:46-157). But the discussion of characterization above shows that Aune inadequately assesses the place of characters in Luke-Acts. He also gives biblical backgrounds short shrift.

Richard Pervo thinks that Acts is of a different genre from Luke and that Acts is an edifying, entertaining historical novel (1987). But the development of narrative schemata across both volumes weighs against their separation into separate genres (see above p. 87). In other words, Pervo makes Acts fit into a given genre rather than discovering the genre that fits Luke-Acts. Further, he neglects backgrounds in the Hebrew scriptures and in fact classifies Acts not so much against its antecedents as among its successors, the apocryphal acts.

David Moessner argues for the primacy of divine event over the person of Jesus and concludes that Luke-Acts is closest in genre to ancient historiography with close parallels to biographically oriented biblical histories (1988b:75-84). But if God is a character in Luke-Acts, then the separation of person and event is an analytical abstraction. Still Moessner points in an important way to the theocentric character of Luke-Acts and, like Barr and Wentling, gives appropriate weight to backgrounds in the Hebrew scriptures.

In fact, Luke-Acts makes explicit and implicit claims to be an extension of the biblical story. Frank Kermode has noted that the way the Gospels use texts from scripture is tacitly to regard themselves as part of the same story (Kermode 1979:98-99). Overtly, Mary's virginal conception is fulfillment of God's covenant with Abraham (Luke 1:54-55). The birth of John the Baptist likewise is a fulfillment of divine promises to forebears (1:72-73). Jesus claims to be a fulfillment of Isaiah (4:21). The suffering Messiah is fulfillment of scripture (24:27, 46).

In Acts 2 Peter declares that the initiation of the Christian mission is fulfillment of scripture, and in Acts 3 he traces the

God who acts in the resurrection of Jesus back to Abraham, Isaac, and Jacob. Further, Peter's audience stands in continuity with the covenant with Abraham (3:25). Stephen's speech in Acts 7 recounts cycles of God's mercy and the people's obduracy from Abraham through Jesus. Paul's sermon in Pisidian Antioch makes God's act in Jesus a part of the same story as the exodus, the conquest, and the monarchy (Acts 13:16-25). Further, Paul claims that his mission is a fulfillment of Moses and the prophets (26:22-23). Thus, biblical backgrounds form an important part of the conventional expectations of the implied reader.

Nevertheless, to ferret out biblical backgrounds alone is also an analytical abstraction. Aretalogies, biographies, successor narratives, novels, Greco-Roman histories, biblical prophetic biographies, and biblical histories together establish the conventional expectations. What is significant about Luke-Acts is not only the way it is similar to all of these but also the way it is different from them. And I drop the suggestion that just as Luke and Acts combine multiple genres (e.g., hymns, miracle stories, speeches), so also part of the innovation of Luke-Acts is that the two volumes fit together in yet another composite genre.

## SOCIOLOGICAL EXEGESIS

One of the major tasks of traditional form criticism is to establish the setting in life. The method analyzes the social conditions for preserving and transmitting tradition. But John Elliott protests that the search has been unimaginatively restricted to didactic, missionary, cultic, or apologetic situations, and he advocates additional sociological methods that also detect implicit evidence (1981:3). That implicit evidence is nothing other than part of the unformulated text. The text may employ strategies to redefine social norms, to integrate implied readers into a new community, to define or redefine the boundaries of the community, or to maintain the community (Esler 1987:16-18).

Sociological exegesis takes over methods developed by the social sciences, especially sociology of religion. For example, in his study of early Christianity John Gager utilizes modern theories about millenarian cults and about missionary efforts in response to disconfirmation of religious beliefs (1975).

On a simpler level, many of the social implications of the text are available for any reader who asks: What is the relationship of the person(s) in need to the larger society? Who or what is keeping that person (those persons) from being integrated into society? How are social boundaries transcended or transformed? And, in order to understand the text from the perspective of the implied reader, when early Christians retold the story, what might it have expressed about their social situation?

Gerd Theissen has helped to elucidate the unformulated text of miracle stories. He points out that characters in miracles can occupy three fields: the demonic, the human, and the divine (1983:43-45). Miracles involve crossing the boundary between the human and the demonic and between the human and the divine (1983:74-80). In miracle stories human beings transcend the barriers of legitimacy in their worlds. They protest against social barriers, and the protests depend on divine omnipotence to become effective. And so crossing the boundaries is faith (1983:134-37). Further, miracle stories give early Christians strength to encounter and combat distress (1983:251).

To take some examples, purity laws isolate the woman with the flow of blood from normal society (Luke 8:42-48). She breaks through the boundary when she violates purity laws and touches Jesus, and Jesus calls her violation of the barrier faith. In Acts 16:16-24, a girl is triply oppressed, estranged from society because she is female, a slave, and demonic. Her owners exploit her economically. In the human field the owners prevent her integration into society, in the demonic field the spirit of divination prevents her integration. Paul appeals to divine power by a command in the name of Jesus, and in this manner he reestablishes the boundary between the human and the demonic, and he breaks through the social barriers of domination of the lower class by the upper class, of the have-nots by the haves, and of a female by men.

Social aspects of the unformulated text go well beyond miracle stories. In Acts there is a repetitive pattern of criteria for entering the community—repentance, baptism, and the gift of the Holy Spirit (Meeks 1983:88). Repentance in Acts is not merely an introspective awareness of sin but an external rejection of social relationships that oppose the messianic community. Repentance undermines the dominant social order. For example, in Acts 2:23 Peter accuses the people of Jerusalem of killing Jesus. Against that background, repentance means repudiating the opponents of Jesus: "Save yourselves from this crooked generation" (2:41). Repentance also means joining the authentic people of God.

When Paul encounters the risen Lord, he receives baptism and the Holy Spirit and undergoes a radical social change (Acts 9:17-18). He abandons relationships with the chief priests and persecutors, a shift so extreme that Paul has difficulty entering the Christian community (9:26).

The criteria for establishing the boundaries of the Christian community receive dramatic emphasis in the story of Cornelius. Cornelius and his household meet the criteria of repentance, baptism, and the gift of the Holy Spirit. Peter's opponents demand circumcision as an additional criterion. They contend essentially that Cornelius must repudiate Gentile relationships and become a Jew in order to be distinguished secondarily from other Jews by baptism and the gift of the Spirit. But Peter's argument in Acts 11 and the Jerusalem council in Acts 15 redefine the social boundaries to include Gentiles on the basis of repentance, baptism, and the gift of the Spirit apart from circumcision. The story of Cornelius embodies a strategy for legitimating and maintaining Christianity as a mixed community of Jews and Gentiles.

## ANGELS AND DEMONS

Most modern readers discover themselves strangers in the literary world of Luke-Acts. The narrative introduces readers into private matters of a childless but pious priestly couple. The unformulated text assumes conventions of the service of priests in the temple and of piety according to God's commandments. Elizabeth's remark that God has taken away her reproach (Luke 1:25) and the joyful celebration at the birth of John provide clues for the cultural value of children in marriage. Moreover, their childlessness is a complicated predicament—presumably Zechariah is impotent, and Elizabeth is past the menopause.

No sooner do readers enter this foreign literary world than they stumble upon an angel. In Luke 1-2 Raymond Brown discovers seven particular allusions to Daniel and catches echoes of the aged childless Abraham and Sarah and reminiscences of the births of Samson and Samuel (1977:270-80). A major part of the reverberations is the appearance of angels to Abraham and Sarah (Gen 18:2, 10; 19:1) and to Manoah and his wife (Judg 13:2-24) and the identification of Gabriel in Dan 8:16; 9:21. Luke-Acts draws on that repertoire.

In the earliest strata of pentateuchal traditions, angels are particular manifestations of God (von Rad 1964:77-78). There is, therefore, an ambiguity in the identification of the angels who come to Abraham and Sarah. The text refers to them both as Yahweh (Gen 18:1, 10) and as men (18:2, 16). In general, however, the angel of God in the Hebrew Bible is the personification of God's assistance to Israel (von Rad 1964:77). In post-exilic Judaism angels take on their own individuality, and they can be distinguished by proper names. Moreover, their function shifts from manifesting the divine to mediating between God and humanity. Specifically, they become messengers and agents of divine aid and judgment (Dan 8:17; 3:28; 6:22).

But the angelology and demonology of Luke-Acts breaks out of the norms of biblical paradigms and draws on a repertoire that permeates the ancient Mediterranean world. *Testaments of the Twelve Patriarchs* develops a very explicit hierarchy of angels. *Testament of Levi* 3:1-10 describes four ranks of angels corresponding to four levels of heaven. In the lowest heaven there are spirits who are instruments of God's judgment upon human beings. In the next there are spirits for vengeance upon the spirits of error and Beliar. Above them are the angels. And in the uppermost heaven archangels are in the presence of God. In addition, a repeated theme in *Testaments of the Twelve Patriarchs* is that Beliar and the spirits of error are the source of evil in human beings (e.g., *T. Judah* 19:4; *T. Sim.* 2:7).

*Ethiopic Enoch* has a full blown angelology. First, angels are agents of the revelation to Enoch (1:2; 40:2; 53:4). Then, as a part of that revelation, readers have access to information about the fall of evil angels and the hierarchy of good angels. *1 Enoch* 6:1-8 tells about angels who fell by having sexual intercourse with human women and names the chiefs of ten among them. *1 Enoch* 69:1-15 names centurions and chiefs of fifty over the evil angels as well. Thus they have rank and organization comparable to military order. Good angels stand over against evil ones as angels of punishment for judgment (66:1). Among these there is also rank and order. *1 Enoch* 20:1-7 names the archangels, and 9:1 singles out Michael, Surafel, and Gabriel as agents of judgment against the evil angels. Moreover, *1 Enoch* 40:9 says that Gabriel is set over all exercise of strength.

Philo is far less precise. He maintains that there are both good and evil angels and that souls, demons, and angels are different names for the same thing (*On the Giants* 16-18). Still he differentiates the highest and purest as angels who are priests in heaven (*On Noah's Work as a Planter* 14, *Special Laws* 1.66). He explains that good angels are ambassadors who mediate between God and human beings (*On the Giants* 16-18, *On Noah's Work as a Planter* 14).

Certain rabbinic literature suggests that angels are differentiated by their behavior rather than by their nature. According to *b. Šabb.* 89a, when Moses ascends to receive Torah, the angels ministering before God confess that the evil tempter is among them. Moreover, according to *b. B. Bat.* 16a, the idea was current during the tannaitic period that Satan, the evil impulse, and the angel of death were all one. Another Talmudic idea is that an evil spirit or Satan seduces human beings into evil (*b. B. Bat.* 16a, *b. 'Erub.* 41b). In one tradition, Satan comes to David like a bird, shatters the screen behind which Bathsheba bathes, and thus seduces David (*b. Sanh.* 107a).

For Josephus (*Ant.* 15.136), angels are agents of the revelation of the noblest doctrines and holiest laws from God (some scholars take this as a reference to prophets). On the other hand, Josephus attributes the suffering of Saul to demons that David charms away with the harp (*Ant.* 6.166-68; 8.45-48). Further, Josephus says that demons are the spirits of deceased wicked people that enter the living with the potential to kill them (*J. W.* 7.185).

Philostratus is in touch with a similar notion. He details an exorcism of a sixteen year old boy by Apollonius. The demon has the character of mockery and lying, does not allow the boy to control his own reasoning, and drives him into desert places. But the demon has informed the boy's mother that he is the ghost of a deceased man who is seeking vengeance for his wife's marriage to another man (*Apollonius* III.38).

In the wider hellenistic world, Hermes is the paradigmatic angel, the messenger of Zeus (Grundmann 1964:75). In the *Odyssey* (5.29) Zeus addresses Hermes as "our messenger," and Hermes conveys a divine decree to Calypso that she must release Odysseus. Plato gives an account where the name of Hermes is supposedly derived from his function as messenger (*Cratylus* 407-408). Luke-Acts assumes something like this in its repertoire when the Lycaonians call Barnabas Zeus and Paul Hermes because Paul is the chief speaker (Acts 14:12). Here Luke-Acts is overturning the conventional belief in Zeus and Hermes but assumes the norm in order to overturn it.

Plato also relates the name of Iris to the verb "to tell" because of her function as a messenger (*Cratylus* 407-408). Further, in writing on the veneration of gods, demons, spirits, heroes, ancestral deities, and living parents, Plato calls Nemesis the messenger of justice (*dikēs angelos*) who watches over these things (*Laws* IV.717d).

The assumption that demons cause suffering in the living is widespread. 1 Samuel 16:14 attributes the torments of Saul to an evil spirit. *Testaments of the Twelve Patriarchs* attributes jealousy, sexual immorality, anger, and murder to Beliar and the spirits of error. Rabbinic literature gives evidence of immorality due to the prompting of the evil impulse or an evil spirit (*b. 'Erub.* 41b; *b. B. Bat.* 16a). Josephus declares that unless demons are exorcised, they will kill the people they inhabit. This is the kind of conventional belief that Lucian seeks to undermine in *The Liar.* In one of his tales Eucrates claims to have seen a thousand apparitions of demons. With such absurdity,

Lucian is redefining the norm of belief in demons. But in order to do so, he also assumes the norm.

The story of the temptation of Jesus in Luke 4 brings together conventional beliefs in the devil as an agent of seductive power and in angels as agents of aid. The devil tempts Jesus to jump off the pinnacle of the temple by appealing to a norm presupposed by Ps 91:11-12 that angels are agents of divine aid. The devil, therefore, proposes a redefinition of the norm by using it to undermine dependence upon the power of God. He attempts to bring the conventional belief in angels into the service of diabolic temptation. Jesus salvages the belief in angels by his own partial redefinition—angels are not agents of divine aid when human beings try to use them as a test of God. Thus, the pericope intensifies the norm that the devil is an agent of seductive power and qualifies the norm that angels are agents of divine aid.

But this qualification of the normative belief in angels comes only after Gabriel has already functioned in a conventional way. Gabriel has been an agent of interrelated revelations (Luke 1:13-20; 1:26-37). He proclaims that John will prepare a people for the Lord (1:17). The message to Mary informs her that Elizabeth has conceived a son (1:36). Then Elizabeth calls Mary the mother of her Lord (1:43). "Lord" here is parallel to the "fruit" of Mary's womb (1:42), and that is a strong clue that Jesus is the "Lord" for whom, according to Gabriel's prediction, John will prepare a people. Then, before the temptations, the fulfillment of Gabriel's predictions in the births of John and Jesus and in John's ministry of preparation has already confirmed the norm that Gabriel is an agent of divine revelation.

This revelatory function of an angel at the beginning of Luke pairs up with similar revelatory functions of angels at the end. The text identifies the two men in dazzling apparel as angels (Luke 24:4, 23). But rather than predict the future, as does Gabriel, their revelation recalls the past. They remind the women of the words of Jesus about his passion, death, and resurrection (24:6-8).

In Acts angels fulfill roles as agents of both revelation and divine aid. Given the identification of the two men in dazzling apparel in Luke 24 and of a man in bright apparel in Acts 10:3, 30 as angels, the reader can identify the two men in white robes in Acts 1:10 also as angels. They predict the parousia. As an agent of divine aid, an angel delivers the apostles from prison (Acts 5:19). Angels give revelation to Cornelius (10:3-6), deliver Peter from prison (12:7-11), and reveal to Paul that he and his companions will survive a shipwreck (27:23-26). In addition, an angel is also an agent of divine judgment in the death of Herod Agrippa (12:23).

Hans Conzelmann contends that the departure of the devil from Jesus in Luke 4:13 implies the devil's absence until the passion (22:3) (1961:16). But the unformulated text shows this to be inaccurate. In Luke 11:15 opponents charge that Jesus casts out demons by Beelzebul, the prince of demons. Jesus equates Satan with Beelzebul and then claims that his exorcisms are manifestations of the kingdom of God against the satanic kingdom (11:15-22). Further, Acts 10:38 summarizes Jesus' healings as releasing people from the bondage of the devil. Thus, every encounter of Jesus with demons is an encounter with the kingdom of Satan.

Luke 4:1-13 also illustrates the sharp antithesis between the divine and the satanic, an antithesis that Werner Foerster claims is absolute in the New Testament (1964:8, 16, 79). As the discussion of Philo above shows, it was possible in antiquity to draw no sharp distinction between the divine and the demonic, and so the radical antithesis redefines the norms. As strong as the antithesis is, however, in Luke-Acts it is not quite absolute. Specifically, the demons have supernatural knowledge of Jesus' identity so that, like angels, they also function as agents of divine revelation (Luke 4:35, 41; 8:28).

In addition, the notion that God and Satan stand in absolute antithesis overlooks the subtlety of satanic temptation. Some of this subtlety is evident in the way Satan uses the conventional belief about angels in the temptation of Jesus (Luke 4:10-11). It is also apparent in the presence of Judas at the last supper. In 22:3 the narrator gives notice that Satan entered Judas and connects this with Judas's complicity in the death of Jesus. And so when Jesus announces that the betrayer is at the table with him (22:21), he alludes back to 22:3, and the reader can hardly miss the irony that in the betrayer Satan is present at the last supper.

Moreover, in Luke 10:18 Jesus tells his disciples, "I saw Satan fall like lightning from heaven." Although some commentators take this as an allusion to Isa 14:12, the passage in Isaiah is a taunt against the king of Babylon (14:4) and makes no reference to Satan. More likely Luke 10:18 presumes a conventional belief that associates phenomena of light with the fall of demons and that projects the downfall of Satan into the eschatological future (Vollenweiden 1988:187-203).[2] In *Testament of Solomon* 20:16-17 the demon Ornias tells Solomon that demons have the capability to fly into heaven. But because they have no place to rest, they become exhausted and fall, and humans watching them think that stars are falling. They fall to earth like flashes of lightning and start fires. Thus, quite likely conventional beliefs in antiquity associated lightning with the fall of demons. Further, *T. Levi* 18:12 anticipates the eschatological time of divine vengeance when the Lord will raise up a new priest who will bind Beliar. Behind this likely lies a conventional belief that the collapse of Satan is an eschatological event. Revelation 20:1-10 alludes to the same type of tradition of the downfall of Satan at the end time. In Luke 10:18, therefore, Jesus redefines the demise of Satan as past rather than future. Thus, the antithesis between God and Satan has its basis in an event of the past and is not absolute historically because at one time Satan was associated with heaven.

To sum up, the angelology and demonology of Luke-Acts draw on biblical but also on wider hellenistic backgrounds. The distinction between angels and demons is largely distinguished by behavior rather than essence. As angels are agents of divine revelation and aid so demons are agents of satanic deception and suffering. But in contrast to Philo's description of a continuum between good and evil angels, Luke-Acts is moving toward an antithesis between them. The antithesis is not a denial of the potency of evil but rather a recognition of it. Evil is so strong that God annihilates it. Therefore, Jesus declares God's sovereignty over the power of evil, and it then is obsolete.

## THE VIOLENT FATE OF THE PROPHETS

Zechariah, filled with the Holy Spirit identifies his son as a prophet who in turn will identify Jesus (Luke 1:76). The prophetic function of John is to prepare the way before Jesus. What Zechariah foreshadows, John carries out by preaching repentance (3:3-14). But what Zechariah does not foreshadow is the opposition that John encounters.

Suddenly, unexpectedly, notice of John's imprisonment breaks into his ministry of preparing a way for Jesus. The seam is so rough as to create the incongruity of John's arrest before Jesus' baptism. That drastic break is part of Conzelmann's evidence for a theology of history that separates the time of Jesus from the time of John (1961:21-27).

On the other hand, there is strong evidence of continuity between Jesus and John. Paul Minear itemizes eight bridges that span the birth narratives and the rest of Luke-Acts (1966: 112-28). Along similar lines, the retrospective recovery of the story shows how narrative needs originating in Luke 1-2 have corresponding competence, performance, and sanction stages in the rest of Luke-Acts (see above, pp. 44-51). In addition, Robert Tannehill extends the continuity by showing that although Jesus surpasses John, his mission continues John's mission and by noting that both Jesus and John suffer as rejected prophets (1986:47-53).

To expand the logic a bit further, the suffering of Jesus and John as rejected prophets is fairly involved with the unformulated text. By the time of the composition of Luke-Acts, a bank of tradition had developed about the violent fate of prophets (Fischel 1946-47:245-80, 363-86). Odil Hannes Steck traces a Jewish tradition that develops out of the Deuteronomistic understanding of the destiny of prophets in which the persistent refusal of people to hear matches God's persistent sending of the prophets (1967:58-99). Jesus alludes to such a tradition in Luke 11:49-51 and 13:34. It is the destiny of a prophet to suffer persecution and martyrdom.

2 Kings 17:13-14 attributes the Assyrian captivity to divine punishment for the stubborn refusal of the people to heed the

prophets. In 2 Chr 24:21 Joash commands that Zechariah be stoned to death because he proclaimed that the Lord had forsaken the people in response to the people forsaking God. Jeremiah complains to his people: "Your own sword devoured your prophets like a ravening lion" (Jer 2:30). Jehoiakim kills Uriah for prophesying against Judah and Jerusalem (26:20-23), and persecution is Jeremiah's own destiny.

Josephus refers to similar traditions. He relates that when Hezekiah purified the temple and invited the Israelites to return to reverence for God, their prophets exhorted them in like manner. But the people spat on them and finally killed them (*Ant.* 9.265-66). Significantly, 2 Chronicles 29-30 parallels Josephus, but the destiny of the prophets in Josephus has no scriptural parallel. Therefore, Josephus is likely drawing on tradition. He also explains the Assyrian conquest of Samaria partially as a result of disregarding the prophets (*Ant.* 9.281).

Comparable views show up in rabbinic literature. In *b. Meg.* 14a there is a tradition that prophets and prophetesses were not able to turn Israel to better courses. The tradition goes on to note that there were actually many more prophets, but only those with lessons for the future were written down. Thus, Israel failed to heed numerous prophets.

The tradition is in full bloom in intertestamental literature. In *Jub.* 1:12 the Lord says to Moses: "I will send them witnesses . . . , but they will not hear. And they will even kill the witnesses." In addition, the *Lives of the Prophets* and the *Martyrdom and Ascension of Isaiah* detail the deaths of some of the prophets at the hands of rulers, family, and the people, although others die in peace.

In the wider Hellenistic domain, Xenophon presents Socrates, at least partially, as an unheeded prophet. He made true prophecies because outcomes verified his predictions (*Recollections of Socrates* I.4-5, *Socrates' Defense Before the Jury* 30-31). Nevertheless, the jury in Athens gave him the death penalty (*Recollections of Socrates* IV.8.2-4). Plato paints a similar portrait. He defends Socrates as obedient to the gods rather than to human beings (*Apology* 29 C-D), and at his death Socrates says: "I would fain prophesy to you; for I am about to die, and that is the time when men are gifted with prophetic power. And I prophesy to you who are my murderers, that immediately after my death punishment far heavier than you have inflicted upon me will surely await you" (*Apology* 39 C-D).

Luke-Acts, then, draws on an unformulated text about the violent fate of prophets. The prophet is so closely associated with suffering that it becomes a constituent of prophetic identity. And thus when the people of Nazareth reject Jesus, they confirm his prophetic identity (see Brawley 1987:17-18). In addition, Jesus dies as a rejected prophet (Luke 13:33-34; 24:19-20). The opposition of the Sanhedrin to the proclamation of the apostles shows that they follow the paradigm of Jesus (Acts 4:1-21; 5:17-41). This helps to explain how the apostles rejoice that they were counted worthy to suffer (5:41), because the suffering verifies the validity of their prophetic proclamation. Against his accusers Stephen appeals to an unformulated text of such a tradition when he asks: "Which of the prophets did not your fathers persecute?" (7:52). Further, Paul's task as a witness entails suffering, and the suffering vindicates his prophetic mission (e.g., see 9:16 and 14:19-20).

The unformulated text about the violent fate of the prophets is a satisfactory explanation for Herod's abrupt interruption of John the Baptist's ministry of preparation. When Zechariah designates John a prophet, it is unnecessary to foreshadow John's suffering because the suffering of the prophets is a part of the unformulated text. John's suffering is one of the criteria for confirming his prophetic identity. Then, in a derivative fashion, John's legitimacy as a prophet confirms Jesus' legitimacy because John prepares for and points to Jesus.

## PUNISHMENT MIRACLES

In sweeping terms, if prophets suffer for standing on the side of God, deceivers suffer because they do not stand on the side of God. In the early Christian community in Jerusalem, Ananias and Sapphira feign their commitment to communal property, but reserve some of their wealth for themselves. Implicitly divine justice strikes both of them dead (Acts 5:1-11). The punishment of Ananias and Sapphira likely offends the sensitivities of most modern readers. It is unlikely, however, that the incident would offend ancient readers because of its relationship to the unformulated text.

Diodorus of Sicily gives a report about the Vaccaei with some noteworthy parallels to the Christian community in Jerusalem. The Vaccaei neighbor the Celtiberians, inhabitants of a mountainous district of ancient Spain. Diodorus recounts that they divide their land among themselves for tilling and then distribute the harvest proportionately. Significantly, they also execute any who appropriate any part for themselves (V.34.3).

The Vaccaei spur Diodorus's interest because their community contrasts with conventional social norms in a broader context. Nevertheless, they reflect a far-reaching standard in antiquity that communal norms take precedence over individual life. The accusations against Socrates boil down essentially to the disruption of communal norms (Plato *Apology* 24 B-C). Therefore, a major part of his defense is that he is a benefactor of the city (Plato *Apology* 36 A-D, Xenophon *Recollections of Socrates* IV). Still the jury rules that the communal norms take precedence over his life.

The same is true in the story of Achan in Josh 7:1-26. Against Joshua's command that the spoils of Jericho be destroyed as dedicated to God, Achan keeps some of the devoted things for himself. As a result, instead of repeating their miraculous victory at Jericho, Joshua's forces are routed at Ai. Joshua is able to discern the offense and the offender, and the people stone Achan and his family and burn them with fire.

The story of Ananias and Sapphira alludes strongly to the story of Achan as a part of the unformulated text. The Septuagint introduces the story of Achan with the Greek phrase *enosphisanto apo tou anathematos* (Josh 7:1). Acts 5:2 uses notably similar language, *enosphisato apo tês timês*.

The verb *nosphizomai* occurs in the Septuagint only in Josh 7:1 and in 2 Macc 4:32 and in the New Testament only in Acts 5:2 and Titus 2:10. There are also close similarities between the encounter of Joshua with Achan and Peter's showdown with Ananias. And like Joshua, Peter divines the deception. Further, the story alludes to passages in Deuteronomy that command purging evil from the midst of the people (Deut 17:7, 12; 19:19; 21:21). Peter draws upon that repertoire when he proclaims that everyone who does not listen to the prophet like Moses shall be destroyed from the people (Acts 3:23). The deaths of Ananias and Sapphira then become manifestations of rooting out the evil from the people (see L. T. Johnson 1977:205-206, Schneider 1980:371-72).

In addition to biblical allusions, the story of Ananias and Sapphira also draws on conventional norms about punishment miracles. Several additional examples occur in Luke-Acts. Zechariah is unable to speak from the time of Gabriel's announcement until the birth of John because he did not believe the angel's words (Luke 1:20). In Acts 13:11 Elymas is unable to see for a time for opposing the straight paths of the Lord, and in 19:16 a man possessed with evil spirits attacks seven sons of Sceva because they undertake exorcism inappropriately in Jesus' name. Lucian gives a case where Eucrates claims that the spirit in a statue cures him of a fever. Tychiades mocks in response. But Eucrates warns him that the spirit will punish him. Then he tells of a servant who stole money offered to the spirit. The man soon died from being flogged every night by the spirit (The Lover of Lies, 19-20).

This is not merely a parallel in that it is a punishment miracle but also in that the punishment is for failing to recognize the presence of the spirit in the statue. When Peter interprets the deception of Ananias and Sapphira as lying not to human beings but to God (Acts 5:4, 9), he shows that the punishment is not merely for violating communal norms but for failing to recognize the presence of God's Spirit in the community.

Paul's shipwreck and viper bite draw on the repertoire of punishment miracles but redefine conventional norms because he miraculously survives. An epitaph recorded by Statyllius Flaccus tells about a man who escaped shipwreck only to be killed by a viper on the shores of Libya (Anthologia Palatina 7.290). Shipwreck and snakebite both reflect norms in antiquity that justice deals out misfortune (Miles and Trompf 1976:260-61). Jonah and the sailors on his ship share the belief that the storm that threatens them is divine judgment. In a rabbinic tradition, R. Gamaliel interprets a storm at sea as divine retribution for his part in banning R. Eliezer b. Hyrcanus (b. B. Meṣ. 59b). In *On the Murder of Herodes* 82-84 Antiphon relates the trial of Helos who is charged with murder during a sea voyage. Helos argues that divine retribution would have resulted in shipwreck if he in fact were the murderer.

Numbers 21:5-6 reflects the view that snakes carry out divine retribution when the people speak against God and Moses. In *t. Sanh.* 8:3, a man witnesses a murder, but because Jewish law requires two witnesses, he cannot bring the murderer to justice. But in the very spot of the homicide a snake bites the murderer, and he dies a victim of divine retribution. A papyrus fragment gives an account of a son who kills his father. When he attempts to flee into the desert, a lion chases him. So he tries to escape by climbing a tree. But in the tree he encounters a snake (Grenfell and Hunt 1897:133-34).

Therefore, the reaction of the people of Malta to Paul's snakebite expresses the cultural norm: "No doubt this man is a murderer. Though he has escaped from the dead, justice (*hē dikē*) has not allowed him to live" (Acts 28:4). But when Paul does not die, their cultural norm is still intact but reversed. "They changed their minds and said that he was a god" (28:6).

In summary, it is the fate of prophets to suffer because they stand on the side of God. It is also the fate of deceivers to suffer because they stand in opposition to God. But God also delivers from suffering some who stand on the side of God. Suffering, therefore, can be a sign of legitimacy, of standing on God's side. Suffering can be a sign of illegitimacy, of not standing on God's side. Deliverance from suffering can also be a sign of the legitimacy of one who stands on God's side. The unformulated text informs and distinguishes all three cases.

## JUDAS

A previous discussion of Judas, under the rubric of the retrospective recovery of the story, concluded that the demise of Judas and the reconstitution of the twelve foreshadow antithetical tensions in the remainder of Acts. According to the principle of homologation, antitheses at the end of a narrative correspond to those at the beginning. Thus, the antithetical tension established in the temptation of Jesus organizes the tensions between the principal axis and the polemical axis for the remainder of Luke-Acts. Along the polemical axis Judas is like a microwave relay tower. He stands in the polemical axis established by the devil's temptation of Jesus, and he renews the power of the signal and becomes a paradigm in the remainder of Acts for Jews who separate from the community judged by the reconstituted twelve and go their own way.

That earlier discussion also shows how the demise of Judas is half of a double fulfillment of scripture, with the reconstitution of the twelve as the other half (see pp. 91). This drawing on biblical texts is a part of the unformulated text. But more is going on than the overt fulfillment of scripture. It is well known that Luke imitates the style of the Septuagint. This style is prominent in Acts 1. The story of Judas and the reconstitution of the twelve begins with a common Septuagint phrase, "And in those days . . ." (Acts 1:15). Fulfillment of scripture and echoes of the Septuagint are hints that the biblical narrative is continuing and reminders of the story of Israel (Tannehill 1986:3, Drury 1987:419-20).

Israel's story, however, continues an even earlier one. Robert Alter's compelling discussion of Genesis 37-39 shows how the account of Joseph and his brothers contains seeds of Israel's later story (Alter 1981:3-12).[3] The treachery of Joseph's brothers in selling him into slavery converges with the story of Joseph and Potiphar's wife. But the episode of Judah and Tamar, or better "Judas" and Tamar by virtue of derivation from the Septuagint, breaks into that story line so that the episodes fall into sharp relief against each other.

The story of Judas and Tamar begins with the notice that Judas separates from his brothers (Gen 38:1). When Judas's son Er dies childless, and Onan rejects the responsibilities of levirate marriage, and when Judas refuses to provide a mate for Er's widow Tamar, Tamar seduces Judas himself. From this union Tamar gives birth to twins who in the act of birth struggle to dominate each other. The firstborn is named Perez who turns out to be an ancestor of David.

These narratives foreshadow the future. When the people split into two kingdoms, the tribe of Judah dominates the Southern Kingdom. Thus the separation of Judas from his brothers is echoed in the division of the kingdoms.

Reminiscences of these stories reverberate in the story of Judas and the twelve appointed by Jesus to judge the twelve tribes of Israel. The Judas of Acts recalls the prototypical Judas and the twelve sons of Israel. Like the first Judas who sells his brother (Gen 37:27), the second sells Jesus (Luke 22:5; Acts 1:18). Similarly, the second separates from the twelve apostles, as the first separates from the twelve brothers, and goes to his own place. And like the story of the first Judas, the story of the second contains seeds of the future. As the Judas of Acts turns aside from his heritage (*klêros*) with the twelve to go to his own place, so also Jews in the remainder of Acts who reject God's salvation align with Judas and turn aside from their heritage with the twelve tribes of Israel.

This is not to suggest that the author of Luke-Acts composed the story of Judas and the reconstitution of the twelve on the basis of Genesis 37-39 anymore than it is to suggest that the story of the division of Israel into two kingdoms was patterned after the patriarchal narratives. Further, this is not to link the two Judases typologically, allegorically, or symbolically. Rather, there is, as E. M. Forster puts it, an extension that joins characters and situations with other people far back (1954:194). Reverberations among the stories tie them together as parts of a larger whole, namely, as parts of a theocentric biblical story.

# 8

# AMBIGUOUS BORDERS: THE SYMBOLIC VOICE

Symbols mark frontiers. They are not that to which they point; they point to that which they are not. In Luke 23:44 darkness accompanies the crucifixion of Jesus. On the one hand, the darkness has a literal referent in the failure of the sun's light. On the other, it refers to the violation of boundaries, day becomes night, God's Christ is killed.

The literal referent to the absence of light is what philosophers of language call the subsidiary subject whereas the new meaning is the principal subject (Berggren 1962:238). A "tensive" symbol mediates between the two. In this way symbols stand between "is" and "is not," between antitheses, half-coursing toward one world, half-coursing toward another, but in neither. Suspended in between, symbols participate in one world and inform the reader about another.

For Hans-Georg Gadamer the modern concept of symbol cannot be understood adequately without comprehending its derivation from the idea that the divine is known through the sensible, a derivation that leaves symbol laden with tension (Gadamer 1975:66-70). The proper meaning of a symbolic expression is negated by the reality to which it points, and yet that reality also affirms the symbolic expression so that it can indeed point beyond itself (Tillich 1951:1.239).

The double-directional nature of symbols enables the reader to construct a symbolic voice that mediates between antitheses. Antitheses by definition are irreducible opposites. But symbols can join irreducible opposites, not annihilating them but mediating them. Symbols link terms that stand in tension.[1]

Because symbols join terms that stand in tension, they may function like a lens to view one side of the antithesis and then the other particularly (1) when the discourse introduces or summarizes an antithesis or (2) when it denotes the site of the conjunction of antitheses (Barthes 1974:21).

In the story of the healing of the paralytic, Jesus abruptly announces the forgiveness of the paralytic's sins (Luke 5:20). (1) Forgiveness encompasses the unnamed antithesis between God and the power of evil, and (2) the text correlates forgiveness with the healing of the paralytic's body as the site of conjunction between the divine and the satanic.[2] In Luke-Acts, although there is a cosmic struggle between God and the powers of evil, the human body is the battleground.

Normally, however, the symbolic voice works the other way around. Rather than focusing on a symbolic term, the text builds up a series of antitheses from which the reader then extrapolates a thematized symbolic meaning, that is, one reinforced by repetition (Culler 1975:203, Martin 1986:164). The discourse gives the reader, as it were, slopes on opposite sides of a mountain from which it is possible to infer a summit. The magnificat (Luke 1:46-55) plays off humility against pride, the hungry against the rich, the powerless against the powerful. From the antitheses the reader infers that Mary is the locus of conjunction of a divine reversal, not a simple reversal—negative becomes positive—but a polar reversal—negative becomes positive, positive becomes negative. God fills the hungry and sends the rich away empty.

In a discussion of positive and negative images, Edgar McKnight avers that negative elements dominate narrative when misfortune brings the action to a low point (tragedy) and positive elements dominate when a fortunate twist brings about a happy ending (comedy) (1988:190). Actually, in the symbolic voice negative and positive elements balance each other. To name darkness is to imply light, to name belief is to imply unbelief. Rather, the manner in which human beings function as the point of conjunction between the antitheses determines whether the movement is tragic or comic. The symbolic voice locates human beings on the borderline, and the direction of their movement determines whether it is toward a low point or toward a fortunate ending.

Thus in Acts 28 the symbolic voice builds upon the oppositions hopelessness/hope, unbelief/belief, brokenness/wholeness, destruction/salvation. The Jews to whom Paul preaches are the sites of the conjunction between the antitheses. Disbelievers move toward a low point, believers take a comic turn.

The antithesis suffusing the discourse is symmetrical, a balance of irreducible oppositions. But mediation upsets the symmetry, and the mediation of antithesis is the essence of narrative (Barthes 1974:28). The narrative of Luke-Acts has to do with breaching the wall separating irreducible antitheses. The crucifixion of Jesus is a satanic act (Luke 22:3), the resurrection is a divine act (Acts 2:24). Thus, the crucified, resurrected Messiah bridges death and life, Satan and God.

Not only do symbols mediate antitheses, they may also have the force of creating a new world. Contrary to the common opinion that symbols merely embellish an existing meaning, symbols have what Douglas Berggren calls an "epiphoric" dimension, that is, they extend meaning beyond its previous non-symbolic boundaries. Further, they have a "diaphoric" dimension where they create meaning by offering a new way of construing reality (1962:241-50). In fact, the new way of construing reality may depend upon the symbol so that it cannot be reduced to a literal level without destroying the new perspective. To give an example from astrophysics, the symbol of a black hole provides a new way of construing the hypothesis of a gravitational field so strong that no light can escape.

In the healing of the woman with a flow of blood (Luke 8:43-48) the discourse juxtaposes the world of the unclean to the world of the socially acceptable—female/male, blood flowing out of the body/blood flowing in the body, malady/health, untouchable/touchable, hidden/revealed, impotence/power, unbelief/faith, distress/peace.

Whereas a child is a socially legitimated issue of the womb (1:58), the issue of this woman's womb is taboo. The two worlds form irreducible oppositions until a touch violates the boundary. That does not yet nettle Jewish purity because it has a way to deal with the breach—reproach for the woman, purification for Jesus. But instead of a reproach this violation of the boundary engenders commendation. Through the touch the woman's body becomes the locus for mediating between the antithesis, and the symbolic voice gives birth to a new world.

The touching body not only symbolizes the new world but constitutes it—a world of commendable touch created out of the world of a prohibited untouchable. The touching body shatters the boundaries and opens a dimension of reality beyond the irreducible oppositions (Heiny 1987:1, 21, Patte 1987:24). Further, that dimension of reality is available only through the touching body. To dispose of the symbol is to destroy the dimension of reality that it makes available, and therefore, the symbol is also irreducible (Berggren 1962:250).

Methodologically, discovering the symbolic voice means analyzing oppositions. Oppositions are contrasting parallels in positive and negative terms (Heiny 1987:2, Patte 1987:28-30). The four Lucan beatitudes balanced by four woes serve as an example—poor/rich, hungry/full, weeping/laughing, excluded (outside)/social celebrity (inside) (Luke 6:20-26). After analyzing a series of oppositions, the reader can then deduce a symbolic theme, here, for example, the divine reversal of human values.

## FOUNDATIONAL ANTITHESES

Unpretentiously, the scene opens upon Zechariah and Elizabeth, profiles in antitheses—pious but fruitless, walking in commandments and ordinances but childless, barren, old (Luke 1:5-25). The prospect for Zechariah and Elizabeth is death. Aged as they are, their lives will end without progeny, cut off. Gabriel's promise of a son is a promise of fruit, issue, continuation, life.

Parallel oppositions build upon this foundation toward an antithesis reinforced by repetition through variation and substitution. There is an outside/inside opposition. People are praying outside the temple without access to the angelic message while Zechariah is inside receiving revelation (Luke 1:10-11). On one side, Zechariah is afraid and correspondingly unbelieving (1:12, 20), on the other, the angel counsels him not to be afraid and promises joy and gladness (1:12-14).

The thematization continues with Elizabeth. Over against her hidden pregnancy (1:24) is the public manifestation of the birth (1:58-59), over against her reproach among human beings (1:25) is the celebration of neighbors and relatives at the birth of her son (1:58). Along one pole Elizabeth keeps crossing deficiency—barren, empty, chagrined. Two notices to the hill country drop the hint that even the landscape is uninviting and bleak (1:39, 65) (Noth 1966:17-19, 55-56, McCown 1962:631). Along the other pole Elizabeth repeatedly experiences fulfillment—pregnant, filled with the Holy Spirit, renowned. And over against the barren hill country, the promise comes from Gabriel who stands in the presence of God (1:19), the promising "landscape" of the God with whom nothing is impossible (1:36).

At the opposite extreme from barren, aged, postmenopausal Elizabeth, Mary is an unfruitful virgin (1:27, 34). Afraid, she has found favor with God (1:29-30). Empty, she judges herself deficient for having no husband (1:34). But the Holy Spirit comes upon her and overcomes the deficiency. Her unfruitful virginal womb bears fruit (1:42). And she is blessed because over against the potential for skepticism, she believes (1:45).

In the two birth stories, the locus of the conjunction of the antitheses—sterility and fruit, fear and confidence, disbelief and faith, death and life—is the human body. Zechariah and Elizabeth stand on the boundary between barren and fruitful, and with the birth of their child the plot takes a fortunate turn from death toward life. The body of Mary likewise is the locus of the conjunction of antitheses. However, the symbolic meaning that the reader constructs also implies that God is father over against Mary as mother. But the discourse attributes no deficiency to

God, unlike the other characters. Therefore, God is not a point of conjunction that summarizes antitheses.

The discourse associates the antithesis between light and darkness with the births of John and Jesus. In Zechariah's prophecy regarding John, darkness parallels oppression, lack of knowledge, and sin (1:68-79). Light corresponds to deliverance, the gift of knowing salvation, and forgiveness. But darkness also explicitly means death (1:79), and so in the thematization of the antitheses the way of peace means life. Simeon's prophecy about Jesus speaks of a light for revelation (2:32) and thus implies opposition between darkness/light and hidden/revealed. As the one who prepares the ways of the Lord (1:76), John is the locus of the conjunction of the antitheses. As God's salvation (2:30), Jesus marks the point of mediation of darkness/light and hidden/revealed. Further, the text states clearly that Jesus is the point of conjunction between the fall and rise of many in Israel, and a sign that is spoken against (2:34).

John the Baptist fulfills Zechariah's prophecy in Luke 3:2-20. Once again the image of bearing fruit stands out in relief against the landscape of the unproductive wilderness. But the wilderness also doubles as the place of preparation and repentance. And so the antithesis shifts from barrenness/fruit to bad fruit/good fruit. The locus of mediation also shifts from John the Baptist to the multitudes who come out to him. Their orientation determines whether the outcome is tragic or comic.

The bad fruit/good fruit opposition overlaps an additional antithesis. The one who is coming after John will gather wheat into the granary and burn the chaff (3:17). Similar is the imagery of cutting down and burning trees that bear bad fruit. But a new spatial dimension comes into play. The wheat is gathered *into* the granary—inside/outside. The person who bears good fruit is the locus of conjunction between inside and outside.

In the baptism of Jesus the discourse implies the opposition heaven/earth but also closed/open (Luke 3:21-22). Both may be understood in spatial as well as transcendent terms. The opened heaven enables the Holy Spirit to descend upon Jesus. Moreover, the opened heaven indicates revelation. A divine voice fulfills the prediction of Gabriel that Jesus will be called Son of

God (1:32, 35). The Son is connected to fruit in two ways. In relation to the birth stories, the Son is the fruit. In relation to the preaching of John the Baptist, the Son bears fruit.

The temptation of Jesus exhibits a complex set of oppositions—hungry/full, tempted by the devil/led by the Spirit (Luke 4:1-13). The landscape again is the wilderness, barren, deficient. The antithesis devil/Holy Spirit is transcendent, but Jesus is the locus of conjunction for the antitheses. All three temptations demonstrate how he is led by the Spirit rather than by the devil. And according to the precedents set in Luke 1-3, Jesus bears fruit in the wilderness as God's Son.

## FROM ANTITHESES TO THEME:
## THE MINISTRY OF JESUS

Jesus' inaugural sermon in the synagogue at Nazareth (Luke 4:16-30) plays off the poor against the rich, captives against the free, the blind against those who see, and the oppressed against those who are at liberty. Three levels of reality underlie these oppositions—physical, social, and transcendent. For example, the blind include those unable to see physically, but they also epitomize the marginalized of society. The captives perhaps represent those in debtor's prison.[3] The oppressed embody social, political, and physical realities. In addition, physical and social maladies manifest the oppression of satanic powers.

As Jesus carries out his ministry, human beings become the locus for the conjunction between these antitheses. In Luke 7:22 Jesus summarizes his ministry primarily in terms of the restoration of the body to wholeness. Further, in Acts 10:38 Peter summarizes the ministry of Jesus as healing all who were oppressed by the devil. Thus, the human body is the point of mediation for these antitheses on all three levels.

The incident in Nazareth also carries on the inside/outside opposition. Jesus is in the synagogue, in Nazareth, in his own homeland. Parallels to Elijah and Elisha demonstrate that a prophet can be in Israel and yet beyond the pale. And so the people of Nazareth cast Jesus outside the city (4:29). But this results in a reversal. The people of Nazareth now are outside with respect to Jesus. Their effort to kill Jesus shows that the issue is a matter of life and death. Tragically, they move toward the side of death.

The outside/inside opposition develops further in the healing of the paralytic (Luke 5:17-26). He is outside, isolated from Jesus, until his companions remove tiles from the roof and let him down before Jesus. The paralytic's body transgresses the boundary between outside and inside, and the violation of the boundary corresponds to his healing and forgiveness.

The sermon on the plain again picks up the imagery of fruit (Luke 6:43-45). The series of oppositions are bad tree/good tree, bad fruit/good fruit, evil/good. Corresponding to the repentant people who bear good fruit in 3:8-9, those who bear good fruit here are the disciples who are like their teacher (6:40). Further, just as in the context of 3:2-22 Jesus is the Son who bears fruit, so also in the context of the sermon on the plain the disciples who are like their teacher are also children of God who bear good fruit (6:35).

The healing of the centurion's slave (Luke 7:2-10) brings together antitheses in a fascinating way—on one side sickness, death, on the other faith, healing, life. Overlying this is an evaluative opposition worthy/unworthy and a partially actualized spatial opposition between inside and outside. Jewish elders evaluate the centurion, not the slave, as worthy. The centurion evaluates himself, not the slave, as unworthy. Jesus heals the slave because the centurion relies on the power of Jesus' word. As a Gentile the centurion is outside, but with respect to faith he swaps places with the people of Israel, more inside than anyone in Israel. The body of the slave is the point of mediation between death and life, whereas the centurion is the locus for the conjunction between disbelief and faith. As a result, this cluster of antipodes reverses the polarity of worthy/ unworthy. Those in Israel who have no faith correspond to the unworthy side. A Gentile who has faith corresponds to the worthy side.

A similar reversal takes place in the house of Simon the Pharisee (Luke 7:36-50). A notorious woman violates the barriers between inside and outside. Jesus treats the woman as an insider. In fact, she replaces the host and becomes the insider who extends hospitality to Jesus. By contrast, Simon withholds hospitality. Rather than Simon and Jesus associating together as insiders over against the woman, Jesus and the woman associate together as insiders, and Simon the inhospitable host is the outsider.

Luke 8 adds to the inside/outside opposition hidden/revealed, darkness/light, secret/manifest. The disciples are insiders who are given the secrets of the kingdom. Parables hide the secrets from outsiders (8:10). But then there is a reversal. What is hidden is to be made manifest, what is secret is to come to light (8:16-17). The secret is that those who hear the word are the point of mediation between barrenness and fruit. If they bring forth fruit, what is hidden becomes manifest, the secret comes to light.

The opposition devil/God overlies the opposition barrenness/fruit. Further, the status of disciples is ambiguous. Insiders may, like germinating seed without root, fall away and become outsiders. Unless they make the secrets of the kingdom manifest, insiders become outsiders. Significantly, the announcement that Jesus' mother and brothers are outside anticipates that Jesus will make them insiders (8:20). Instead, he makes those who hear the word of God and do it insiders, that is, those who, according to the parable, bear fruit (8:21; see 11:27-28).

The Gerasene demoniac is an outsider to the extreme—demonic, naked, dwelling not in the habitation of the living but among tombs (the habitation of the dead, taboo), unclean, chained, fettered, driven into the desert (Luke 8:26-39). When Jesus exorcises the demons, the man crosses barriers—seated, clothed, in his right mind, healed, commanded to return home (the habitation of the living), one for whom God has acted. Now he is to bear fruit by declaring how much God has done for him. He is the locus of the conjunction between the antitheses, the battleground in the struggle between the demonic and the divine.

With the first passion prediction that battleground shifts to Jesus. When Jesus foretells his passion, suffering, rejection, and death stand on one side, resurrection on the other (Luke 9:22).

And the body of Jesus is the locus of mediation between the antithesis.

But like teacher, like disciple, Jesus' followers are equally the locus. The sayings of Luke 9:23-27 locate losing life, forfeiting self, and shame on the side of death. On the other side stand salvation, denying oneself, following Jesus, and the kingdom of God. Superimposed on these antitheses is a chronological opposition—present/future ". . . when the Son of man comes in his glory . . ." (9:28). The present is the time of bearing fruit or remaining an insider. The future is the time of judgment but also of fulfillment of the kingdom of God.

The problem of the status of the disciples continues with the second passion prediction. According to Luke 8:10 the disciples have been given the secrets of the kingdom. Further, the voice at the transfiguration commands the disciples to listen to Jesus (9:35). But when Jesus predicts his passion, it is concealed from them (9:45)—an opposition between hidden and revealed, misunderstanding and understanding, fear and faith. Are the disciples insiders or outsiders?

Luke 9:51 gives notice that the time is drawing near for Jesus' assumption into heaven. This implies an opposition heaven/earth. Luke 10:17 establishes a kind of negative parallel in the fall of Satan from heaven. In between 9:52 and 10:17 Jesus' disciples wish to call down fire from heaven upon the Samaritans (9:52), and Jesus announces judgment on Capernaum in terms of the antithesis heaven/hades (10:15). Further, immediately after reporting the fall of Satan, Jesus tells the seventy that their names are written in heaven.

There is, thus, a strong spatial thematization earth/heaven, hades/heaven reiterated in the spatial opposition far/near. Other antitheses overlie the spatial antitheses—rejection/acceptance, dead/alive, woe/peace, homeless/housed, sick/healed, Satan/God. The antitheses locate those who encounter Jesus and his emissaries on the borderline, and their response determines whether they take a tragic or a comic turn, whether the kingdom of God, which has come near, is indeed near or far.

In the monologue in Luke 10:21-22 Jesus is the point of conjunction between hidden and revealed. But hidden/revealed also corresponds to wise and understanding/babes, an antithesis that encompasses all other human beings. They too, therefore, form a point of mediation between the antitheses.

On their own, these sayings appear to make knowing God arbitrarily dependent upon God's act of hiding and revealing and Jesus' sheer choice. But in the context, nothing is hid that shall not be made manifest (8:17). Further, the sayings fit closely with the success and failure of the mission of the seventy (10:6-20). Accordingly wise and understanding/babes parallels outside/inside, rejection/acceptance, unbelief/belief. In addition, the revelation of God as Father stands over against the fall of Satan (10:18-22).

Knowing God is thus dependent upon three interdependent characters and functions. God reveals. But God reveals that Jesus is the revealer. As the revealer Jesus reveals that the revelation is hidden from the wise and understanding, but available to babes. Hence Jesus' revelation is a demand for people to become babes and so recipients of the revelation.

Thus, the blessedness of "seeing" and "hearing" (Luke 10: 23-24) is not agonistic. It requires no struggle with Satan, who has fallen, no wrestling with God. Rather, it entails adopting the stance of a child—dependence upon God. The point is reiterated under the image of a child again in 11:9-13. Asking, seeking, knocking imply a negative side of silence, refusal, resistance. Similarly, receiving, finding, opened have their antipodes in spurning, losing, closed. But the positive pole means asking and receiving as a child from a father whereas the negative pole presumably coincides with both fainthearted indifference and aggressive independence.

In contrast to God's children who see and hear, some of Jesus' contemporaries contend that he casts out demons by the prince of demons (11:14-26). In the antithesis Satan/God, Jesus' detractors align him with Satan. But Jesus violates the barrier between the satanic and the divine and storms the kingdom of Satan as an invader from the side of God. By aligning with Jesus other human beings have the same option. Otherwise, they are the ones in league with the prince of demons.

In focusing on aligning with Jesus, Luke 11:14-52 recapitulates 7:36-8:39. The repetition is structural as well as thematic. Luke 11:14-52 follows the sequence of 7:36-8:39 in reverse:

---

(A) Dining with a Pharisee (7:36-50)
    (B) Bearing fruit (8:4-15)
        (C) Lamp and light (8:16-18)
            (D) Mother and brothers (8:19-21)
                (E) Lack of faith among disciples (8:22-25)
                    (F) The healing of a demoniac (8:26-39)
                    (F´) The healing of a demoniac (11:14)
                (E´) Lack of faith among the people (11:15-26)
            (D´) Mother (11:27-28)
        (C´) Lamp and light (11:33)
    (B´) The whole body full of light (11:34-36)
(A´) Dining with a Pharisee (11:37-52)

---

Further, Luke 11 reiterates the antitheses darkness/light, hidden/manifest, to disregard/to hear, blindness/sight. Against Jesus/with Jesus replaces the outside/inside opposition of Luke 8. Bearing fruit (8:11-15) and the body full of light (11:34-36) make humans the sites of conjunction between the antitheses.

In the incident in the home of a Pharisee (Luke 11:37-52), the opposition between inside/outside is a variation on unclean/clean, wickedness/righteousness. Cup and dish correspond to the exterior of the Pharisees, clean, artificial; unseen graves correspond to the interior, unclean, factual. On the other hand, inside/outside is a variation on knowledge/nescience. The lawyers take away the key of knowledge for themselves and for others (11:52). The nescient correspond, however, to those who reject the prophets and apostles whom God sends. In short, inside/outside reflects the attitude toward Jesus. Human beings stand on the border between antitheses, and the steps that they take away from the borderline determine whether the turn is tragic or comic.

Luke 12:2-21 summarizes the antithesis between fidelity and apostasy in the symbol "possessions." To lay up treasure for oneself is apostasy, death. To be rich toward God is fidelity, life. Fidelity, however, is not first of all the character of humans but of God (12:22-31). Accordingly, human fidelity corresponds to faith in God's fidelity, apostasy to anxiety. The discourse reiterates the antithesis spatially and chronologically. Heaven and earth stand over against each other as permanent and temporal (12:33) but also as future and present (12:35-48).

Interpreting the present (12:56) means repenting (13:2, 5) like settling with an accuser before facing the judge (12:57-59). As in the call of John the Baptist (3:8-9), repenting means bearing fruit (13:6-9). Inasmuch as Jesus is the Son who bears fruit, he exemplifies bearing fruit in the healing of the woman bent with a spirit of infirmity. She is the locus of conjunction between malady/health, bound/loosed, satanic/divine. Jesus and the ruler of the synagogue are also the points of conjunction between conventional propriety and impropriety, although they move from the borderline in opposite directions. Jesus is also the locus of conjunction between God and Satan. Conventional propriety corresponds to binding, to malady, to the satanic, to an unfruitful tree that is to be cut down (13:9). (See 14:1-6.)

The parable of the great banquet (Luke 14:15-24) renews the opposition outside/inside and correlates it with the chronological antithesis present/future. Invited guests are insiders in the present, outsiders in the future. The poor, maimed, blind, and lame are outsiders in the present, insiders in the future. (Compare 13:22-30.)

The outsiders who become insiders parallel the toll collectors and sinners who draw near to Jesus in 15:1-2. The discourse reiterates the outside/inside opposition with resentment/joy, sin/repentance, lost/found, death/life. The lost son's environment is bleak—far country, loose living, famine, hunger, sin, forfeited sonship. But brightness and celebration balance the bleakness—home, reasonableness, embrace, confession, restored sonship, banquet, cheer. Luke 15:1-2 locates the toll collectors, sinners, Pharisees, and scribes on a boundary, and the direction in which they move determines that outsiders become insiders and insiders outsiders.

Similar antitheses continue in the parable of the dishonest steward (Luke 16:1-9). On one side there is dishonesty, waste, outside—"You can no longer be steward." On the other side there is shrewdness, a prudently thrifty use of possessions, inside—"So that people may receive me into their houses when

I am put out of the stewardship." The following pericope adds the oppositions dishonest/faithful, unrighteous mammon/true riches, hate/love, mammon/God (16:10-13). Here possessions mediate the antitheses, but the locus of the mediation is the human being who takes a tragic or comic turn on the basis of his or her use of possessions.

The healing of ten lepers in Luke 17:11-19 violates the boundary between outside/inside in two ways. The boundary is emphasized by distance, malady, and pollution on the one hand and proximity (at Jesus' feet), healing, and cleansing on the other. But there is another boundary—the border between Judea and Samaria. Ten outsiders become insiders because Jesus cures a malady of pollution in the Jewish purity system. That is parallel to the foreigner who becomes an insider. With respect to faith, he swaps places with the nine (presumably Israelites). An outsider becomes an insider, freshly franchised insiders become outsiders.

A present/future opposition pervades the remainder of Luke 17. For Jesus, present suffering is played off against the revelation of the future. For this generation, the alleged normality of the present is played off against destruction, losing life against gaining life (17:25-33). Jesus and this generation are points of conjunction between losing life and gaining it. Jesus assuredly takes a comic turn. Luke 18:8 leaves the direction others take up in the air: "When the Son of man comes, will he find faith on earth?" The discourse illustrates the ambiguity of the borderline with another polar reversal in the parable of the Pharisee and the toll collector (18:9-14). Initially, inside corresponds to Pharisee, righteous, outside to toll collector, sinner. In the end, the toll collector is the insider, humble, vindicated; the Pharisee is the outsider, arrogant, liable.

In Luke 18:18-30 the rich ruler and the disciples play comparable roles. On its own the story of the rich ruler is a simple reversal, positive becomes negative. But in context the story of the rich ruler is part of a larger chiastic structure: (A) rich ruler (18:18-27), (B) the twelve (18:28-34), (B') a blind man (18:35-43), (A') Zacchaeus (19:1-10). And so in connection with Peter's remark, "We have left our homes and followed you" (18:28), the rich ruler becomes part of a polar reversal. Rule, wealth, and commitment to commandments stake out the claim on one side, subservience (following Jesus), homelessness, and commitment to the kingdom of God on the other.

A passion prediction then threatens the place of the twelve as insiders (Luke 18:31-34). The prediction implies the antithesis hidden/revealed. But the twelve do not understand so they stride away from the borderline toward the hidden, the outside.

A blind man functions as a contrast to the twelve who are deficient in understanding (18:35-43). A beggar by the roadside, he is the point of conjunction for poverty/wealth, far/near, blindness/sight, unbelief/faith. He is brought near to Jesus, and by the command of Jesus he breaks through the boundary between blindness and sight—healed, saved, a person of faith, an insider who follows Jesus.

As the final part of the chiastic pattern, Zacchaeus contrasts with the rich ruler (19:1-10). Socially unacceptable, he is the point of mediation for outside/inside, sin/virtue, poverty/wealth, lost/saved. In contrast to the rich ruler who refuses to sell his possessions and give to the poor, Zacchaeus dedicates his possessions to reparation and to distribution to the poor. He becomes, therefore, an insider.

As Jesus moves to Jerusalem the symbolic voice builds on the oppositions rejection/acceptance, unfaithfulness/fidelity, hidden/revealed, unknown/known. Jesus weeps over Jerusalem because his kingship is hidden from their eyes (19:38-42). Thus he is an outsider—rejected, unknown—who enters the temple and drives out the insiders (19:45). This leads authorities to question Jesus' authority, setting up the antithesis unauthorized/authorized, from human beings/from God (20:1-8). Moreover, the parable of the vineyard portrays the chief priests and scribes as producing no fruit—barren (20:9-19). There is, therefore, a polar reversal. The authorities become unauthorized, the rejected one becomes divinely authorized.

The saying that the rejected stone has become the head of the corner (20:17) invites a comparison with the temple. Jesus predicts its destruction (21:5-6) and sets beauty against ugliness, building against destruction. The chronological antithesis present/future overlies this so that the present beautiful building becomes the future ugly rock pile—one pole of the reversal. But the rejected stone becomes the head of the corner—the other pole.

In contrast to God's care for persecuted disciples (21:12-19), in the distress of Jerusalem the populace will experience wrath (21:20-24). Jesus advises those inside the city to depart—insiders become outsiders. Others will be made captives among the Gentiles—insiders become outsiders.

In the passion of Jesus, initially Judas is an insider. But Satan enters inside Judas, and he betrays Jesus for money (Luke 22:3-6). Here, money is the symbolic term summarizing the antitheses Satan/God, death/life, inside/outside. Judas goes "away" from the twelve, becomes an outsider with them, and becomes an insider with the high priestly party (22:4).

Nevertheless, Judas is with Jesus at the last supper (22:7-30). In the meal Jesus becomes the locus of conjunction between incomplete and fulfilled, between present and future, between death and life. Simultaneously Judas takes a tragic turn toward the incomplete, the present, death.

The discourse also locates Simon on the borderline between Satan and God, unbelief and faith, denial and confession, death and life (Luke 22:31-34). Instead of following Jesus to death, he denies Jesus (22:54-62). From the ideological point of view of Luke-Acts, to seek to save one's life is to lose it, whereas to die for the sake of Jesus is to gain life. Therefore, Peter turns from life toward death.

Twice the passion narrative plays off darkness against light, and this is mixed with the antithesis present/future. Jesus' arrest is the power of darkness (Luke 22:53). At the crucifixion darkness covers the earth from the sixth until the ninth hour (23:44). On the one hand the covert arrest contrasts with Jesus' public appearances in the temple, and so darkness/light implies secret/open. In addition, darkness contrasts with God's time when the power of darkness will be overcome, and so darkness/light parallels present/future, Satan/God (22:69).

The darkness in 23:44-45 is not merely the antithesis of light but a symbolic term matching the torn curtain of the temple.

The two symbolic terms summarize the violation of boundaries, day becomes night, secret precincts are thrown open, the sacred becomes profane, God's Christ is killed.

Comparably, the tomb summarizes the transgression of boundaries (Luke 24:1-12). Two angels appear in a sepulcher—taboo. When the living enter the tomb, they do not find the dead body. The crucified one is the risen one, a dead man is alive (24:5). The resurrection shatters the boundary between life and death.

In spite of shattering boundaries, the risen Jesus vies in a world where his disciples still straddle ambiguous borderlines. The report of the women to the apostles plays on the antithesis unbelief/belief (24:9-11). The walk to Emmaus (24:13-32) implies the oppositions hidden/revealed, closed/open, despair/hope, unbelief/belief. Presence/absence interweaves with these oppositions in a fairly complicated way. Initially, Jesus is present but hidden, and so in spite of his presence the two disciples founder in despair and unbelief. When their eyes are opened, Jesus is revealed but absent.

Even when the two disciples report to the eleven, and when the eleven proclaim that the Lord has risen, the risen Jesus still contends with disciples on ambiguous borderlines (24:33-49). They are the points of mediation between fear and confidence, unbelief and belief, lacking understanding and having understanding, closed and open. Jesus has taken a comic turn. The disciples are poised for an upward turn, but they wait for that as they wait for the promise of Jesus' Father (24:49).

## FROM ANTITHESES TO THEME:
## AMONG DISCIPLES OF JESUS

Acts 1:1-11 contrasts the presence and absence of Jesus. Presence/absence is parallel to down/up, seen/hidden, earth/heaven. The chronological antithesis present/future is superimposed on this cluster, and the future reverses the oppositions. Jesus will come from heaven to earth, no longer hidden but seen, no longer absent but present.

Acts quickly reiterates the opposition between inside and outside, life and death. It is when the company of believers is together (1:12-15) that the narrator explains the separation of Judas from the twelve. The thematization extends to his field. The place of habitation, living, become uninhabitable, desolate (1:20). Judas forfeits his place of ministry and apostleship to go to his own place (1:25). An insider becomes an outsider.

On Pentecost inside/outside is parallel to empty/full, earth/ heaven, passive/active (Acts 2:1-42). Inside a place of gathering, the Holy Spirit fills believers. The Holy Spirit is inside believers but has an outside manifestation that drives them from inside to outside, from quietistic waiting to active witnessing. Moreover, there is a past/present opposition. A prophecy from the past is a present description of the last days. The conjunction of death and life in Jesus becomes the occasion for Peter to offer his hearers the possibility of moving one way or the other from the borderline between resisting and receiving, impenitence and repentance, death and life. When insiders (believers) become outsiders (witnesses), outsiders (hearers) can become insiders (believers).

In the early Christian community, possessions are symbolic terms that embrace the antitheses associated with rejection/ acceptance (Acts 2:43-47). In contrast to Judas who used his money to buy his own place, believers have a community of goods (L. T. Johnson 1977:126, 180, 183-190). Thus possessions summarize outside/inside, impenitence/repentance, death/ life, and the use of possessions is an index of the direction in which one moves away from the borderline. The case of Ananias and Sapphira illustrates the point (4:32-5:10). Their use of possessions separates them, like Judas, from the community (Johnson 1977:206). And in contrast to the blessedness of the community (4:32-34), Ananias and Sapphira, like Judas, incur catastrophe. Insiders become outsiders.

The use of possessions as an index for catastrophe or blessing is truncated in the healing of the lame man (Acts 3:1-10). The lame man anticipates alms as potential blessing. But rather than make a dole out of the community of goods, Peter shifts the focus from possessions to the lame man's body—a body that bridges the antitheses carried/walking, weakness/ strength, malady/healing. Peter's explanation of the healing sets unbelief against faith, human power against divine power, human malice against divine good, death against resurrection.

Further, Peter insinuates that the healing of the lame man has parallels in (1) the resurrection of Jesus, (2) the repentance and forgiveness of Peter's audience, and (3) the blessing of all the families of the earth in the fulfillment of the Abrahamic covenant. That is, Peter's audience has access to the divine power promised to Abraham and manifested in Jesus' resurrection and the healing of the lame man. And Peter, the lame man, and the audience are points of conjunction for the antitheses. In so many words, like possessions, Peter's proclamation has the double potential for catastrophe or divine blessing.

Opposition provides Peter and the apostles an opportunity to test the double potential for catastrophe or divine blessing. The high priestly party and the Sadducees first arrest Peter and John (Acts 4:1-22) and then all the apostles (5:17-42), and the sanhedrin prohibits their teaching. With this the reader recalls Jesus' warnings of divine judgment for apostasy and his promises of divine care for fidelity (Luke 12:1-12; 21:12-19).

But the reader also remembers Jesus' brush with the chief priests, scribes, and elders about authority (20:1-8). And so the incidents implicitly raise the opposition unauthorized/authorized. Divine authorization undercuts human authority (Acts 4:19-20; 5:29). On one level divine authorization for the apostles overrules the authority of the sanhedrin. But Peter's remarks make it equally applicable to Jesus—killed by authorities, authorized by the God who raised him from the dead (4:10; 5:30-31).

Thus, in these incidents unauthorized and authorized reverse poles, and those who threaten the apostles stand on the borderline between catastrophe and blessing, impenitence and repentance, liability and forgiveness. As far as the apostles are concerned, God proves the correlation between fidelity and blessing over against apostasy and catastrophe. Subtly (and sublimely) the apostles are examples already of Gamaliel's criterion: "If it is of God, you will not be able to overthrow them" (5:39).

Does the discourse then subvert its own subtlety with the catastrophe of Stephen's martyrdom (Acts 6:8-7:60)? Stephen is full of the Holy Spirit. His opponents are full of rage. Stephen's speech reflects a similar dichotomy in Israel's history and aligns him with God's acts of grace and the opponents with recalcitrant people who rejected God's acts of grace. Stephen's opponents murdered the Righteous One sent as an act of God's grace.

Up until this point in Acts, the announcement of God's raising of Jesus has counterbalanced the attribution of his death to human beings. Here there is no proclamation of Jesus' resurrection. Rather, the incident plays on the antitheses heaven/earth, opened/closed, and Stephen's vision of the risen Jesus replaces the resurrection and aligns him with God's act of vindication. But Stephen's announcement of the vision also places his auditors on the border between heaven and earth, opened and closed. The lynching of Stephen indicates that their turn is tragic. And so the poles of catastrophe/blessing reverse.

One of those auditors is Paul, and another revelatory act makes him the locus of conjunction between earth/heaven, darkness/light, hidden/seen, blindness/sight, empty/full (Acts 9:1-19; 22:3-16; 26:9-18). The notice that Paul has letters from the high priestly party fits into the opposition authorized/unauthorized. Initially, he moves away from the borderline in a tragic direction—from the ideological perspective of Acts, catastrophe. But he proves the possibility of repentance, and so he regains his sight, eats food, and is filled with the Holy Spirit.

All three accounts of Paul's conversion juxtapose the revelatory event to his activity as persecutor so that the pair of oppositions bound/unbound, imprisoned/free not only traverse his victims but also Paul himself. Furthermore, just as he moves from darkness to light, his mission is to turn Jews and Gentiles from darkness to light. Significantly, 26:17-18 also parallels the oppositions closed/opened, sin/forgiveness, unbelief/faith to Satan/God. The antitheses locate Paul, and in Acts 22 and 26 also his auditors, on borderlines from which one has a double potential for death or life, catastrophe or blessing.

Two miracle stories reinforce the thematization of the reversal of catastrophe/blessing. In the healing of Aeneas (Acts 9:33-34), through Peter's announcement, Jesus crosses the boundary between malady and healing. And in place of Aeneas's paralyzed body, the pallet is covered by a spread. In the restoration of Tabitha (9:36-42), the christological focus, so evident in Peter's words to Aeneas, falls out. Nevertheless, Peter's prayer and the response of belief imply a divine dimension (9:40-42). Peter and Tabitha break through the boundaries between malady and health, closed eyes and opened eyes, death and life. Significantly, Peter places the weeping widows outside, and with the restoration of life, he calls in the saints and widows (outside/inside). Thus, the poles catastrophe/blessing reverse.

The conversion of Cornelius is a reversal of another sort (Acts 10:1-11:18). The discourse plays on hidden/revealed, unclean/clean, Gentiles/Jews, outside/inside, unlawful/lawful, human/divine, earth/heaven, unbelief/belief, guilt/forgiveness, impenitence/repentance. Paralleling the revelation in the visions, the Holy Spirit's manifestations are a revelation to Jewish Christians. Consequently, the relationship between Jews and Gentiles reverses. Clean/unclean receives a new, divine definition, and criteria for becoming an insider shift radically.

The discourse also connects the extension of belief among Gentiles to the persecution inaugurated by Stephen's martyrdom (Acts 11:19). Thus, not only Stephen's vision of the risen Christ but also the extension of God's salvation reverses the catastrophe of Stephen's death. Gamaliel's criterion legitimates Stephen's death and its consequences: "If it is of God, you will not be able to overthrow them" (5:39).

According to Gamaliel's criterion, the execution of James in Acts 12 could imply that the messianic movement has only human authority, but the notice in 12:24 that the word of God grew and multiplied forestalls a negative argument from providence. Further, the execution of James shows Herod's alignment against God, and Peter's miraculous release from prison overshadows the death of James. Peter is the point of conjunction between imprisoned/at liberty (inside/outside), enemies/allies, Herod/God. The movement away from the borderline, however, centers not on Peter but on God's angel. The account is a theocentric demonstration of divine providence and God's reversal of catastrophe and blessing. And according to Gamaliel's criterion in 5:39, Peter's release shows the inability of opponents to stop God's undertaking.

Central to the resumption of Paul's mission is the antithesis between the devil and the Holy Spirit (Acts 13:1-13). Paul, filled with the Holy Spirit, confronts Elymas, a son of the devil. That antithesis parallels true/false, straight/crooked, righteousness/ iniquity, belief/unbelief. And so the blindness of Elymas is not merely a punishment miracle but a part of the symbolic voice. Elymas is blind in comparison with Paul who was likewise blind but received his sight (9:17).

Paul's sojourn in Antioch of Pisidia provides parallels to the opposition blindness/sight (13:16-52). The people of Jerusalem and their rulers exhibit a tragic turn from the borderline recognition/lack of recognition, understanding/lack of understanding (13:27). There is a further variation in the antitheses sin/forgiveness, bound/free, unbelief/belief, wrath/salvation, and darkness/ light (13:38-47). Additionally, the antithesis death/resurrection (13:28-37) impinges on the other oppositions so that it is possible for the auditors to move away from the negative pole toward the positive. Still, unbelief incurs catastrophe even for Jews. Belief leads to blessing even for Gentiles. And as 13:48 shows, the double potential is a matter of life and death.

This double potential applies to both Jews and Gentiles in Acts 14. In contrast to the Gentiles and Jews who attempt to stone Paul and Barnabas, Paul and Barnabas heal a lame man—the locus of conjunction between unbelief and belief. Paul's explanation to counter the Lycaonians' pagan interpretation pits vain things against God, evil against good, barren against fruitful, sorrow against gladness. Echoing Luke 8, where insiders bear fruit, the healing of the lame man is bearing fruit both from the perspective of God's agents and from the perspective of the God who gives fruitful seasons from heaven (Acts 14:17).

The Jerusalem council centers on a debate about criteria for inside/ outside (Acts 15:1-35). In Peter's speech the criteria are two—faith and the gift of the Holy Spirit. The final outcome, however, adds an additional criterion in terms of clean/unclean, not on the basis of the law of Moses but on the basis of apostolic mores (Wilson 1983:71-101).[4] Under the new criteria outsiders can become insiders.

Acts 16 makes a double play on hidden/revealed and closed/open. When Paul, Silas, and Timothy attempt to go into Asia, the way is closed. But God reveals the divine purpose in a vision—hidden/revealed. Reiterating the opened way, the Lord opens Lydia's heart. To the contrary, when Paul liberates a slave girl, her owners appeal to magistrates who close Paul and Silas inside a prison. But an earthquake opens the prison, and correspondingly the jailer believes—another opened heart. The magistrates then wish to keep their illegal imprisonment of Roman citizens secret. But Paul forces an open escort. There is thus a reversal of closed/open, imprisoned/free.

In Thessalonica Paul sets resurrection over against death (Acts 17:1-9). Therefore, when Jews attack the house of Jason and drag him and some other believers before authorities, the paradigm of death/resurrection already reverses the persecution. And so there is ironic truth in the complaint of the opponents that these people have turned the world upside down (17:6). With the resurrection suffering becomes vindication, death becomes life.

In the address at Athens the antithesis unknown/known dominates the symbolic voice (Acts 17:22-31). But it stands in parallel with near/far, ignorance/repentance, judgment/salvation, death/resurrection. Paul's proclamation substitutes the true God for the unknown, and places his auditors on the border between near and far. Belief and unbelief determine the way Paul's auditors move away from the borderline (17:34).

Paul's relationship with the synagogue in Corinth plays on inside/outside (Acts 18:1-11). At the beginning he is in the synagogue. But opposition drives him outside, matching his declaration to go to the Gentiles. Initially, inside is a place of rejection. Therefore, it becomes outside. The house of Titius is the place of belief, and it becomes inside. A similar reversal occurs in Ephesus (19:8-10). Paul is inside the synagogue, but unbelief drives him outside. Then the hall of Tyrannus becomes the place where the word of the Lord is heard, and so it becomes inside.

The incident concerning the sons of Sceva manifests the basic conflict between the satanic and the divine (Acts 19:13-20). On the border between the divine and satanic, known and unknown (and tacitly authorized and unauthorized), the sons of Sceva have no access to divine power, and so they become victims of the evil spirit rather than victors. Furthermore, the man who is possessed by the evil spirit cannot break through the boundary between the satanic and the divine. The upshot is that Paul is authorized, practitioners of magic unauthorized.

In the riot at Ephesus, confusion summarizes the ambiguous border between paganism and Christianity, no god and God, nothing and greatness (Acts 19:23-43). On its own, this incident does not adjudicate the confusion. But Demetrius's charge that Paul has said that gods made with hands are not gods recalls Paul's words on the Areopagus (17:24). Further, possessions return as a sign of how one moves away from the borderlines. The concern of Demetrius for wealth contrasts with the community of goods of the early Jerusalem congregation and aligns the silversmiths with the rich ruler, Judas, Ananias and Sapphira, and Simon Magus. That is, the ideological perspective does adjudicate the confusion.

In connection with Paul's farewell at Troas, Ernst Haenchen warns against taking the name Eutychus ("Lucky") symbolically (1971:585). But the conjunction of antitheses in Eutychus hardly permit the reader to take it any other way.[5] The story builds on oppositions light/darkness, upper/lower, inside/outside, awake/asleep, life/death. Sitting in the window, Eutychus mediates between outside and inside. The inside is the upper room, a place of light and Paul's speech. The fall from upper to lower parallels the passage from life to death. Paul restores Eutychus to life and goes back up and resumes his speech inside the upper room (cf. Trémel 1980:359-69, Schneider 1982:284-85, Tannehill 1990:249-50). Eutychus marks the point of conjunction between life and death and demonstrates sequentially the movement away from life toward death (tragic) and the movement away from death toward life (comic).

The tacit opposition authorized/unauthorized comes around again in Paul's speech at Miletus (Acts 20:18-35). The implication of his legitimacy lies in the antithesis innocent/guilty and the parallels humility/pride, public/secret, bound/free, suffering/comfort, boldness/trepidation, Paul/ wolves. Again possessions are an index of the direction in which one moves away from the borderlines. Paul's freedom from coveting, his willingness to work, and his commitment to help the weak locate him on the side of divine authorization.

Such authorization vindicates Paul before his detention in Jerusalem. Prophecies of imprisonment (Acts 20:23) and binding (21:11) foreshadow events in Jerusalem so that Paul's location on the side of "bound" in the antithesis bound/free (bound with two chains, 21:33) is a fulfillment legitimated by a prophecy, a legitimation further supported by Paul's location in the antithesis divine will/human will (21:14). Paul is legitimated as an innocent righteous person who suffers for God's sake. The reader knows Paul's genuine location in the antithesis purified/defiled (21:26, 28; 24:7, 18), and that matches his location in the opposition innocent/guilty. Possessions surface again as an index—Paul makes an offering for four men under a vow (21:26), a sign of his righteous innocence.

Paul's autobiographical account in Acts 22 not only expresses a reversal from catastrophe to blessing, but also plays on the oppositions bound/unbound and inside/outside. As a persecutor who binds believers Paul is an insider with the high priest and the sanhedrin (22:4-5). Ironically, he is bound at the very time he tells of binding others (21:33). There is a corresponding shift from inside to outside. When Paul relates that Jesus instructed him to leave Jerusalem and go to Gentiles, the crowd rejects Paul again. Inside with respect to the high priestly party is linked to binding people of the way, outside is joined to being bound and rejected.

An engaging detail is that Paul is unbound when he comes before the sanhedrin in Acts 22:30-23:10. According to the reversal of 22:5, the reader expects Paul to be an outsider with respect to the sanhedrin, and so he is. But in locating himself with the Pharisees in the antitheses despair/hope, death/

resurrection, he claims to be an insider in relation to a part of the sanhedrin. His ambiguity as bound or unbound, outside or inside reflects his ambiguous identification with the sanhedrin. From the ideological perspective of Luke-Acts Paul's agreement with the Pharisees on belief in the resurrection, angels, and spirits is a part of the authorization of Paul. And so the Pharisees explicitly exonerate Paul: "We find nothing wrong in this man" (23:9)—guilt/innocence (Brawley 1987:90).

On three additional occasions Paul's imprisonment is qualified. Felix keeps him in custody but with some liberty (Acts 24:23). Agrippa declares that Paul could have been set free if he had not appealed to Caesar (26:32). In Rome Paul is under house arrest, preaching and teaching quite openly and without hindrance (28:16, 20, 31). He is the point of conjunction between custody and liberty in parallel with guilt/innocence (25:25; 28:17-20), rejection/acceptance (25:24-25; 28:24). His custody corresponds to opposition, his liberty to divine authorization. Further, according to Gamaliel's criterion in 5:39, Paul's limited freedom demonstrates the inability of opponents to put a stop to an undertaking from God.

On a symbolic level the storm on the sea and the snakebite on Malta reinforce the locus of conjunction between catastrophe and blessing, unauthorized and authorized in Paul (Acts 27:1-28:10). The incidents also embrace the parallel antitheses despair/hope, lost/saved, hungry/nourished, misfortune/good fortune, injustice/justice, death/life. The people of Malta express how the shipwreck and snakebite locate Paul on ambiguous borderlines. Initially the incidents combine with Paul's custody to imply divine retribution—catastrophe, unauthorized. But ultimately Paul's survival signifies divine providence and vindicates him—blessing, authorized.

In Acts 28:17-31 Paul anticipates that his location in the antithesis between bound and free will convey to the Roman Jews that he is on the deficient side of catastrophe/blessing and thus also on the deficient side of unauthorized/authorized. The discourse then locates the Roman Jews on the border between catastrophe and blessing, unauthorized and authorized with the parallel antitheses unwilling to hear/willing to hear, unwilling to see/willing to see, unwilling to understand/willing to understand, malady/health, perdition/salvation, unbelieving Jews/believing Gentiles.

Paul argues explicitly that his bondage is no sign that he is unauthorized. Rather, the hope of Israel authorizes him in spite of his bondage. But he also decertifies unbelieving Jews by associating them with their forebears whom the Holy Spirit rebuked through Isaiah. Paul, believing Jews in Rome, and believing Gentiles break away from the borderlines toward authorized and blessing. Unbelieving Jews in Rome move toward unauthorized and catastrophe.

## CONCLUSION

The wide array of oppositions suffusing the discourse maps out a boundary between the antitheses. Variety and diversity create the illusion that the discourse is mapping out multiple boundaries, but in reality the multiplicity is reiteration of but one boundary. Oppositions run over the same tracks and reinforce each other. In other words, variation and substitution allow the discourse to repeat antitheses, and the repetition builds up the symbolic voice in equivalences.

This understanding of the relationship among pairs of opposites bears some resemblance to Claude Lévi-Strauss's analysis of oppositions in mythic structure (1955:428-44). According to him, in myth secondary oppositions mediate between primary opposites that are irreconcilable. For example, agriculture and warfare may replace life and death—irreconcilable opposites for Lévi-Strauss. Hunting mediates between agriculture and warfare. Like agriculture, hunting produces food, like war, it produces death. In hunting, death sustains life, so that life and death no longer appear as opposites.

Elizabeth Struthers Malbon has adapted Lévi-Strauss's theory of mythic mediation of oppositions for the study of spatial order in Mark. She develops a logical hierarchy of geographical antitheses and sees it as corresponding to a mythological hierarchy in which the fundamental antithesis is chaos and order. The fundamental opposition chaos/order is replaced by sea/land, replaced in turn by foreign land/home-land, replaced in turn by Judea/Galilee (1986: esp. 1-14).

Further, Daniel and Aline Patte build on Lévi-Strauss's theory of progressive mediation of a primary opposition. They have developed a method for determining the semantic universe underlying a narrative by matching a series of semiotic squares to a series of interrelated oppositions among narrative states. Their product is the deep values of the semantic universe of the narrative (1978:1-38).

But in spite of some similarities, the analysis of the symbolic voice in this book has to be distinguished from the work of Lévi-Strauss, Malbon, and the Pattes in that it makes no effort to reduce the symbolic voice to another fundamental level. In fact, the diaphoric function of symbol means that the world of the symbol is accessible only through the symbol, and therefore, the symbol is irreducible.

The symbolic voice develops out of antitheses that can replace other antitheses. The variation and substitution form a network of parallels that thematizes the symbolic voice. The text expresses antitheses spatially, socially, chronologically, morally, psychologically, visually, physically, decisionally, transcendently, and existentially. It interchanges outside/inside, hades/heaven, rich/poor, mourning/rejoicing, old/new, present/future, evil/good, darkness/light, unbelief/belief, Satan/God, death/life. Variation and substitution are means of reiterating and reinforcing the symbolic voice rather than replacing irreconcilable antitheses with oppositions that permit mediation.

Moreover, antitheses in the symbolic voice do not fit into a hierarchy. All are fundamental. There is no primary irreconcilable antithesis. On the contrary, the symbolic voice is the mediation between antitheses that correspond to the distance between human beings and God. Thus Gadamer specifies that religious symbols divide what is one and reunite it again. Specifically, religious symbols both sustain the tension between humanity and God and unite humanity with God (1975:70).

Thus, in the temptation of Jesus (Luke 4:1-13), the saying, "One shall not live by bread alone," implies a parallel between life/death and led by the Spirit/led by the devil. The possibility of Jesus being led by the devil preserves the tension between God and human beings. But the fact that he is led by the Spirit is a manifestation of the unity between God and human beings. The existential border between life and death is a reiteration of the transcendent borderline between God and Satan.

Characteristically, human beings are the sites of conjunction between antitheses. That is, the discourse locates human beings on the borderlines, and their orientation away from the borderlines determines whether the turn is tragic or comic. In Luke-Acts, however, a comic turn is theocentric. The God with whom nothing is impossible—no deficiency—enables unfruitful human beings to bear fruit.

Because the comic turn is theocentric, it always has a twist. It is a reversal. Outside becomes inside, death and life reverse. In Luke 7, by his orientation in the antithesis unbelief/belief, a Gentile centurion violates the boundaries of inside/outside. Correspondingly, outside and inside reverse. Not only do characters move from one pole to another, but the poles move. Negative becomes positive, positive becomes negative.

Most especially the resurrection of Jesus is a dramatic reversal. The crucifixion of Jesus is a satanic act (Luke 22:3), the resurrection is a divine act (Acts 2:24). A crucified, resurrected Messiah is the site for the conjunction of the antitheses, death/life, Satan/God. By the hand of God the resurrection is a breakthrough to a new reality, and aligning with the Messiah places human beings on the same threshold, and the God with whom nothing is impossible enables them to break their subjection to the powers of evil in order to participate in the eternal. God turns the world upside down, outside becomes inside, death becomes life (cf. Malbon 1986:130-31, 140).

But if the world is turned inside out, inside is a precarious position. As outside may become inside, so inside may become outside. Not only may a tragic turn be reversed into a comic turn, a comic turn may be reversed into a tragic turn. Freshly franchised insiders may become outsiders. Thus the inside is fraught with irony. Inside has the potential of instability, especially in the face of Jesus' passion and the suffering of disciples.

But where does the reversal of outside/inside stop? Wayne Booth has an intriguing theory that infinite irony insinuates that the universe is absurd, meaning is forever undercut. On the other hand, infinite but somehow stable irony suggests that there is after all a Supreme Ironist. The universe is, therefore, not absurd, only the arrogant human stance of being in the know, the stance of being on the inside (1974:253-69). Because of the instability of inside in Luke-Acts, the reader does not know where to stop an infinite reversal of outside/inside short of a divine bedrock, short of the ultimate subjection of all to the Lordship of Jesus (Acts 2:34).

The ironic reversal of outside/inside hits stability only in God. Because the reversal is theocentric, the tragic turn also always has a twist. Insiders who become outsiders can once again become insiders. A case in point is the captives in Luke 21:20-24. Announcing the destruction of Jerusalem, Jesus predicts that insiders will become outsiders, led captive among the nations. In Luke 4:18 Jesus claims that the Spirit of the Lord has anointed him to proclaim release to the captives (*aichma-lôtos*). The only other place in Luke-Acts where the text employs the same Greek root is in reference to the future captives of Jerusalem (*aichmalôtizô*, 21:24). Are they not among the captives to whom the Lord has sent Jesus to proclaim release?

What goes on in the symbolic voice is also what goes on in the retrospective discovery of the story. Both unveil a double potential for catastrophe/blessing. Therefore, in a state of blessedness there remains a potential for catastrophe. One remains in a state of blessedness only so long as one lives under the dominion of God. Equally, in a state of catastrophe there remains a possibility for blessing. The God with whom nothing is impossible enables barren, unfruitful people to produce fruit. And so human fidelity ultimately is faith in God's fidelity.

The outsider who becomes an insider is not finished with God. God is not finished with the insider who becomes an outsider. God reverses the poles and enables human beings to become a part of the divine reversal. Thus, the possibility of a comic turn from the ambiguous borderlines of the symbolic voice is theocentric and world-encompassing.

# 9

# THE
# CHALLENGE
# OF
# SYNTHESIS

"All the king's horses
And all the king's men
Couldn't put Humpty
together again."

To turn to a synthesis of the foregoing analysis is to raise the paradoxical problem of how the parts fit into the whole—a whole which assumes the unity of Luke-Acts. The meaning of the whole depends upon the function of its parts; the function of the parts depends upon the meaning of the whole. The parts may be dissonant and contradictory. Nevertheless, the goal of interpretation in this book is to arrive at a coherent understanding, an utterance arising out of a unitary point of intersection of the operations of understanding.

A coherent understanding does not eliminate the tensions of the discourse. As an analysis of the symbolic voice shows, from the tensions the reader discovers mediation. Mediation unites what is fragmented. The reader's mediation between antitheses is precisely the way the text assumes wholeness.

The relation of part to whole, however, is not merely a problem of the text but also of life (Gadamer 1975:167, with respect to Schleiermacher), provided there is another postulate that life also has wholeness, meaning. Luke-Acts becomes a hermeneutical problem in that it is a "part" that the reader must fit into the "whole" of existence. There is a tension between the text and modern existence that demands mediation ever anew between a Lucan view of the world and our own. Progressive discovery of what is true in the narrative world (chapter 2) requires a constant revision of expectations. But the hermeneutical problem is that our own existence continues to unfold for us so that we do not know the "whole," and, therefore, the relationship between the biblical text and our own situation also requires a constant revision (Gadamer 1975:175).

If, as Paul Ricoeur claims, the world of God in relation to humanity comes to expression through models that produce figures of God accompanying humanity rather than through descriptive language (see above, p. 39), then God in relation to humanity is available only indirectly. But indirectly, God in relation to humanity is available. The *indirect* availability of the world of God in relation to humanity imposes upon interpreters at least a modicum of humility. They will be unable to claim to uncover the "real" world of the text. But the indirect *availability* of the world of God in relation to humanity gives interpreters a dash of audacity. Glimpsing God in relation to humanity through models that produce figures of God accompanying humanity may motivate us to revise our vision of what it is to live in our everyday world.

After an appeal in chapter 1 for a unitary point of intersection, which is understanding, and after proposing a synthesis that fits the parts into the whole, I have one more defense of partiality. My interpretive synthesis and my hermeneutical appropriation of the text are quite incomplete. I choose a portion of Luke-Acts—the well-known parable of the good Samaritan—to serve as an illustration of the direction of a synthesis and hermeneutical appropriation of the entire text. There is humility in my attempt to give some semblance of synthesis to my own analysis. There is also brashness in my venture to relate the Lucan world to my own.

## REDEFINING GOD IN RELATION TO HUMANITY

To facilitate identifying the voices of the text, Roland Barthes suggests a division of the "smooth" text into lexias, that is, a few words or several sentences that form manageable units of reading (1974:13). This sort of methodology remains analytical, but it maintains the sequential flow of the text, and it sustains a focus on the text. Moreover, such a procedure avoids the fragmentation of the foregoing analysis where the reading under distinct voices falls into separate chapters. The product is a set of interpretative notes following a stream of consciousness.

In the retrospective recovery of the story, Jesus' encounter with the captious lawyer consists of two basic narrative schemata in sequence. The lawyer asks Jesus two separate questions that put him to the test. The need, competence, performance, and sanction stages of each of these tests constitute the narrative schemata. (For the purpose of identifying schemata in the following discussion, I arbitrarily designate some of the schemata with numbers.)

But the narratives are intricate (see above, p. 64). When the first test comes to completion (schema 1), its performance and sanction create a narrative need for the lawyer to understand who his neighbor is. Therefore, the second basic schema (schema 2) is a diverging narrative. But in each of the primary schemata there are also converging narratives. Jesus' first question to the lawyer creates a secondary narrative need for an answer, and the lawyer's answer is a converging narrative (schema 1a) that provides the competence for Jesus to meet the first test (schema 1).

The lawyer's second question creates a new narrative need for Jesus to give an answer (schema 2). The parable of the good Samaritan is another converging narrative that becomes a part of the performance stage of Jesus' answer. Within the parable another narrative schema develops from the need to restore the wounded man (schema 2a). As part of the performance of giving an answer to the lawyer, Jesus asks the lawyer to identify the neighbor in the story. That creates another need for an answer, and the lawyer's identification of the neighbor is another converging narrative (schema 2b). Finally, Jesus' command, "Go and do likewise," sanctions the lawyer's identification of the neighbor but also establishes the need phase for yet another diverging narrative in which the lawyer needs to fulfill Jesus' mandate, a narrative schema that remains incomplete.

**Lexia 1**. *And behold . . .*
Progressive discovery: This introduction provides transition and continuity. It signals a transition from the return of the seventy(-two) from a successful ministry, that is, they bear fruit in terms of Luke 8:15. The seventy(-two) also correspond to babes who see that which is hidden from the wise (10:21, 23). Thus, the introduction also indicates continuity in that a new case implicitly is to be compared with the sending of the seventy(-two). Will the discourse give another example of a babe who sees or of one of the "wise and understanding" (sarcasm) from whom Jesus' relationship to God and his ability to bring others into a relationship with God are hidden (10:21)?

**Lexia 2**. *. . . a lawyer stood up to put him to the test, saying . . .*
Retrospective recovery: In the confrontation of the lawyer with Jesus, the narrative is organized on a polemic principle (Greimas and Cortés 1982: "Polemic," "Narrative Schema").

Characterization: A reliable narrator's internal view (psychological point of view) characterizes the lawyer as an antagonist. A title identifies him as a legal expert. In the context of Luke 10:21 he is one of the wise and understanding. Elsewhere, Luke-Acts associates lawyers with scribes and Pharisees. In Luke 5:17, 21 "teachers of the law" is used interchangeably with "scribes," and in 11:45-52 the woes against the Pharisees apply also to the lawyers.

Progressive discovery: What test will the lawyer concoct? Will Jesus pass the test?

**Lexia 3**. *"Teacher, . . ."*
Characterization: The lawyer characterizes Jesus by epithet. But because his reliability is under question, the reader must make a judgment as to the accuracy of his view. In the thematization of Jesus' character, repetitions reinforce the identity of Jesus as a teacher. Nevertheless, on the level of the phraseo-

logical point of view, the lawyer stops short of calling Jesus "Lord," a title only on the lips of disciples and sincere suppliants. Thus, the term teacher on his lips further characterizes him as duplicitous.

Progressive discovery: The lawyer's identification of Jesus as teacher picks up the developing theme that disciples when fully taught will be like their teacher.

**Lexia 4**. ". . . *what must I do to inherit eternal life?*"

Retrospective recovery: The question creates a narrative need for an answer that will meet the test (schema 1). Further, the lawyer creates a subsidiary narrative need to do something himself, and anticipates Jesus' answer as the competence stage of that subsidiary schema.

Progressive discovery: "What must I do" anticipates a future course of action.

Unformulated text: Nowhere does Luke-Acts define "eternal life." The future tense in the lawyer's question implies joyful, honorable existence beyond death as divine vindication for the righteous. Such a view is prominent in intertestamental Jewish literature. For example, Wisdom 5:15 says, "But the righteous live forever."[1]

Symbolic voice: The lawyer's question "What must I do?" implies deficiency. According to the cultural norms, the antithesis of eternal life is death, punishment. But in this narrative, the antithesis of eternal life is deficiency.

**Lexia 5**. *He said to him, "What is written in the law? How do you read?"*

Retrospective recovery: In the competence phase of the schema of Jesus' test (schema 1), he solicits an answer from the lawyer. His question creates a narrative need for the lawyer to answer (schema 1a).

Progressive discovery: Jesus' response in the form of a question modifies expectations that he will give an answer. He tests the tester, the legal expert.

Characterization: Action shows that Jesus is astute.

Unformulated text: The "law" is the Jewish scriptures.

**Lexia 6**. *"You shall love the Lord your God with all your heart, and with all your soul, and with all your strength, and with all your mind; and your neighbor as yourself."*

Unformulated text: The lawyer conflates Deut 6:5 and Lev 19:18.

Progressive discovery: The conflation is a redefinition of norms. Two commandments become one.[2] Love of neighbor is an integral part of love of God, love of God is incomplete without love of neighbor. Originally anthropocentric ("What must I do?"), the focus becomes theocentric.

Retrospective recovery: The conjunction of the lawyer with OT texts constitutes the competence phase of the narrative schema of the question to him. His answer fulfills the performance stage (schema 1a).

Characterization: From the ideological point of view, the lawyer agrees with the narrator with regard to the value of scripture.

Symbolic voice: Love implies disdain as its opposite, God stands over against Satan, and neighbor is antithetical to enemy.

**Lexia 7**. *And he said to him, "You have answered right; do this, and you will live."*

Retrospective recovery: Jesus sanctions the performance of the lawyer's test (schema 1a). In so doing, he fulfills the performance stage of his own test (schema 1). Thus, the conjunction of Jesus with the lawyer's answer is the competence phase in the schema of Jesus' test. The narrative trajectory expressed in the formula for narrative programs, S1 (S2 ∩ Ov), is as follows.

$$\text{Jesus (Lawyer} \cap \text{Answer)}$$
$$|$$
$$\text{Lawyer (Jesus} \cap \text{Answer)}$$
$$|$$
$$\text{Lawyer (Lawyer} \cap \text{Scriptures)}$$

Jesus' evaluation of the lawyer's answer as "right" sanctions the lawyer's performance, and the agreement implies the lawyer's sanction of Jesus'.

Progressive discovery: Jesus and the lawyer agree on what to do, but Jesus' response is a subtle restatement. The lawyer's term "eternal life" implies future divine vindication beyond death. Jesus does not repeat verbatim the term "eternal life" but says, "Do this and you will live," a variation that insinuates that the experience of living is coexistent with loving God and neighbor—a realized eschatology.[3]

Characterization: The relationship indicated by their agreement mutually characterizes Jesus and the lawyer.

Symbolic voice: Jesus' command "do this" implies deficiency.

**Lexia 8**. *But he, desiring to justify himself, said to Jesus, "And who is my neighbor?"*

Characterization: The narrator gives an inside view of the lawyer's motivation. His desire to show that he was right in testing Jesus originally (Fitzmyer 1985:886) demonstrates that he is still an antagonist. Further, his question shows that he presupposes discriminating among people (Danker 1988:220).

Retrospective recovery: The lawyer's desire to justify himself motivates his action in asking another question. The question establishes a new narrative need for an answer and reestablishes a test for Jesus (schema 2).

Progressive discovery: The question anticipates clarification of the identity of the neighbor.

Symbolic voice: Neighbor stands over against enemy.

**Lexia 9**. *Jesus replied, "A man was going down from Jerusalem to Jericho, and he fell among robbers, who stripped him and beat him, and departed, leaving him half dead."*

Retrospective recovery: The conjunction of Jesus with the knowledge of a story [? (Jesus ∩ story)] is the competence phase in the schema of his answer (schema 2). Telling the story and soliciting the lawyer's conclusion is the performance. Within the parable, the robbery and beating create a narrative need for restoration (schema 2a). The man is conjoined with the undesir-able state of being half dead: bandits (traveler ∩ half dead).

Unformulated text: The road from Jerusalem to Jericho leads through sparsely inhabited wilderness where the danger of surprise attacks constantly menaced travelers (Jeremias 1972: 203). The bandits perhaps are fervent nationalists who finance insurrection by robbery as the equivalent of taxation (Rengstorf 1967:261, Schweizer 1984:186)—a heightening of the irony that the wounded man's compatriots do not act for his well-being.

Characterization: Jesus functions as a parabler.

Symbolic voice: The issue is life or death.

**Lexia 10**. *"Now by chance a priest was going down that road; and when he saw him he passed by on the other side. So likewise a Levite, when he came to the place and saw him, passed by on the other side."*

Retrospective recovery: The priest and the Levite have the potential of becoming agents of the restoration of the man who fell among thieves. Because they fail to come to his aid, howev-er, that potential aborts. The narrative schema remains at the need stage (schema 2a).

Unformulated text: A closed group determined by heredity, ordinary priests ranked lower that the high priestly party but still occupied a place of status (Schrenk 1965:262, Jeremias 1969: 180).[4] Levites were lesser temple functionaries, who, like the priests, were restricted by heredity (Schrenk 1965:262).

Progressive discovery: With respect to genre the story is following a folkloric triad. The triadic structure anticipates a Jewish layperson to follow the priest and the Levite (Jeremias 1972:204).

**Lexia 11**. *"But a Samaritan, as he journeyed, came to where he was; and when he saw him, he had compassion, and went to him and bound up his wounds, pouring on oil and wine; then he set him on his own beast and brought him to an inn, and took care of him. And the next day he took out two denarii and gave them to the innkeeper, saying,*

*'Take care of him; and whatever more you spend, I will repay you when I come back.'"*

Retrospective recovery: The conjunction of the Samaritan with compassion, with the ability to bind wounds, and with the possession of oil, wine, a beast of burden, and money constitutes the competence phase of the narrative schema (schema 2a). Binding the wounds, pouring on wine, transporting the wounded man to the inn, and paying the innkeeper make up the performance stage. The story breaks off without a sanction phase to verify the restoration of the wounded man.

Unformulated text: Historically, Jews regarded Samaritans with varying degrees of disdain. Jews considered Samaritans to be descendants of Assyrian colonists with no legitimate claim to the Jewish heritage. Two major indicators of antipathy are the destruction of the Samaritan temple on Gerizim by John Hyrcanus about 128 BCE and the scattering of bones in the Jerusalem temple by Samaritans during passover about 6-9 CE (Josephus *Ant.* 18.29-30, 13.255-56, Jeremias 1971:90-91).

Progressive discovery: Therefore, the appearance of the Samaritan on the scene initially introduces a further threat for the wounded man (Scott 1981:29). Further, the appearance of the Samaritan radically revises the reader's anticipations of a Jewish layperson following the folkloric triad. Equally radical is the revision of anticipations that the Samaritan will prove to be an enemy. A wounded man finds himself, not altogether happily, receiving help from a despised outsider.

Characterization: An inside view of the Samaritan, from Jesus as narrator, characterizes him as compassionate toward a Jew, a characterization incompatible with cultural norms of the unformulated text (cf. Crossan 1973:64).

Symbolic voice: Outside and inside reverse. The Samaritan who comes to the aid of the wounded man is an outsider. But in effect he swaps places with the priest and Levite, franchised insiders. He is an insider with respect to the wounded man, they are outsiders.

Lexia 12. *"Which of these three, do you think, proved neighbor to the man who fell among the robbers?"*

Retrospective recovery: Jesus' question creates a need for the lawyer to give an answer (schema 2b).

Progressive discovery: The reader anticipates that the answer to Jesus' question will resolve the lawyer's original question, "Who is *my* neighbor?" (10:29, emphasis added).

**Lexia 13**. *He said, "The one who showed mercy on him."*

Retrospective recovery: The conjunction of the lawyer with the parable constitutes the competence phase in the schema for the lawyer to answer Jesus' question (schema 2b). The lawyer's identification of the neighbor is the performance stage in the same schema. But the parable and the lawyer's answer together also constitute the performance stage in the schema in the lawyer's second test of Jesus, that is, the schema in which Jesus must answer the lawyer's question, "Who is my neighbor?" (schema 2). The lawyer's identification of the neighbor in the story is the sanction stage.

Progressive discovery: Rather than force an answer on the lawyer, Jesus creates a narrative world in which the lawyer brings the Samaritan into conjunction with "neighbor" and "showing mercy," a conjunction that is incongruous with cultural norms in his own world (Crossan 1973:64). In the course of the encounter between Jesus and the lawyer, there is a shift in the understanding of "neighbor." When the lawyer cites Lev 19:18, and when he asks, "Who is my neighbor?" the neighbor is the object of the lawyer's love (Luke 10:27, 29). But when the lawyer identifies with the wounded man in the parable and names the Samaritan as the neighbor, the neighbor is the one who extends mercy, and the lawyer identifies with the one who receives it (so Crossan 1973:59).

Symbolic voice: The Samaritan is the point of mediation between love and disdain, outside and inside, life and death, the divine and the satanic. One who shows mercy mediates between enemy and neighbor, no longer irreconcilable antitheses.

**Lexia 14**. *And Jesus said to him, "Go and do likewise."*

Retrospective recovery: Jesus meets the second primary test. He provides an answer to the lawyer's question (schema 2). His command for the lawyer to go and do likewise sanctions the lawyer's answer as the performance in schema 2b. The narrative trajectory in formulaic fashion is:

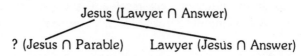

Jesus (Lawyer ∩ Answer)

? (Jesus ∩ Parable)    Lawyer (Jesus ∩ Answer)

Progressive discovery: There is another reversal in the perspective of understanding "neighbor." The command to go and do identifies the lawyer with the Samaritan, and the neighbor once again is the object of mercy.

Symbolic voice: The command to do implies deficiency.

At the point of returning to an overall consideration of the encounter between Jesus and the lawyer, perhaps a personal confession is in order. In earlier stages of my work, I attempted, unsuccessfully, to align narrative programs into principal and polemic axes (see above, pp. 75, 91). The method would not yield the positive results that it had with Jesus' temptation or with the demise of Judas. But as I continued to work, the solution became clear—the lawyer is ambiguous. Unquestionably, the narrator characterizes him as an antagonist intent on testing Jesus.

*Principal*          *Polemical*
Jesus (Lawyer ∩ Life)   Lawyer (Jesus ∩ Test)

But then he becomes a helper aiding Jesus to meet the tests.

(Schema 1)    Jesus (Lawyer ∩ Answer) (10:28)
|
Lawyer  (Jesus ∩ Scripture) (10:27)

(Schema 2)    Jesus (Lawyer ∩ Answer) (10:36-37)
|
Lawyer  (Jesus ∩ Identity of Neighbor) (10:37)

The symbolic voice confirms the ambiguous status of the lawyer. In the cultural norms the opposite of eternal life is destruction or eternal punishment. But in this case life stands over against deficiency. Although he is a duplicitous antagonist, the lawyer stands on the borderline between deficiency and life. His ambiguous location creates an open possibility that he may undergo a transformation from one of the "wise and understanding" to one of the "babes" to whom God gives revelation.

The parable is a narrative within a narrative. But the parable resonates with its Lucan setting. The parable is not merely a case of commendable human kindness. It is a part of the double-pronged vision of loving God and neighbor. Love of neighbor is a part of love of God; love of God is incomplete without love of neighbor. Love of God is so integral to love of neighbor, love of neighbor so integral to love of God, that the revision of the character of the Samaritan is also a revision of the character of God.

By E. M. Forster's criteria, God is a flat character who undergoes no change (1954:105-106). But God repeatedly acts in surprising ways that reverse expectations. In the context of the double commandment, the Samaritan's action derives from love of God—a striking theological reversal from Jewish cultural norms. Therefore, the reader's perception of God undergoes dramatic revision. Thus, the world of God in relation to humanity comes to expression in a model that produces figures of God in relation to humanity (Ricoeur 1977:21-27, 1979:215-27, see above, p. 39). In the theocentric orientation of his encounter with the lawyer, Jesus creates a literary world that challenges the lawyer's own world. Dare he venture the bizarre gamble that the world of the parable alters his own?

In 1983 Roman Catholic Bishop Francis Stafford, now Archbishop of the Archdiocese of Denver, spoke at the Protestant seminary where I teach. By chance his visit coincided with our celebration of the five hundredth anniversary of the birth of Martin Luther. Bishop Stafford began his address by commending us for our celebration of Luther's birth. He confided that the celebration of Luther's birth had been an occasion for him to read Luther. He then told us that in his reading he had been captivated by Luther's question: "What can I do to please God?" "I think I know," Bishop Stafford said.

At that point, I have personal knowledge that at least one of his auditors thought skeptically that he had misunderstood Luther. I thought that whereas Luther had abandoned his anthropocentric concern with himself in his experience of God's

grace, Bishop Stafford had reverted to the early Luther's an-
thropocentricity. "I think I know," he said, "God be merciful to
me a sinner!" Bishop Stafford shifted the anthropocentric
question into its theocentric counterpart in a way that is similar
to what goes on in the encounter between Jesus and the lawyer. The lawyer asks an anthropocentric question, "What must
I do?" But when Jesus' reciprocal question forces him to provide his own answer, he shifts to a theocentric affirmation:
"You shall love the Lord your God with all . . . and your
neighbor as yourself."

If analysis fragments the text, synthesis reunites it. But the
synthesis is not merely a reunion of the parts of the text but also
a reunion of the text with the interpreter. The problem of
synthesis is ultimately how interpreters integrate the experience
of the text into their own view of the world. The part is known
in the context of the whole not only textually but also in the
context of human life (Gadamer 1975:167, in a discussion on
Schleiermacher). In chapter 1 I suggested three particular ways,
not to exclude others, in which interpreters may integrate the
world of the text into their own world—analogy, identification
with characters, and extension of the story. Some of all of these
have occurred in my own reading of Luke 10:25-37. (There are
surely additional ways in which I correlate the world of the text
to my own that escape my analysis.)

Never do I read the parable of the good Samaritan without
vivid recall of an analogous personal experience. The last week
of December, 1966, when I was teaching in a theological
seminary in Mexico, an adjunct professor, my wife, our infant
daughter, and I were driving through the rugged mountains of
the Sierra Madre Oriente from Valles to Mexico City, a trip that
would take us all night.

We began driving late on a Sunday evening in order to
arrive in Mexico City early Monday morning. Around midnight
we were driving through a section of Mexico populated by
indigenous Huastecas. I reveal a prejudice that impinged upon
me that night by relating that I had learned by rumor and
personal observation that a large number of the male popula-
tion of Huastecas habitually became intoxicated on Sundays.

Largely for that reason I was already quite wary when I slowly negotiated a curve and began to climb a steep incline in dense fog. Ahead there appeared in the dense fog what I supposed was a log in the road. At the last instant before we passed, I realized that it was a man, likely dead. But that I do not know, because I did not stop. I put on brakes to stop. But the adjunct professor said, "Let's get out of here." I thought at first that he had in fact seen some bandits. But then I realized he was afraid as I myself was. "Have you never heard of the parable of the good Samaritan?" I asked. "Yes," he said, "but let's get out of here." And we did. Never do I read Luke 10:25-37 without identifying with the priest and the Levite who failed to become agents of restoration for the man who fell among thieves and with the lawyer who presumed to discriminate among people.

I can appeal that there were extenuating circumstances on my trip to Mexico City, some stemming from my own prejudicial fear, perhaps not unfounded. But I have no reason to assume that the Samaritan was exempt from extenuating circumstances—nationalistic, racial, social, religious. The lawyer's identification of Jesus as "teacher" fits into the development in the progressive discovery of the theme that disciples will be like their teacher. Already in Luke 9:23-24 that means taking up their cross and losing their lives for Jesus' sake. But the disciples are fully taught only after the resurrection when Jesus opens their minds to understand the scriptures (24:45-46). Specifically, they understand the necessity of the Christ to suffer. Then, although they are within the providential care of God, they too suffer in Acts. That is to say, to live under the dominion of God's love is for the disciples to give themselves sacrificially without banking on their own terms of security.

In this connection, I recall another event in Mexico. On September 18, 1966, my wife, our infant daughter, and I were driving in Cuernavaca in midday, when we witnessed a garbage truck hit two little girls and leave the scene of the accident. This time we took the two girls and their mothers to the hospital. But that, I know all too well, was under my own terms of security. And the world of Luke-Acts challenges my devices to modify love of God and neighbor with my own terms of security.

If, however, I identify only with the priest and the Levite, I run the danger of making them negative role models and thus also the hazard of an anthropocentric hermeneutic—neither theocentric nor world-encompassing. As a methodological reminder, I recall James Sanders's strategy of identifying with all the characters. That is possible for me through another graphic reminiscence.

In the late 40s, the only world my twin brother and I had known, at the age of seven, was the west side of Charlotte, North Carolina. The war was over, but we Americans had cultivated hostilities against the Germans and the Japanese, and a gang of teenagers in my community began to redirect some of those warring hostilities toward Hoskins, the next neighborhood on the other side of the P & N railroad tracks. My brother and I watched with both envy and relief as the band of teenagers began to prepare for a gang war with Hoskins, which rumors held to be imminent. We were envious because we were far too young to take on this alleged mantle of manhood. But we were also relieved, because there was something altogether too serious about the arsenal of homemade weapons that began to appear, stuck into pockets and tucked under shirts, sometimes carelessly hidden in order to be seen—monstrously heavy bolts about 6 inches long, 5/8 of an inch thick, screwed down into about ten inches of flexible garden hose, clubs carved out of broken baseball bats, switchblades, brass knuckles, and one zip gun. It had to be done, the most eager ones argued, because rumor had it that the Hoskins boys had a head start—my first memory of an arms race.

Curiously adventuresome, one day during those times of heightened tensions my twin brother and I walked the ambiguous borderline between the two neighborhoods. We took a hike down the middle of the P & N railroad tracks. When we were within 100 yards of getting back onto our own turf, the tracks cut between some banks high on each side. That is when those Hoskins boys zoomed down the banks, eight of them, all older, bigger, faster, shouting and chasing us, and one of them was carrying a 22 rifle. My brother and I bolted with sheer fear, I a few yards ahead, hoping desperately that we could make it to safe territory. But my brother's screams brought me to a halt. He was down, fallen on a track meant only for a train to run on. I wheeled around and saw the Hoskins boys grab my brother. My heart pounded. Hysterical sobs convulsed my chest. And I stood there frozen between running away and turning back to help.

In my vivid reminiscence of that tension, when I read Jesus' parable, I am unable to split it into good guys against the bad. Whose face in the story is mine? Priest's? Levite's? Samaritan's? Frozen between running away and turning back to help my brother, I try on the mask of all three.

Some of the tensions of our modern world may correspond. The Soviet Union and the United States have missiles with nuclear warheads pointing toward each other. Fanatical Muslims declare that they are prepared for *jihad* against the great American infidel. Mobsters convey drugs to our streets promising quick highs, producing wasted Americans. *Fortune* magazine publishes a celebrated list of the 400 richest citizens of a land where 3 million blear-eyed homeless people and 10 million gaunt hungry people lie, as if it were, at our roadsides half dead. Our world is, so to speak, threatened by Hoskins boys.

In face of the threats and dilemmas that we face, we may sense that we stand on ambiguous borderlines similar to the tension that I felt between running away and turning back to help my brother. How could I run away? They had my brother. But how could I go back? There were eight of them, older, bigger, faster, and one of them had a gun. Then my worst fears began to be realized when I saw the biggest one of all lay his hands on my brother. But the biggest one of all picked up my brother, brushed off his clothes, picked cinders out of his elbows, held him in his arms, and comforted him so that he would not cry.

When we stand in the tension between running away and turning back to help, we may suppose that God's grace is available only if we do turn back. At that moment we may be prime candidates to receive the grace of God. When I stand in the tension between running away and turning back to help, I not only try on the mask of the priest, the Levite, and the

Samaritan. I also put on the face of the wounded man lying in the ditch. Frozen between running away and turning back to help, I become a victim who may receive the grace of God from Hoskins boys, so to speak—from the most unlikely.

In the traditional allegorical interpretation of the parable, the Samaritan lost his identity and became a cipher for Jesus. I have suggested that such a move lacks genuine correspondence to the text because it substitutes a secondary text for the original. Nevertheless, there are lines of correspondence between Jesus and the Samaritan. Jesus is an unlikely messianic figure. Incredibly, the grace of God comes through the agency of a Galilean Jew who was crucified. To see Jesus as Messiah is, therefore, to see messianism turned on its head. It is likewise to see the God of the Messiah with an inverted vision. Such a God turns our world upside down. The wise and understanding become babes.

# NOTES

## NOTES TO CHAPTER 1
### THE CHALLENGE OF ANALYSIS

1. On the complexity of a literary work and the dangers of distortion from analytical procedures that overemphasize or underemphasize, see Ingarden 1973:277, 315-17, 362.

2. Tolbert (1979:93-114) attempts a revival of allegory using psychoanalytic theory to provide equivalents for the parable of the prodigal son. This too rewrites the text.

3. Ingarden (1973:85, 315-17) theorizes that the "idea" of a literary work of art is clarified and conceptually determined by analysis and then, ultimately, synthesis. "The 'idea' of the literary work of art is a 'demonstrated,' synthetic, essential complex of mutually modulated, aesthetically valent qualities which is brought to concrete appearance either in the work or by means of it" (85).

4. The same surface structure may have the potential for different deep structures. Cf. Rimmon-Kenan 1983:10.

5. See a similar argument in Sternberg 1985:6-23.

6. On the validity of intentions embodied in the text, see Sternberg 1985:8-9.

7. While Wink interprets the admonitions on the level of the historical Jesus, his interpretation also holds for the context in Luke.

8. Schweizer (1984:61) translates "in [the world] of my Father."

9. The promise that Jesus will come in a manner comparable to his ascension (Acts 1:11) is another external prolepsis. On prolepsis and analepsis, see Genette 1980:33-85.

10. Rimmon-Kenan (1983:37-38) expands Barthes's categories similarly. Her terms *world view*, *manner of speech*, and *actions* correspond closely to what I mean by *evaluation*, *information*, and *actions*.

11. Ricoeur (1977:5) suggests that biblical narrative designates God as one of the personages signified by the narration itself. Cf. Tannehill 1986:29.

12. I borrow the imagery from Martin 1986:164.

13. I follow Uspensky extensively in my explainations of points of view.

14. Different perspectives may mutually reinforce each other, but they may also conflict. Ordinarily, the dominant point of view establishes the norms for evaluation and others are subordinate to it. Cf. Rimmon-Kenan 1983:81-82.

15. This raises the issue of the genre of Luke-Acts. On the view that Luke writes as a hellenistic historian, see Gasque 1975; Aejmelaeus 1987:16-31. On the debate about the genre of Luke-Acts, see Talbert 1974: esp. 125-35; Smith 1971:174-99; Barr and Wentling 1984:63-80; Pervo 1987. Talbert (1988:53-7) argues that focus on personages indicates that Luke-Acts corresponds to ancient biography. In response, Moessner (1988b:75-84) argues that Luke-Acts focuses on God rather than on personages, and thus, that Luke-Acts corresponds to hellenistic historiography. Whatever the genre, Luke-Acts makes claims for the independent reality of its literary world (Luke 1:4). Cf. Auerbach 1953:15.

16. For Aejmelaeus, the exhortation is for the readers to imitate Paul in the face of Gnostic or pre-Gnostic opposition. Cf. Lambrecht 1979:309, 316-18.

17. Schneider (1982:293) divides the speech into two parts, the first having to do with Paul and his behavior, the second offering direct paraenesis.

18. On closure and openness in Luke-Acts, see Tannehill 1986: 298-301; 1990:353-57; Parsons 1987:69-111.


# NOTES TO CHAPTER 2
## PROGRESSIVE DISCOVERY:
## TRUTH IN THE NARRATIVE WORLD

1. This paragraph is based on my distillation of Ricoeur 1977:21-27 and 1979:215-27. Cf. Ricoeur 1976:37, and Petersen 1978:39-40.

2. Here I am largely following Völkel 1973-74:293-95. Cf. Tannehill 1986:11-12.

3. Tannehill (1990:146-47) explores the possibility that Peter's mission to Cornelius and the preaching to Gentiles in Antioch occurred during the same period of time.

4. In my opinion there is a more positive response of many in Israel to God's salvation than Tannehill allows.

5. Moessner's appeal to Isaiah's suffering servant and the Deuteronomistic view of the rejection of the prophets seems to me to depend too heavily on texts outside Luke-Acts.

6. Their discussion is indirect discourse in the optative corresponding to the potential optative in the direct discourse denoting what is thought but not yet put into practice. Blass, Debrunner, Funk § 386(1).

7. Conzelmann (1961:49-50) sees this incident as ". . . of fundamental importance for the Gentile mission."

8. Though quite overdone in my opinion, Radl (1975) describes extensive parallels between the sufferings of Jesus and Paul.

# NOTES TO CHAPTER 3
## RETROSPECTIVE DISCOVERY:
## LUKE

1.   Forster (1927:130) sees causality as essential to plot. While modern theorists may not demand strict causality, a logic of relationships exists among actions in a plot. Cf. Chatman 1978:47, 53.

2.   On conventional assumptions as the context for interpretation, see Fish 1980:vii, 10-14, and passim.

3.   Calloud (1976:28) calls the competence, performance, and sanction stages qualifying, main, and glorifying tests respectively.

4.   The discussion and the schematic representation depend heavily upon Patte and Patte 1978:24-26. They use the term "narrative hierarchy" to refer to the narrative trajectory.

5.   Miscall (1986:xx-xxi) critiques structuralism for granting primacy to one pole of oppositions and considering the other irrelevant. Against Miscall, structural analysis helps to confirm the value of the polemical pole. But the investment of a narrative in overcoming a lack or need does establish one pole as primary.

6.   Talbert approaches the text from a perspective of a principle of promise/fulfillment. I arrive at similar conclusions by analyzing the narrative need. In narrative schemata, prediction creates narrative need for fulfillment.

7.   For a thoroughgoing debate on the interpretation of Luke 4:16-30 and for a close analysis of logic of the argument, see Brawley 1987:6-27.

8.   On the background of an eschatological Jubilee, see Sanders 1975:88, 91, and Strobel 1972:42-44.

9.   On the literary relationship between the transfiguration and the journey to Jerusalem, see Moessner 1989:66-70, 133.

10. On the Lucan dramatic episode style as it is manifested in Acts, see Plümacher 1972:80-136.

11. Lohfink (1975:17-31) shows how Luke 1-2 anticipates the gathering and sifting of God's people. Surprisingly, Lohfink attends little to the prediction of John the Baptist in Luke 3:17.

# NOTES TO CHAPTER 4
## RETROSPECTIVE RECOVERY:
## ACTS

1.   On the repetition of themes and literary patterns, see Talbert 1974.

2.   Jervell (1972:79) shows that the promise that the twelve will judge Israel is the legacy of Jesus' farewell address.

3. Although this discussion of Judas reflects my own analysis, I follow extensively Panier 1981a:20-43, and Panier 1981b:111-122. Panier and J. Giroud have written a series of articles on the narrative structure of Acts in *Sémiotique et Bible* from 1982-85.

4. Haenchen (1971:99-100) and L. T. Johnson (1977:203-204) note the relationship between Barnabas and the apostles as a factor in his role in the story of Paul. But the same logic pertains here. Cf. Haenchen 1971:366.

5. For example, Tannehill (1985:69-85) argues that Acts ends with the hope of the fulfillment of the promises to Israel pathetically crushed. But he fails to assess adequately belief as well as unbelief at the end of Acts.

6. Haenchen (1971:723), Conzelmann (1987:227), Sanders (1984:108), and Pesch (1986:2.309) argue that Acts 28:24 does not actually mean that some Roman Jews believe. That is a direct contradiction of the text as the antithesis between *epeithonto* and *êpistoun* shows.

7. Haenchen (1971:722) points out that *egô* forms the theme of Paul's speech. Dupont (1979:372) argues that Acts 28:17ff. turns from Paul to the hope of Israel. But against Dupont 28:30-31 shift squarely back to Paul.

8. In Acts 8:21 Peter warns Simon that he has forfeited his *klêros*. Foerster (1965:759-60) shows that in the LXX *klêros* and *klêronomia* coincide when they refer to the land of Canaan as a God-given possession. The way *klêros* functions in Acts also suggests its connection with the heritage of Israel.

# NOTES TO CHAPTER 5
## CHARACTERIZATION:
## GOD AND JESUS

1. In a forthcoming Ph.D. dissertation, D. Gowler (Southern Baptist Theological Seminary) helpfully surveys this development.

2. Some structuralists recognize the interplay between character and action. Cf. Calloud 1976:13; Barthes 1975:252.

3. On prolepsis and analepsis, see Genette 1980:33-85.

On the indirect function of epithets and their relation to action and evaluation, see Sternberg 1987:331, 342-44, 476.

On relational epithets, see Alter 1981:126-27.

4. On repetition with variation and shifts in perspective and judgment, see Sternberg 1987:390-428, 438-39.

5. God thus fits Northrop Frye's category of a divine hero who is superior both to others and to the environment (1957:33).

6. A character can be individualized only if set in a particular time and place (Watt 1961:68).

7.   Schweizer (1984:345) refers to the connection between Son of man and the betrayal as a fixed idiom.

8.   Dawsey (1986:6) groups together characters from the multitudes who address Jesus as "teacher" and classifies them as mildly curious, mildly antagonistic, and mildly respectful.

9.   These are cases of dramatic irony that invite the reader to compare Jesus and his counterparts. Cf. Booth 1974:63.

10.   Jesus' prayer for the forgiveness of his executors does not appear in some early prominent MSS from a wide geographical distribution.

## NOTES TO CHAPTER 6
## CHARACTERIZATION:
## PETER AND PAUL

1.   Luke 4:44 summarizes Jesus' activity as centered in Judea and creates problems for a strict geographical sequence. Conzelmann (1961:38-43) argues that for Luke Capernaum is not located by the lake. True, the text never specifies such a location, but Luke 4:38 and 5:1 assume it.

2.   Peter's occupation as a fisherman associates him with the class of manual laborers and traders—rather low in the social order. Cf. Wuellner 1962:338-39.

3.   As a qualifier for Luke 6:14, Luke 6:48 puts restraints on attempts to interpret Luke in light of Matt 16:17 (as does Cullmann 1962) or in light of Simon's founding of the Jewish and Gentile missions (as does Schneider 1976:204).

4.   On construing *adelphos* in the plural as an inclusive term, see Danker 1988:351-52; Bauer, Arndt, Ginrich, and Danker 1979:16.

5.   Dillon (1978:66-67) argues that Peter's marveling is not perplexity but the appropriate human reaction to the messianic *mysterium*. But Peter's reaction is not merely to what had happened but perplexity *within himself*.

6.   For Burchard (1970:118-25) and Löning (1973:11-18) the discrepancies distinguish tradition from redaction.

7.   I cannot agree with Lewycky that Paul turns to Gentiles because Jews refuse him hospitality.

8.   Negative evaluations assist the reader in fixing the character. See Iser 1974:48.

9.   Many commentators fail to recognize Tertullus as unreliable and inaccurately assess his characterization of Paul. Recently, Robinson 1987:476.

10.   The author molds the reader to judge character by establishing norms (Booth 1961:182-83). Redundancy provides a corrective against errors of communication (Iser 1978:94).

11. E.g., Acts 9:22, 29; 13:45; 15:39; 17:2 (iterative), 17; 18:4; 19:9.

12. Acts 13:2, 4; 16:6-10; 19:2; 20:22. Cf. 22:21; 23:11; 27:24-24.

13. Conzelmann (1987:72) declares that Paul's blindness is not punishment. Contextually, however, it aligns with the inability of Zechariah to speak (Luke 1:20), the deaths of Ananias and Sapphira (Acts 5:1-10), and the blindness of Elymas (13:11).

14. From blindness to sight is stereotypical conversion language (Gaventa 1986:86-87).

15. Acts 13:44, 48, 49; 14:3, 25; 15:35; 16:6, 32; 17:11, 13; 18:5, 11; 19:10, 20; 20:2, 7.

16. Schille (1979:14, 22) views Paul as representative of the five Antiochenes (Acts 13:1). The Antiochenes function to legitimate Paul's mission, but never does Paul function as their representative.

17. On status and profession as marks of individuation, see Berlin 1983:36.

18. For the opinion that Paul is a model for conversion, see Schille 1979:31; S. Wilson 1976:399.

19. Roloff (1965:206) notes that what Ananias does he does as an agent of Christ rather than as an agent of the church.

20. A corrective on the thesis of Klein (1961) that Paul is subordinated to the apostles to protect against gnostic appropriation of Paul and on the thesis of Burchard (1970) that Paul is not subordinate to the twelve but independently equal.

## NOTES TO CHAPTER 7
### SHARED PRESUMPTIONS
### AND THE UNFORMULATED TEXT

1. Hermogenes uses *diêgêsis* to refer to the history of Herodotus and the *suggraphê* of Thucydides, but *diêgêma* to speak of *to kata Ariôna* and *to kata Alkaiôna.*, see Güttgemanns 1983:14-15. Güttgemanns discovers at least five technical terms from ancient rhetoric in the prologue to Luke. *Diêgêsis* refers to a comprehensive, complex narrative, *diêgêma* to a narrative of an episode.

2. This paragraph depends heavily on Vollenweiden.

3. My discussion of Genesis 37-39 relies heavily on Alter.

## NOTES TO CHAPTER 8
### AMBIGUOUS BORDERS:
### THE SYMBOLIC VOICE

1. On the symbolic voice, see Barthes 1974:17-18, 21, 27, 65-66.

2. According to Barthes (1974:28, 65-66) the human body is frequently the site where opposites meet.

3.   In antiquity prison was otherwise ordinarily used as a place of detention before trial or execution or as punishment for minor offenses. Severe offenses usually incurred execution (Greenberg 1962:892, Fitzmyer 1981:532, Tannehill 1986:65).

4.   Wilson doubts that the apostolic decree derives from Lev 17-18.

5.   Compare the explicit attention to the symbolic character of the name Barnabas, for example (Acts 4:36).

## NOTES TO CHAPTER 9
### THE CHALLENGE OF SYNTHESIS

1.   Cf. 1 Enoch 103:3-4, Pss. Sol. 3:12; 13:11; 14:10; 15:13, T. Benj. 10:7-8, Bertram 1964:853-54, Bultmann 1964:865-66, Nickelsburg 1962:349.

2.   On whether or not there is a pre-Christian conflation of the two commands, see Fitzmyer 1985:879.

3.   The progressive discovery of the present reality of salvation undergoes further development in Luke-Acts (see, e.g., Luke 19:9, cf. Fitzmyer 1981:222).

4.   The social class of ordinary priests is high enough for Josephus to use his priestly genealogy to advance his own status (*Life* 1-2).

# BIBLIOGRAPHY

Aalen, Sverre. 1961-62. "'Reign' and 'House' in the Kingdom of God in the Gospels." *New Testament Studies* 8:215-40.

Adams, David. 1979. "The Suffering of Paul and the Dynamics of Luke-Acts." Ph.D. dissertation, Yale Univ.

Aejmelaeus, Lars. 1987. *Der Rezeption der Paulusbriefe in der Miletrede (Apg 20:18-35).* Helsinki: Suomalainen Tiedeakatemia.

Alter, Robert. 1981. *The Art of Biblical Narrative.* New York: Basic Books.

Auerbach, Erich. 1953. *Mimesis: The Representation of Reality in Western Literature.* Princeton: Princeton Univ.

Aune, David. 1987. *The New Testament in Its Literary Environment.* Philadelphia: Westminster.

Barr, David & Wentling, Judith. 1984. "The Conventions of Classical Biography and the Genre of Luke-Acts: A Preliminary Study." In *Luke-Acts: New Perspectives from the Society of Biblical Literature Seminar,* ed. Charles Talbert. New York: Crossroad.

Barr, James. 1980. *The Scope and Authority of the Bible.* Philadelphia: Westminster.

Barthes, Roland. 1975. "An Introduction to the Structural Analysis of Narrative." *New Literary History* 6:237-72.

—— 1986. *S/Z.* New York: Hill & Wang.

Berggren, Douglas. 1962-63. "The Use and Abuse of Metaphor." *Review of Metaphysics* 16:237-58, 450-72.

Berlin, Adele. 1983. *Poetics and Interpretation of Biblical Narrative.* Sheffield: Almond.

Bertram, G. 1964. *"zaô."* *Theological Dictionary of the New Testament* 2:851-54.

Blass, F. & Debrunner, A. 1961. *A Greek Grammar of the New Testament and Other Early Christian Literature,* translation and revision by Robert Funk incorporating supplementary notes of A. Debrunner. Chicago: Univ. of Chicago.

Boers, Hendrikus. 1985. "Polarities at the Roots of New Testament Thought: Methodological Considerations." In *Perspectives on the New Testament; Essays in Honor of Frank Stagg,* ed. Charles Talbert. Macon, GA: Mercer Univ.

Booth, Wayne. 1961. *The Rhetoric of Fiction.* Chicago: Univ. of Chicago.

—— 1974. *A Rhetoric of Irony.* Chicago: Univ. of Chicago.

Brawley, Robert. 1984. "Paul in Acts: Lucan Apology and Conciliation." In *Luke-Acts: New Perspectives from the Society of Biblical Literature Seminar,* ed. Charles Talbert. New York: Crossroad.

—— 1987. *Luke-Acts and the Jews: Conflict, Apology, and Concilia-tion.* Atlanta: Scholars.

Bremond, Claude. . "Morphology of the French Folktale." *Semiotica* 2:248-76.

Brill, Earl. 1966. "Sex Is Dead!" *Christian Century* 83:957-59.

Brook, Peter. 1984. *Reading for the Plot: Design and Intention in Narrative.* New York: Alfred A. Knopf.

Brown, Raymond. 1977. *The Birth of the Messiah: A Commentary on the Infancy Narratives in Matthew and Luke.* Garden City, NJ: Doubleday.

Brown, Robert McAfee. 1984. *Unexpected News: Reading the Bible with Third World Eyes.* Philadelphia: Westminster.

Bultmann, Rudolf. 1964. "*zaô.*" *Theological Dictionary of the New Testament* 2:849-51, 855-72.

Burchard, Christoph. 1970. *Der dreizehnte Zeuge: Traditions- und kompositionsgeschichtliche Untersuchungen zu Lukas' Darstel-lung der Frühzeit des Paulus.* Göttingen: Vandenhoeck & Ru-precht.

Burnett, Fred. 1988. "Exposing the Implied Author in Matthew: The Characterization of God as Father." Unpublished paper pre-sented to the Literary Aspects of the Gospels and Acts Group of the Society of Biblical Literature.

Cadbury, Henry. 1933. *The Beginnings of Christianity,* vol. 4, ed. F. J. Foakes Jackson & Kirsopp Lake. London: Macmillan.

—— 1956-67. "'We' and 'I' Passages in Luke-Acts." *New Testament Studies* 3:128-32.

Calloud, Jean. 1976. *Structural Analysis of Narrative.* Philadelphia: Fortress.

Chatman, Seymour. 1978. *Story and Discourse: Narrative Structure in Fiction and Film.* Ithaca: Cornell Univ.

Conzelmann, Hans. 1961. *The Theology of St. Luke.* New York: Harper & Row.

—— 1987. *Acts of the Apostles.* Philadelphia: Fortress.

Crane, R. S. 1961. "The Concept of the Plot." In *Approaches to the Novel: Material for a Poetics,* ed. R. Scholes. San Francisco: Chandler.

Crossan, John Dominic. 1973. *In Parables: The Challenge of the Historical Jesus.* New York: Harper & Row.

Culler, Jonathan. 1975. *Structuralist Poetics: Structuralism, Linguistics and the Study of Literature.* Ithaca: Cornell Univ.

Cullmann,. Oscar. 1962. *Peter: Disciple, Apostle, Martyr.* Philadelphia: Westminster.

—— 1963. *The Christology of the New Testament.* Philadelphia: Westminster.

Dahl, Nils. 1957-58. "'A People for His Name' (Acts XV.14)." *New Testament Studies* 4:319-27.

Damrosch, David. 1987. *The Narrative Covenant: Transformation of Genre in the Growth of Biblical Literature.* San Francisco: Harper & Row.

Danker, Frederick. 1988. *Jesus and the New Age: A Commentary on St. Luke's Gospel.* Philadelphia: Fortress.

Dawsey, James. 1986. *The Lukan Voice: Confusion and Irony in the Gospel of Luke.* Macon, GA: Mercer Univ.

Dibelius, Martin. 1956. *Studies in the Acts of the Apostles.* London: SCM.

Dillon, Richard. 1978. *From Eye-Witnesses to Ministers of the Word: Tradition and Composition in Luke 24.* Rome: Biblical Institute.

Docherty, Thomas. 1983. *Reading (Absent) Character: Towards a Theory of Characterization in Fiction.* Oxford: Clarendon.

Drexler, Hans. 1968. "Die grosse Sünderin: Lucas 7.36-50." *Zeitschrift für die neutestamentliche Wissenschaft* 59:159-73.

Drury, John. 1987. "Luke." In *The Literary Guide to the Bible*, ed. Robert Alter & Frank Kermode. Cambridge: Harvard Univ.

Dunning, Al. 1988. "Biblical All-Stars Abound." *Memphis Commercial Appeal*, Dec. 20:D1.

Dupont, Jaques. 1959-60. "Le salut des gentils et la signification théologique du Livre des Actes." *New Testament Studies* 6:132-55.

—— 1979. "La conclusion des Actes et son rapport a l'ensemble de l'ouvrage de Luc." In *Les Actes des Apôtres: Traditions, rédaction, théologie*, ed. J. Kremer. Gembloux: Duculot.

Elliott, John. 1981. *A Home for the Homeless: A Sociological Exegesis of 1 Peter, Its Situation and Strategy.* Philadelphia: Fortress.

Esler, Philip. 1987. *Community and Gospel in Luke-Acts: The Social and Political Motivations of Lucan Theology.* Cambridge: Cambridge Univ.

Fiorenza, Elisabeth Schüssler. 1983. *In Memory of Her: A Feminist Theological Reconstruction of Christian Origins.* New York: Crossroad.

Fischel, H. 1946-47. "Martyr and Prophet (A Study in Jewish Literature)." *Jewish Quarterly Review* 37:245-280, 363-86.

Fish, Stanley. 1980. *Is There a Text in This Class? The Authority of Interpretive Communities.* Cambridge: Harvard Univ.

Fitzmyer, Joseph. 1981. *The Gospel According to Luke I-IX: Introduction, Translation, and Notes.* Garden City, NY: Doubleday.

—— 1985. *The Gospel According to Luke X-XXIV: Introduction, Translation, and Notes.* Garden City, NY: Doubleday.

Foerster, Werner. 1964. "daimôn," "diabolos." *Theological Dictionary of the New Testament* 2:1-20, 75-81.

—— 1965. "klêros," "kurios." *Theological Dictionary of the New Testament* 3:758-69, 1038-58, 1081-98.

Forster, E. M. 1927. *Aspects of the Novel.* New York: Harcourt, Brace, & World.

Frye, Northrop. 1972. "The Critical Path: An Essay on the Social Context of Literary Criticism." In *In Search of Literary Theory*, ed. Morton Bloomfield. Ithaca: Cornell Univ.

Funk, Robert. 1988. *The Poetics of Biblical Narrative.* Sonoma, CA: Polebridge.

Gadamer, Hans-Georg. 1975. *Truth and Method.* New York: Continuum.

Gager, John. 1975. *Kingdom and Community: The Social World of Early Christianity.* Englewood Cliffs, NJ: Prentice-Hall.

Gasque, Ward. 1975. *A History of the Criticism of the Acts of the Apostles.* Grand Rapids: Eerdmans.

Gaventa, Beverly Roberts. 1985. "The Overthrown Enemy: Luke's Portrait of Paul." *Society of Biblical Literature Seminar Papers*, ed. Kent Richards. Atlanta: Scholars.

—— 1986. *From Darkness to Light: Aspects of Conversion in the New Testament.* Philadelphia: Fortress.

—— 1988. "Toward a Theology of Acts: Reading and Rereading." *Interpretation* 42:146-57.

Genette, Gérard. 1980. *Narrative Discourse: An Essay in Method.* Ithaca: Cornell Univ.

González, Justo & González, Catherine. 1980. *Liberation Preaching: The Pulpit and the Oppressed.* Nashville: Abingdon.

Gowler, David. Forthcoming. Ph.D. dissertation. Southern Baptist Theological Seminary.

Greenberg, M. 1962. "Prison." *The Interpreter's Dictionary of the Bible* 3:891-92.

Greenwood, David. 1985. *Structuralism and the Biblical Text.* New York: Mouton.

Greimas, A. & Cortés, J. 1982. *Semiotics and Language: An Analytical Dictionary.* Bloomington: Indiana Univ.

Grenfell, B. & Hunt, A., eds. 1897. *New Classical Fragments and Other Greek and Latin Papyri.* Oxford: Clarendon.

Gros Louis, Kenneth R. R. 1982. "Some Methodological Considerations." In *Literary Interpretations of Biblical Narratives*, vol. 2, ed. Gros Louis with J. Ackerman. Nashville: Abingdon.

Grundmann, W. 1964. "*angelos.*" *Theological Dictionary of the New Testament* 1:74-76.

Güttgemanns. 1983. "In welchem Sinne ist Lukas 'Historiker'? Die Beziehungen von Luk 1,1-4 und Papias zur antiken Rhetorik." *Linguistica Biblica* 54:9-26.

Hadas, Moses & Smith, Morton. 1965. *Heroes and Gods: Spiritual Biographies in Antiquity.* New York: Harper & Row.

Haenchen, Ernst. 1961. "Das 'Wir' in der Apostelgeschichte und das Itinerar." *Zeitschrift für Theologie und Kirche* 58:329-66.

—— 1971. *The Acts of the Apostles: A Commentary.* Philadelphia: Westminster.

Harvey, W. J. 1965. *Character and the Novel.* Ithaca: Cornell Univ.

Hayes, John & Holladay, Carl. 1982. *Biblical Exegesis: A Beginner's Handbook*. Atlanta: John Knox.

Heiny, Stephen. 1987. "2 Corinthians 2:14-4:6: The Motive for Metaphor." In *Society of Biblical Literature Seminar Papers*, ed. Kent Richards. Atlanta: Scholars.

Hengel, Martin. 1980. *Acts and the History of Earliest Christianity*. Philadelphia: Fortress.

Hochman, Baruch. 1985. *Character in Literature*. Ithaca: Cornell Univ.

Ingarden, Roman. 1973. *The Cognition of the Literary Work of Art*. Evanston: Northwestern Univ.

Iser, Wolfgang. 1974. *The Implied Reader: Patterns of Communication in Prose Fiction from Bunyan to Beckett*. Baltimore: Johns Hopkins Univ.

—— 1978. *The Act of Reading: A Theory of Aesthetic Response*. Baltimore: Johns Hopkins Univ.

James, Henry. 1961. "The Art of Fiction." In *Approaches to the Novel: Materials for a Poetics*, ed. Robert Scholes. San Francisco: Chandler.

Jaynes, Julian. 1977. *The Origins of Consciousness in the Breakdown of the Bicameral Mind*. Boston: Houghton Mifflin.

Jeremias, Joachim. 1969. *Jerusalem in the Time of Jesus: An Investigation into Economic and Social Conditions During the New Testament Period*. Philadelphia: Fortress.

—— 1971. "Samaritês." *Theological Dictionary of the New Testament* 7:88-94.

—— 1972. *The Parables of Jesus*. New York: Scribner's Sons.

Jervell, Jacob. 1972. *Luke and the People of God: A New Look at Luke-Acts*. Minneapolis: Augsburg.

—— 1986. "Paulus in der Apostelgeschichte und die Geschichte des Urchristentums." *New Testament Studies* 32:378-92.

Johnson, Luke Timothy. 1977. *The Literary Function of Possessions in Luke-Acts*. Missoula: Scholars.

—— 1982. "The Lucan Kingship Parable (Lk. 19:11-27)." *Novum Testamentum* 24:139-59.

Johnson, S. 1962. "Lord." *The Interpreter's Dictionary of the Bible* 3:150-51.

Jülicher, Adolf. 1910. *Die Gleichnisreden Jesu*, vol. 2. Tübingen: J. C. B. Mohr (Paul Siebeck).

Karris, Robert. 1986. "Luke 23:47 and the Lucan View of Jesus' Death." *Journal of Biblical Literature* 105:65-74.

Kawin, Bruce. 1972. *Telling It Again and Again: Repetition in Literature and Film*. Ithaca: Cornell Univ.

Kennedy, George. 1984. *New Testament Interpretation through Rhetorical Criticism*. Chapel Hill: Univ. of North Carolina.

Kermode, Frank. 1967. *The Sense of an Ending: Studies in the Theory of Fiction*. New York: Oxford Univ.

—— 1979. *The Genesis of Secrecy: On the Interpretation of Narrative*. Cambridge: Harvard Univ.

Klein, Günter. 1961. *Die zwölf Apostel: Ursprung und Gehalt einer Idee*. Göttingen: Vandenhoeck & Ruprecht.

Kort, Wesley. 1975. *Narrative Elements and Religious Meanings*. Philadelphia: Fortress.

—— 1988. *Story, Text, and Scripture: Literary Interests in Biblical Narrative*. University Park: Pennsylvania State Univ.

Lambrecht, J. 1979. "Paul's Farewell Address at Miletus (Acts 20,17-38)." In *Les Actes des Apôtres: Traditions, rédaction, théologie*, ed. J. Kremer: Gembloux: J. Duculot.

Lévi-Strauss, Claude. 1955. "The Structural Study of Myth." *Journal of American Folklore* 68:428-44.

Lewycky, David. 1985. "Paul's Turning from the Jews to the Gentiles in Luke-Acts." Ph.D. dissertation, Marquette Univ.

Lohfink, Gerhard. 1975. *Die Sammlung Israels: Eine Untersuchung zur lukanischen Ekklesiologie*. München: Kösel.

Lohmeyer, Ernst. 1937. "Vom urchristlichen Abendmahl." *Theologische Rundschau* 9:168-94, 195-227, 273-312.

Löning, Karl. 1973. *Die Saulustradition in der Apostelgeschichte*. Münster: Aschendorf.

—— 1974. "Die Korneliustradition." *Biblische Zeitschrift* 18:1-19.

Luedemann, Gerd. 1988. "Acts of the Apostles as a Historical Source." In *The Social World of Formative Christianity and Judaism; Essays in Tribute to Howard Clark Kee*, ed. Jacob Neusner et al, pp. 109-125. Philadelphia: Fortress.

McCown, C. C. 1962. "Palestine, Geography of." *The Interpreter's Dictionary of the Bible* 3:626-39.

McKnight, Edgar. 1988. *The Post-Modern Use of the Bible: The Emergence of Reader-Oriented Criticism*. Nashville: Abingdon.

Malbon, Elizabeth Struthers. 1986. *Narrative Space and Mythic Meaning in Mark*. San Francisco: Harper & Row.

Martin, Wallace. 1986. *Recent Theories of Narrative*. Ithaca: Cornell Univ.

Meeks, Wayne. 1983. *The First Urban Christians: The Social World of the Apostle Paul*. New Haven: Yale Univ.

Metzger, Bruce. 1971. *A Textual Commentary on the Greek New Testament*. Stuttgart: United Bible Societies.

Miles, Gary & Trompf, Garry. 1976. "Luke and Antiphon: The Theology of Acts 27-28 in the Light of Pagan Beliefs about Divine Retribution, Pollution, and Shipwreck." *Harvard Theological Review* 69:259-67.

Minear, Paul. 1966. "Luke's Use of the Birth Stories." In *Studies in Luke-Acts; Essays in Honor of Paul Schubert*, ed. Leander Keck & J. Louis Martyn. Nashville: Abingdon.

—— 1973. "Dear Theo: The Kerygmatic Intention and Claim of the Book of Acts." *Interpretation* 27:131-50.

Miscall, Peter. 1986. *1 Samuel: A Literary Reading*. Bloomington: Indiana Univ.

Moessner, David. 1988a. "The Ironic Fulfillment of Israel's Glory." In *Luke-Acts and the Jewish People*, ed. Joseph Tyson. Minneapolis: Augsburg.

—— 1988b. "And Once Again, What Sort of 'Essence'?: A Response to Charles Talbert." *Semeia* 43:75-84.

—— 1989. *Lord of the Banquet: The Literary and Theological Significance of the Lukan Travel Narrative.* Philadelphia: Fortress.

Nickelsburg, George. 1964. "Future Life in Intertestamental Literature." *The Interpreter's Dictionary of the Bible* S.V.:348-51.

Noth, Martin. 1966. *The Old Testament World.* Philadelphia: Fortress.

Panier, Louis. 1981a. "Comprenez pourquoi vous comprenez! Actes 1,15-2,47." *Sémiotique et Bible* 23:20-43.

—— 1981b. "La mort de Judas: Elements d'analyse sémiotique du recit de la pentecote." *Lumiere et vie* 30, no. 153/54:111-122.

Parsons, Mikeal. 1987. *The Departure of Jesus in Luke-Acts: The Ascension Narratives in Context.* Sheffield: Sheffield Academic.

Patte, Daniel. 1987. "A Structural Exegesis of 2 Corinthians 2:14-7:4 with Special Attention on 2:14-3:6 and 6:11-7:4." In *Society of Biblical Literature Seminar Papers*, ed. Kent Richards. Atlanta: Scholars.

Patte, Daniel & Patte, Aline. 1978. *Structural Exegesis: From Theory to Practice: Exegesis of Mark 15 and 16: Hermeneutical Implications.* Philadelphia: Fortress.

Perrin, Norman. 1976. *Rediscovering the Teaching of Jesus.* New York: Harper & Row.

Pervo, Richard. 1987. *Profit with Delight: The Literary Genre of the Acts of the Apostles.* Philadelphia: Fortress.

Pesch, Rudolf. 1986. *Die Apostelgeschichte,* 2 vols. Zürich: Benziger.

Petersen, Norman. 1978. *Literary Criticism for New Testament Critics.* Philadelphia: Fortress.

Plümacher, Eckhard. 1972. *Lukas als hellenistischer Schriftsteller: Studien zur Apostelgeschichte.* Göttingen: Vandenhoeck & Ruprecht.

Plunkett, Mark. 1985. "Ethnocentricity and Salvation History in the Cornelius Episode (Acts 10:1-11:18)." *Society of Biblical Literature Seminar Papers*, ed. Kent Richards. Atlanta: Scholars.

Rad, Gerhard von. 1965. "*angelos.*" *Theological Dictionary of the New Testament* 1:76-80.

Radl, Walter. 1975. *Paulus und Jesus im lukanischen Doppelwerk: Untersuchungen zu Parallelmotiven im Lukasevangelium und in der Apostelgeschichte.* Frankfurt: Peter Lang.

Reicke, Bo. 1973. "Jesus in Nazareth—Lk 4,16-30." In *Das Wort und die Wörter; Festschrift Gerhard Friedrich*, ed. H. Balz & S. Schulz. Stuttgart: Kohlhammer.

Rengstorf, Karl. 1964. "*hamartôlos.*" *Theological Dictionary of the New Testament* 1:324-27.

—— 1967. "*lêstês.*" *Theological Dictionary of the New Testament* 4:257-62.

Ricoeur, Paul. 1976. *Interpretation Theory: Discourse and the Surplus of Meaning.* Fort Worth: Texas Christian Univ.
—— 1977. "Toward a Hermeneutic of the Idea of Revelation." *Harvard Theological Review* 70:21-27.
—— 1979. "Naming God." *Union Seminary Quarterly Review* 34: 215-27.
Rimmon-Kenan, Shlomith. 1983. *Narrative Fiction: Contemporary Poetics.* London: Methuen.
Robinson, James. 1987. "Acts." In *The Literary Guide to the Bible,* ed. Robert Alter & Frank Kermode. Cambridge: Harvard Univ.
Roloff, Jürgen. 1965. *Apostolat-Verkündigung-Kirche: Ursprung, Inhalt und Funktion der kirchlichen Apostelamts nach Paulus, Lukas und den pastoral Briefen.* Gütersloh: Mohn.
Sanders, Jack. 1984. "The Salvation of the Jews." In *Luke-Acts: New Perspectives from the Society of Biblical Literature Seminar,* ed. Charles Talbert. New York: Crossroad.
—— 1985. "The Pharisees in Luke-Acts." In *The Living Text; Essays in Honor of Ernest W. Saunders,* ed. Dennis Groh & Robert Jewett. Lanham, MD: University Press of America.
—— 1987. *The Jews in Luke-Acts.* Philadelphia: Fortress.
Sanders, James. 1975. "From Isaiah 61 to Luke 4." In *Christianity, Judaism and Other Greco-Roman Cults; Studies for Morton Smith,* ed. Jacob Neusner. Leiden: E. J. Brill.
—— 1984. *Canon and Community: A Guide to Canonical Criticism.* Philadelphia: Fortress.
Savaran, George. 1988. *Telling and Retelling: Quotation in Biblical Narrative.* Bloomington: Indiana Univ.
Schille, Gottfried. 1979. *Das Älteste Paulusbild: Beobachtungen zur lukanischen und zur deuteropaulinischen Paulus-Darstellung.* Berlin: Evangelische.
Schneider, Gerhard. 1976. "'Stärke deine Brüder!' (Lk 22,32)." *Catholica* 30:200-206.
—— 1980. *Die Apostelgeschichte,* 1. Teil, *Einleitung, Kommentar zu Kap. 1.1-8.40.* Freiburg: Herder.
—— 1982. *Die Apostelgeschichte,* 2. Teil, *Kommentar zu Kap. 9,1-28,31.* Freiburg: Herder.
Schrenk, G. 1965. "*hiereus.*" *Theological Dictionary of the New Testament* 3:257-65.
Schubert, Paul. 1968. "The Place of the Areopagus Speech in the Composition of Acts." In *Transitions in Biblical Scholarship,* ed. J. Rylaarsdam. Chicago: Univ. of Chicago.
Schweizer, Eduard. 1984. *The Good News According to Luke.* Atlanta: John Knox.
Scott, Bernard. 1981. *Jesus, Symbol-Maker for the Kingdom.* Philadelphia: Fortress.
Shklovsky, Victor. 1965. "La construction de la nouvelle et du roman." In *Théorie de la littérature,* ed. Tzevetan Todorov. Paris: Seuil.

Smith, Morton. 1971. "Prolegommena to a Discussion of Aretalogies, Divine Men, the Gospels, and Jesus." *Journal of Biblical Literature* 90:174-99.

Steck, Odil Hannes. 1967. *Israel und das gewaltsame Geschick der Propheten: Untersuchungen zur Überlieferung des deuteronomistischen Geschichtsbildes im Alten Testament, Spätjudentum und Urchristentum.* Neukirchen-Vluyn: Neukirchener Verlag.

Sternberg, Meir. 1985. *The Poetics of Biblical Narrative: Ideological Literature and the Drama of Reading.* Bloomington: Indiana Univ.

Strobel, August. 1972. "Die Ausrufung des Jubeljahrs in der Nazarethpredigt Jesu: Zur apocalyptischen Tradition Lc 4:16-30." In *Jesus in Nazareth,* ed. Walther Eltester. Berlin: Walter de Gruyter.

Suleiman, Susan. 1980. "Redundancy and the 'Readable' Text." *Poetics Today* 13:119-42.

Talbert, Charles. 1974. *Literary Patterns, Theological Themes, and the Genre of Luke-Acts.* Missoula: Scholars.

—— 1977. *What Is a Gospel? The Genre of the Canonical Gospels.* Philadelphia: Fortress.

—— 1982. *Reading Luke: A Literary and Theological Commentary on the Third Gospel.* New York: Crossroad.

—— 1984. "Promise and Fulfillment in Lucan Theology." In *Luke-Acts: New Perspectives from the Society of Biblical Literature Seminar,* ed. Charles Talbert. New York: Crossroad.

—— 1988. "Once Again: Gospel Genre." *Semeia* 43:53-73.

Tannehill, Robert. 1985. "Israel in Luke-Acts: A Tragic Story." *Journal of Biblical Literature* 104:69-85.

—— 1986. *The Narrative Unity of Luke-Acts: A Literary Interpretation,* vol. 1, *The Gospel According to Luke.* Philadelphia: Fortress.

—— 1990. *The Narrative Unity of Luke-Acts: A Literary Interpretation,* vol. 2, *The Acts of the Apostles.* Minneapolis: Fortress.

Theissen, Gerd. 1983. *The Miracle Stories of the Early Christian Tradition.* Philadelphia: Fortress.

Thomas, Cal. 1988. "Bible Suggests a Punishment for Thievery." *Memphis Commercial Appeal.* Dec. 15:A8.

Tiede, David. 1988. "'Glory to Thy People Israel': Luke-Acts and the Jews." In *Luke-Acts and the Jewish People,* ed. Joseph Tyson. Minneapolis: Augsburg.

Tillich, Paul. 1951. *Systematic Theology,* vol. 1, *Reason and Revelation, Being and God.* Chicago: Univ. of Chicago.

Tolbert, Mary Ann. 1979. *Perspectives on the Parables: An Approach to Multiple Interpretations.* Philadelphia: Fortress.

Torgovnick, Marianna. 1981. *Closure in the Novel.* Princeton: Princeton Univ.

Trémel, Bernard. 1980. "Apropos d'Actes 20,7-12: Puissance du thaumaturge ou du témoin." *Revue de Théologie et de Philosophie* 112:359-69.

Tyson, Joseph. 1986. *The Death of Jesus in Luke-Acts*. Columbia, SC: Univ. of South Carolina.

Uspensky, Boris. 1973. *A Poetics of Composition: The Structure of the Artistic Text and Typology of a Compositional Form*. Berkeley: Univ. of California.

Vökel, Martin. 1973-74. "Exegetische Erwägungen zum Verständnis des Begriffs *kathexes* im lukanischen Prolog." *New Testament Studies* 20:289-99.

Vollenweiden, S. 1988. "'Ich sah den Satan wie einen Blitz von Himmel fallen' (Lk 10:18)." *Zeitschrift für die neutestamentliche Wissenschaft* 79:187-203.

Watt, Ian. 1961. "Realism and the Novel." In *Approaches to the Novel: Materials for a Poetics*, ed. Robert Scholes. San Francisco: Chandler.

Wilder, Amos. 1983. "Story and Story-World." *Interpretation* 37:353-64.

Wilson, Stephen. 1973. *The Gentiles and the Gentile Mission in Luke-Acts*. Cambridge: Cambridge Univ.

—— 1976. "The Portrait of Paul in Acts and in the Pastorals." *Society of Biblical Literature Seminar Papers*, ed. Kent Richards. Missoula: Scholars.

—— 1983. *Luke and the Law*. Cambridge: Cambridge Univ.

Wink, Walter. 1988. "Neither Passivity nor Violence: Jesus' Third Way." In *Society of Biblical Literature Seminar Papers*, ed. David Lull. Atlanta: Scholars.

Wuellner, W. H. 1962. "Fishermen." *The Interpreter's Dictionary of the Bible* S.V.:338-39.

Zahn, Theodor. 1919. *Die Apostelgeschichte de Lucas*. Leipzig: A. Deichertsche Verlagsbuchhandlung Werner Scholl.

Zehnle, Richard. 1969. "The Salvific Character of Jesus' Death in Lucan Soteriology." *Theological Studies* 30:420-44.

—— 1971. *Peter's Pentecost Discourse*. Nashville: Abingdon.

# INDEXES

## AUTHORS

## SUBJECTS

# BIBLE WITH APOCRYPHA

## PSEUDEPIGRAPHA

# RABBINIC LITERATURE

# AUTHORS OF ANTIQUITY